BI   STUDIES:
MEETING GROUND OF JEWS AND CHRISTIANS

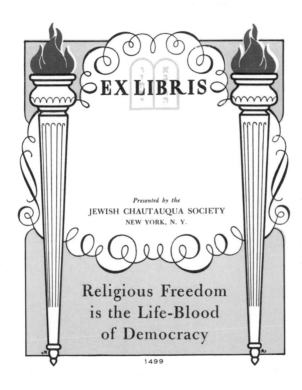

Studies in Judaism and Christianity

*Exploration of issues in the
contemporary dialogue between Christians and Jews*

Editors
Lawrence Boadt, C.S.P.
Helga Croner
Leon Klenicki
Kevin A. Lynch, C.S.P.

BIBLICAL STUDIES: MEETING GROUND OF JEWS AND CHRISTIANS

Edited by

Lawrence Boadt, C.S.P.
Helga Croner
Leon Klenicki

A Stimulus Book

Paulist Press ■ New York ■ Ramsey

Library of Congress
Catalog Card Number: 80-82812

ISBN: 0-8091-2344-4

Published by Paulist Press 545 Island Road, Ramsey, N.J. 07446

Printed and bound in the
United States of America

Contents

Part III
THE BIBLE AS RECORD AND REVELATION

Dedication

This volume is dedicated to the memory of Rabbi Samuel Sandmel, long-time Distinguished Service Professor of Bible and Hellenistic Literature at Hebrew Union College—Jewish Institute of Religion in Cincinnati. His untimely death on November 4, 1979 prevented him from contributing an article to this collection as he had planned. Throughout his eminent career as a scholar, Dr. Sandmel's sympathetic and enlightening studies of early Judaism, Jesus, and the beginnings of Christianity marked him as a pioneer. In many instances he created dialogue where none had existed.

זכר צדיק לברכה

"May his memory be a blessing"

Foreword

This is the fourth volume of STIMULUS BOOKS (see inside cover for previous publications in this series).

The editors wish to make available with this series material of interest not only to those immediately involved in scholarly work on Judaism and Christianity but also to educators and leaders of discussion groups at large. The index of authors and subjects was compiled to assist in such use of the book.

The essays here presented are original copyrighted material that has not been published elsewhere. Christian and Jewish scholars were asked to write on specific aspects of Bible research, from their own points of view as scholars and as exponents of their respective religious affiliation.

Helga Croner

Introduction: Biblical Studies on the Fifteenth Anniversary of Nostra Aetate

Lawrence Boadt, C.S.P.

I

October 28, 1980 marked the fifteenth anniversary of the promulgation of the Second Vatican Council's *Declaration on the Relation of the Church to Non-Christian Religions,* often simply called by its Latin title *Nostra Aetate* from its first words, which mean "In our age. . . ."[1] The five brief sections of this document affirm the Catholic Church's respect for all religions which search for God and which offer their followers a way of life in that search. Individual mention is made of the great religions Hinduism and Buddhism, and special sections are devoted to Islam and to Judaism. It concludes with a call for a world community of peace and an end to all discrimination and deprival of human rights and dignity.

The background history of this document is complicated and can only be summarized here.[2] It began with the wish of Pope John XXIII that the Secretariat for Promoting Christian Unity prepare a statement for the bishops of the Vatican Council on the question of Catholic relations with the Jews. Originally intended as a clear statement by the Church repudiating all antisemitism and any Christian claims that the Jewish people should be held responsible for the death of Christ, the first draft was modified and discussed and gradually enlarged in its contextual setting. By the final session it had been united with the present wider schema on all non-

1

Christian religions. This was due both to the political sensitivity of the issue involving both Arab Christians and the State of Israel, and to the need for a better theological framework within which the Church could address the question. This latter point centered on how best to express the belief that Israel, both old and new, bears a unique relationship to Christianity. Not only are they united in the common human search for God, but they are related to one another as two branches of one family who proudly share common roots, great ancestors, and most of their early traditions and insights into that God.

The final form of the Council's Declaration on the Jews, now found as paragraph #4 of *Nostra Aetate,* is an important landmark for the Catholic Church. It is too much, of course, to say that it pleased everybody. Some expected much more, while others, particularly Eastern Rite bishops, felt that it went too far. On one side, it repudiates all forms of antisemitism on the part of Christians and proscribes any reading of the New Testament that blames the death of Christ on all Jews, or presents the Jews as cursed, or suggests that God has broken his special covenantal relationship with them. On the positive side, *Nostra Aetate* explores the Church's continuity with Israel, using language such as "the people of God," "stock of Abraham," "election," "promise" and "covenantal revelation." By avoiding divisive categories, as, e.g., the "body of Christ," the document openly extends an invitation to Christians to reconsider the biblical roots of their faith in terms of the common heritage, and to rediscover and cherish those New Testament passages, such as Romans 11 or Ephesians 2, that wrestle with the mystery of unity between Christian and Jew. Although this Council Declaration is primarily the Catholic leadership speaking to other Catholics, it also clearly represents a public gesture to the Jews welcoming further dialogue. In fact, the document distinctly declares:

> This sacred Council wishes to encourage and further mutual understanding and appreciation. This can be obtained, especially, by way of biblical and theological inquiry and through friendly discussions.

In order that the Council fathers' seriousness in this matter would not be underestimated, further steps were soon taken to underscore the need for *contemporary* interaction between Christians and Jews, and not just for a better knowledge among Catholics of the Hebrew Scriptures, i.e., the Christian Old Testament. The plenary session of the bishops of the Commission for Promoting Christian Unity stated in November 1969 that

Christianity cannot be understood except by reference to Jewish *tradition* in which it took root and which is *still alive* today.[3] The working paper from that session noted in December 1969 how the Jewish tradition had developed beyond the Scriptures and so must be considered a rich source for the on-going interpretation of *Torah,* i.e., Law, the gift confided to Israel, a word that endures forever (Is. 40:8).[4] Finally, in October 1974, Pope Paul VI established a special Commission for Religious Relations with the Jews, attached to the Secretariat for Promoting Christian Unity and not to the Secretariat for Non-Christian Religions.[5] This decision emphasized the special relationship of Judaism to Christianity and guaranteed the Catholic Church's commitment to the continuation and development of dialogue. Soon, in January 1975, this Commission issued guidelines for implementing *Nostra Aetate* which repeated and strengthened the call for dialogue and warned Catholics to diligently correct and improve liturgical and educational books to reflect the Council's teaching.[6]

In all these decrees and guidelines of Vatican offices, as well as in the many statements of bishops' committees in the United States, Canada, France, Germany and elsewhere,[7] the dominant note has continually been the call to Christian scholars to explore the Scriptures more deeply in a spirit of dialogue and collaboration with their Jewish peers. To mark the tenth anniversary of *Nostra Aetate,* in November 1975 the bishops of the United States devoted special attention to this aspect of the on-going relationship, calling on Catholic scholars to "address themselves in a special way to the theological and scriptural issues raised by these documents which deal with the relationship of the Church with Judaism."[8] It is a fitting way to now celebrate the fifteenth anniversary of the Declaration by offering this volume in response to that call—a volume which brings together Jewish and Christian scholars in just such a collaborative effort. The succeeding articles will focus primarily on those aspects of the Hebrew Scriptures which are our common heritage, and on the place of the New Testament in the Jewish-Christian dialogue. These essays are the fruit of long reflection by respected religious thinkers, but each brings fresh insight to what the author's particular faith holds in common with the other and raises honest questions about the problems and the divergences.

Such a volume is possible today not only because of the increased openness of ordinary Jewish and Christian believers to talk to one another, but also because of the tremendous gains in the study of Scripture itself in this century. Most of these stem from our vastly enlarged knowledge of ancient history and civilization. This in turn has led to a deepened understanding of the manner of expression and the literary output of the semitic world, and has created a scientific passion for capturing the original setting and sense of the biblical books. This movement has perhaps been strongest on the Christian side, but it has also found broad support among Jewish biblical scholars.

I would like to take this opportunity to single out a few areas of modern biblical study that have been significant in kindling *Christian* interest in undertaking such a *mutual* re-examination of the Scriptures:

1. The use of the historico-critical method in biblical study, which includes form criticism, source criticism, redaction criticism and transmission history approaches, has opened up the multiplicity of understandings about God in ancient Israel and stressed the constant growth and development in thought.[9] The Hebrew Scriptures do not reflect a monolithic statement of faith, but a dynamic process of reinterpretation and reformulation of the earlier levels of understanding. Theological themes such as promise or election, salvation events such as the Exodus or conquest, bodies of Law such as the Holiness Code or Leviticus, are never frozen creeds, but always a source for further reflection within the Scriptures themselves.

2. Modern archaeology has brought Jewish and Christian scholars together in a shared research task, and has resulted in basic agreements on the available data about the history of Israel.[10] Further, it has challenged Christians to respect the setting of Scripture in its own times, rather than to see in it only a prediction or foreshadowing of the New Testament.

3. Especially important has been the attention paid to the post-exilic period. Unlike nineteenth-century critical scholarship which generally viewed anything after the Exile as a regression in religious development, recent Christian research has begun to take seriously the centuries from 539 to the time of Christ as a creative and vital period of biblical formation.[11] No longer may Christians characterize the developing Judaism of this period as a breakdown of the biblical faith of the prophets, but more and more must they come to appreciate it as an integral and faithful response to God's continuing action for his people.

4. This better understanding of the world of the Hebrew Scriptures is mirrored in our better understanding of the world of Jesus and the rabbis. The discovery of the Qumran scrolls and other writings from the same era has revealed the dynamism and richness of first-century Judaism.[12] For example, we have gained much more information on the sects within Judaism of the time of Christ and particularly of the achievements of the Pharisees.[13] At the same time, the vibrancy of first- and second-century thought has come alive through renewed Christian attention to the Talmud and the Targums, Josephus and other Greek and Roman writers.

This has helped to situate Jesus more clearly as a Jew among Jews, and to redeem Paul from the ranks of Greek Gentile religious thinkers.[14] It is no longer possible for Christian theologians to write off the Talmud in particular as sterile formalism.

5. Another aspect that has engaged the attention of biblical students today is the question of the canonization of the Scriptures and the realization that this process involved decisions on both sides about the inclusion or exclusion of books determined in large part by the counter-claims of the other side. This is in a special way true of the so-called "Deutero-canonical Books" found in the Septuagint (the Jewish diaspora collection of Alexandria, Egypt) which were certainly Palestinian in origin, namely Sirach, Judith, Tobit and 1 Maccabees. Concretely, this rules out any simplistic definition of the closing of the Old Testament canon for Christians. A facile distinction between the closing of the Hebrew Scripture canon from the fourth to the second centuries before Christ and the rabbinic writings after Christ cannot be maintained. The whole question of canon study and its development as a theological touchstone is one of the most productive and alive areas of biblical research today.[15]

6. Also, the aims and methods of Christian "Old Testament theology" have come under increasing scrutiny. Promise and fulfillment, salvation history, law versus grace, typology, or even replacement ("old" covenant by "new") schemas, all have severe shortcomings as a means of organizing the traditions in the Hebrew Scriptures. Most problematic is their total interpretive orientation toward the New Testament.[16] The relationship of the Hebrew Scriptures to the New Testament, especially in reference to continuity and discontinuity, must begin with the premise that each speaks from its own complete integrity.

7. Finally, from the Jewish side, the response has been warm and open to Christian efforts. Not only do many Jewish scholars publish in what began as exclusively Christian learned journals,[17] but cooperative exchanges on theological and biblical issues are becoming a regular occurrence.[18]

II

The present vitality of the Jewish-Christian dialogue and its interest in biblical sources is reflected in the steady output of important articles and books in the last fifteen years. There is only space here to mention a few of the notable book-length studies that have appeared.[19]

Several prominent Jewish scholars have addressed major areas of Jewish-Christian tension rooted in biblical considerations. The person of Jesus has been sensitively treated in Samuel Sandmel's *We Jews and Jesus* (Oxford University Press, 1965), in David Flusser's *Jesus* (Herder and Herder, 1969) and in Geza Vermès' *Jesus the Jew* (Collins, 1973). The English translation of Jules Isaac's original French work, *Jésus et Israel* (Paris, 1948), has made available a most important critique of the New Testament from a Jewish perspective (*Jesus and Israel;* Holt, Rinehart and Winston, 1971). Rabbi Pinchas Lapide's *Juden und Christen: Verleitung zum Dialog* contains some valuable meditations on the shared aspects of biblical faith (Benziger, 1976). Samuel Sandmel's *Ancient Judaism and Christian Origins* (Oxford Press, 1978) brings together the fruit of forty years of pioneering work by the leading Jewish authority on the Christian Bible. And, recently, two significant studies have appeared: Helga Croner and Leon Klenicki, eds., *Issues in the Jewish-Christian Dialogue: Jewish Perspectives on Covenant, Mission and Witness*, Stimulus Book (Paulist Press, 1979), and Eugene Borowitz, *Contemporary Christologies* (Paulist Press, 1980).

Meanwhile, Christian scholars have not been idle. Clemens Thoma, *A Christian Theology of Judaism* (Paulist Press, 1980) brings together all the significant issues from a Catholic standpoint in an attempt to present a synthetic Christian theology on the Church's relation to Judaism. Protestant volumes of note range from A. Roy Eckhardt's *Elder and Younger Brothers: The Encounter of Jews and Christians* (Scribner's, 1967) up to Jürgen Moltmann's *The Crucified God* (Harper and Row, 1974) and Franklin Littell's *The Crucifixion of the Jews: The Failure of Christians To Understand the Jewish Experience* (Harper and Row, 1975).

In recent years, too, the number of studies that wrestle directly with the problem of antisemitism in Christian theology and biblical interpretation has multiplied. Works such as Rosemary Ruether's *Faith and Fratricide: The Theological Roots of Antisemitism* (Seabury Press, 1974) and Charlotte Klein's *Anti-Judaism in Christian Theology* (Fortress Press, 1978) have even had the distinction of creating a mild controversy within the normally stolid theological community. Recently, Alan Davies has edited a new volume of twelve studies on the roots of theological antisemitism entitled *Antisemitism and the Foundations of Christianity* (Paulist Press, 1979).

Equally important are the collaborative works in which both Jews and Christians contribute their different points of view on specific problems. The 1966 volume *Torah and Gospel: Jewish and Christian Theology in Dialogue,* edited by Philip Scharper (Sheed and Ward, 1966), has been one such significant attempt. A second is Volume #98 of *Concilium* (Seabury Press, 1974), edited by Hans Küng and Walter Kasper, which is dedicated to presenting a Christian and a Jewish statement on several key issues of dialogue. Representative of current interest is the popular presentation of the Jewish-Christian dialogue gathered in *Jewish/Christian Relations,* edited by Robert Heyer (Paulist Press, 1975).

Since all of these studies have appeared since the issuance of *Nostra Aetate,* it would be fair to judge that the Vatican Council's expressed concern for more dialogue has borne fruit already, and that we are presently participants in what will prove to be a far-reaching re-evaluation of many of our most cherished religious stereotypes and characteristically polemical language. At the same time, a beginning has been made in the mutual exploration of a shared biblical heritage. But for all that has been accomplished, much remains. A brief sketch of the tasks ahead indicates how many miles still lie before us.

1. Christians must continue to root out and condemn the practical antisemitism that has become ingrained in the *preaching* and popular *presentation* of the New Testament, and which has by no means fully responded to the rarefied summons from on high of the Vatican Council.[20]

2. Along with this, Christian theology must pay more attention to Talmudic studies and to later Jewish tradition. Rarely does a Christian theological work take into account Jewish thought *after* the lifetime of Jesus and Paul. Major sourcebooks, such as Kittel's *Theological Dictionary of the New Testament* (8 volumes; Eerdmans Publishing Company, 1964) and Strack and Billerbeck's *Kommentar zum Neuen Testament aus Talmud und Midrasch* (3. Auflage; Munich: 1961; 6 vols.), treat the Hebrew Scriptures merely as a prelude to New Testament interpretation, and rabbinic thought mainly as an illustration of the Jewish cultural standards and literary canons of the time.

3. Christians need to familiarize themselves with modern Jewish thought, and particularly with Jewish understanding of the relationship of the Bible vis-à-vis the oral and written tradition. They must learn what such concepts as *Torah* and *Halakhah* really mean to a Jew.

4. More seminaries and theology schools will have to develop Jewish studies programs which incorporate the history of biblical interpretation according to Jewish tradition if the cycle of misunderstanding and misuse of the Hebrew Scriptures, as though they were primarily Christian documents, is to be broken.[21]

5. For their part, Jews must simply learn more about the New Tes-

tament if any dialogue is to take place. Since Judaism in no way recognizes the New Testament as Scripture for herself, the internal religious motive is lacking for such a study. Yet no fruitful discussion is possible as long as Jews are not willing to take seriously the religious claims of Christians nor to look at and appreciate the real areas of continuity between the two religions. If Christianity is seen essentially as a Gentile rejection of Judaism, then Christian protestations of love and obedience to the Hebrew Scriptures will fall on deaf ears.

6. Jews will have to complement their rich tradition of biblical study based on the authority of the rabbis and the Jewish interpreters through the centuries by a broader acceptance of the historico-critical method employed by almost all Christian scholars to one degree or another.[22] Just how such statements as "God gave the Torah to Moses on Mount Sinai" and similar ones are to be understood by historians and scientific religious critics needs more treatment by Jewish writers. But it also requires some modicum of acceptance of the legitimacy of the method within the Jewish community. Christian scholarship views much of the Talmudic tradition to be highly uncritical in its transmission and considers its internal methods of interpretation of the Scriptures to be as artificial and as far from the original meaning of the biblical text as is the so-called "spiritual sense" employed by Christian fathers up through the Middle Ages.[23]

7. Although there has been considerable analysis of the hermeneutical methods employed both by New Testament authors such as Paul or Matthew and by the rabbis of the Talmud, there has been little serious joint discussion among Christians and Jews about the implications of such an analysis. In many cases, the interpretive criteria employed by both sides have not primarily served to engage the original sense of the Scriptures, but to adapt their use to later community positions and self-understandings, many of which were consciously adopted in opposition to those of the other faith.[24]

8. In the case of the Jewish and Christian *canons* of Scripture, recognition of the dynamic process of development should lead, as in the previous two points, to a deeper and more respectful appreciation of each other's faith tradition. Knowledge of the canonization process will counteract the tendency of both sides to view their own tradition as an absolute revelation handed down as a unified whole which stands in almost complete opposition to the way of faith of the other party.

9. Theologians of both traditions now see the need to work together on the significance of the *covenant* concept. Christians have already devoted significant debate to how they can best describe their faith as a "new"

covenant in Christ in relation to the original covenant. The usual answers are often broken down into either a "one-covenant" school which understands Jews and Christians sharing the same covenant in different modes, or a "two-covenant" school, which envisions a different but interrelated and truly complementary covenant for each.[25] To be productive, this debate calls for reflections and responses from Jewish thinkers, especially in suggesting elements from their tradition which allow some room for Gentiles within the definition of the covenant.

10. *Creation* as a topic for theological reflection is closely tied to re-examining the subject of covenant.[26] On the one hand, fresh thinking about the implications of the Noachide and Abrahamic covenant references in both Talmudic and New Testament sources could open up new zones of common agreement; on the other, wider consideration of the import of creation theology in Genesis 1 and in the Wisdom writings could lead to a better foundation for interchange on the concepts of *promise, election* and *covenant.*

11. The subject of *revelation,* especially its continuity, its openness to God's on-going activity, and its historical formulation into beliefs, doctrines and traditional statements, offers excellent opportunities for common considerations on both the particularity of God's self-revelation and its multiplicity/plurality.

12. Christians will need to ponder their theology of the *mission* of the Church, derived from New Testament demands to bring the "Good News" to the world, in order to best relate it to the covenantal fidelity of a God who promised he would not abandon Israel. And Jews will need to examine their theology of *witness* in relation to the challenge that they are not the only group who lays claim to the Hebrew Scriptures and its revelation of God. Respectful but frank discussion on this issue can clear a lot of ground between us.[27]

13. Finally, similar remarks could easily be made about several other biblical themes that are ripe for further exploration and reciprocal exchange: (a) *messianism,* (b) the *promise of land,* (c) *prophecy* as a function of both promise and prediction, (d) *election,* (e) the "people of God" as a *pilgrim people.*[28]

III

The foregoing survey reveals how many subjects need our attention in dialogue, and at the same time indicates how lively the current interest is. A volume of this size can tackle only a few of these vital questions. In light of the importance of *Nostra Aetate* for raising the basic issues and insisting on theological and biblical replies, the Jewish and Christian contributors here focus on the fundamentals in three related areas: (1) the implications of modern biblical research for mutual biblical dialogue; (2) the relationship of the Hebrew Scriptures to the New Testament; (3) the ramifications of the concept of revelation for understanding one another's faith.

The first article by David Sperling, "Judaism and Modern Biblical Research," explains the Jewish response to modern critical methods of biblical study. Sperling traces Jewish emphasis on the Talmud and rabbinic literature which overshadowed Bible study. He notes how recent is any significant Jewish attention to the historico-critical method as practiced by Christian scholars. As a second step, he evaluates the Wellhausen thesis from a Jewish point of view and sketches the contributions of pioneer Jewish scholars such as Arnold Ehrlich, Abraham Kahana, Tur-Sinai, M. D. Cassuto, and Y. Kaufmann. In a third part, he deals with Jewish contributions to philology, singling out Harry Orlinsky, H. L. Ginsberg and others, and with the archaeological discoveries and their implications, surveying Ugarit, Mari, Alalakh, Akkad, Hittite Turkey, Ebla, Egypt and Palestine. He concludes with thoughts on how all this affects traditional Jewish methods, and how Jews will differ from Christians in their major concerns.

In the matching Christian contribution, Jorge Mejia presents a Catholic evaluation of the critical method in Bible study. First he addresses the problems it has raised pastorally for the traditional faith, for bridging the gap between the ordinary believer and the scholar, for developing a biblical theology, and for answering the demands for "committed reading" of the Scriptures made by new movements such as liberation theology. Next he follows the history of Catholic reaction to modern biblical criticism from Loisy and Modernism through source criticism, form criticism, tradition criticism, redaction criticism and archaeological developments. His third section outlines the growing acceptance of these methods in Church documents beginning with the pontificate of Pope Pius XII. In a concluding section, he discusses some of the most important theological aspects of Scripture study, such as the mystery of God, inspiration, tradition, the analogy of faith and the unity between critical exegesis and theological use. He ends with some reflections on needed directions for present study.

Leonard Kravitz' study, "A Jewish Reading of the New Testament," opens Part II with an overview of Jewish reactions to the New Testament considered as Scripture. He looks at the problems a Jew faces trying to understand the claims of another religion's book and shows the many road-blocks raised by Christian polemics against Judaism within the New Testament. He details the differences from Palestinian Judaism in cultural understanding present in the New Testament and its movement away from the major ideas of the Hebrew Scriptures. He uses the change in the idea of the messiah as a good example. Another is the meaning of Torah, to which he devotes a full treatment in the Jewish tradition of the Scriptures. He shows how Christianity consciously separated itself from Judaism over this point, a process which involved some very polemical attacks on the authority of the Law and, more concretely, on the actual persons of authority at the time. His last section describes some of the ways a modern Jew sees Jesus: as a miracle worker and teacher, as ambivalent in his attitude toward the Law, as strongly eschatological in approach. He concludes that much of this puzzles a Jew, but the effort does lead to a better appreciation of the Christian position.

In "Tanakh and the New Testament: A Christian Perspective," Joseph Blenkinsopp focuses the problem of the relationship between the Testaments on two major Christian concerns: the development of the canon and the evolution of biblical theology. On the first topic he shows the difficulties encountered in pinning down a first-century canon of the Hebrew Scriptures and notes how Christian use of the Septuagint, the stress on prophetic fulfillment in Jesus, and the diversity of New Testament attitudes toward the Old Testament all played important roles in the process. On the topic of biblical theology, he chronicles the developments of the nineteenth century which led to a weakened biblical theology and a strengthened history of Israel. This included an emphasis on salvation history which neglected the post-exilic period and thus forced a discontinuity between the New Testament and an Israel whose apparent value had ceased centuries before. He illustrates this by examining the theologies of Schultz, König, and Eichrodt. In his summary, he delineates some present needs for Christians doing biblical theology, e.g., better integration of the Wisdom tradition, more attention to the post-exilic period and rabbinic Judaism, avoidance of any salvation history schema which sees a radical break after the Exile, and a necessity to include the canonization process within Old Testament theology.

In the third article on the place of the New Testament in the dialogue, André Lacocque brings some specifically Protestant insights to the Christian outlook on reading the Old Testament. He first depicts the ambiguity of Christian attitudes, especially among the Reformers, and then addresses the difficulties of a "New" Testament which seems to supersede the "Old."

Taking a different aspect of the canon from that of Dr. Blenkinsopp, he describes the effects of a Christian "spiritual interpretation" of the Bible which allows all other meanings to be swallowed up in Christ, opposes the "Old" to the "New" as appearances to inner reality, and sets Synagogue over against Church. He then briefly delineates the basic attitudes of fundamentalism, liberalism and neo-orthodoxy that have developed among Protestants. This leads him into an evaluation of the hermeneutical methods of allegory and typology employed by Christians for Old Testament interpretation. Besides the distortions possible in such exegesis, he adds the danger of Christian interpretation which neither knows the world of the Hebrew Scriptures nor seeks rapport with them. For Lacocque, the crux of the problem is in the Christian understanding of history. Instead of a tendency to see the discontinuity between Christ and all previous history of revelation, Christianity needs to stress the continuity and organic unity of a history involving God's will for both Jews and Christians.

Part III particularizes the discussion with two views of revelation. Martin Cohen presents four aspects of the question from the Jewish side. First, he points out that the idea of revelation itself raises questions about the divine or human origins of belief. Moreover, any admission of divine communication puts some of the claims beyond the critique of reason. This is not to mention that on our human language level the formulations of traditional revelation claims are mostly either apologetic or confessional in nature. His second section presents the Jewish idea of *Torah,* and, in particular, the *Torah min ha-shamayim* in Jewish tradition. This history pinpoints the many reassessments and reformulations of the concept within Judaism itself. His third section surveys the effects of modern secularism on Jewish belief in revelation and how the Jewish community has responded with different accommodations. His fourth part works out suggestions for a modern recovery of *Torah min ha-shamayim* involving Judaism's search for its uniqueness, an apologetic from a rational, scientific and heuristic methodology for the value of Torah, and the creation of a value system based on it. Above all, it is the reaffirmation of the value system which has revealed the strength of Jewish witness through suffering. Finally, he proposes a four-part schema for holiness based on this Torah value system: *theoretically* by consistency, *practically* by conduct, *intellectually* by conviction, and *spiritually* by conversion of self.

The second article on revelation comes from the Christian perspective. Monika Hellwig begins with observations on the use of Scripture texts for the formulation of doctrines within the Christian Church. She then treats the possible Christian approaches to the Hebrew Scriptures in the context of dialogue. For the Christian, revelation has both a universal and a particular aspect; it combines recognition that God works in all that happens in the world along with a specific understanding of Jesus as the central experience in which God speaks. Next she concentrates on the two themes of *election* and *covenant* as central to the dialogue. She gives special attention to the question of models for relating Jewish and Christian views of the covenant, pointing out some of the problems inherent in both the one-covenant model and in the two-covenant model. She develops the difficulties that face the two faiths over the covenant issue. These areas of contention include the distinction between "Old" and "New" in the covenant, continuity versus discontinuity, the dangers of literal interpretations of texts, and the diversity of revelation language between Christians and Jews and even among Christians themselves. She ends with her own preference for a one-covenant model and the acknowledgment that we all have a long way to go as we follow God's will in this search.

NOTES

1. Available in *The Documents of Vatican II,* edited by Walter M. Abbott, S.J. (Herder and Herder/Association Press, 1966) 660–671, or in *Vatican Council II: The Conciliar and Post-Conciliar Documents,* edited by Austin Flannery, O.P. (Costello Publishing Company, 1975) 738–742.

2. The history of the deliberations are popularly presented in the commentary of René Laurentin in *Declaration on the Relation of the Church to Non-Christian Religions of Vatican Council II* (Paulist Press, 1966) 17–58, and in the remarks of Thomas Stransky, C.S.P. in *Vatican II: An Interfaith Appraisal* (University of Notre Dame, 1966) 343–348.

3. *Secretariat for Promoting Christian Unity Information Service* #9 (February 1971) now available in Helga Croner, *Stepping Stones to Further Jewish-Christian Relations* (Stimulus Books, 1977) 2–5.

4. *Ibid.,* 6–11.

5. "Guidelines on Religious Relations with the Jews," issued by the Commission for Religious Relations with the Jews, December 1, 1974, in Flannery, *op. cit.,* 743–749.

6. See Croner, *op. cit.,* 11–16.

7. Jorge Mejia, "Survey of Issues in Catholic-Jewish Relations," *Origins,* Volume 7, #47 (May 11, 1978) 744–748, discusses the various statements of Bishops' Conferences.

8. See Croner, *op. cit.,* 29–34.

9. See particularly the comments of David Sperling and Jorge Mejia in their articles in this volume.

10. See the remarks of Sperling in his article below. A useful survey of the more important finds that affect biblical studies appears in Edwin Yamauchi, "Documents from Old Testament Times: A Survey of Recent Discoveries," *Westminster Journal of Theology* 41 (1978) 1–32.

11. See the comments of Joseph Blenkinsopp in his article below. An example of such serious restudy of the post-exilic period by Christian exegetes and historians is Ralph Klein, *Israel in Exile: A Theological Interpretation* (Overtures to Biblical Theology: Fortress Press, 1979) and David Petersen, *Late Israelite Prophecy* (Scholars Press, 1977).

12. The Qumran texts are available for the general reader in Theodor Gaster, *The Dead Sea Scriptures* (3rd ed., Anchor book, Doubleday, 1976). Other documents would include the various papyri from the caves of Murabba'at and from the revolt of Bar Kokhba; compare the remarks of Frank Cross, *The Ancient Library of Qumran,* Anchor book (Doubleday, 1958), 16–19.

13. Examples include Ellis Rivkin, *A Hidden Revolution* (Abingdon Press, 1978) who treats the question from a Jewish view with many new insights into the first century. See also the recent survey of advances in our knowledge of the Essenes, in Jerome Murphy-O'Connor, "The Essenes in Palestine," *Biblical Archaeologist* 40 (1977) 100–124.

14. See, for example, Geza Vermès, *Jesus the Jew* (Collins, 1973) and E. P. Sanders, *Paul and Palestinian Judaism: A Comparison of Patterns of Religion* (Fortress Press, 1977).

15. Note the comments of André Lacocque in his article below. James Sanders has written several important studies in this area, e.g., his "Adaptable for Life: The Nature and Function of Canon," in *Magnalia Dei: The Mighty Acts of God,* edited by F. M. Cross *et al.* (Doubleday, 1976) 531–560. Brevard Childs has recently published a most important study, *Introduction to the Old Testament as Scripture* (Fortress Press, 1979) which traces the canonical shape of the Scriptures.

16. A helpful survey of the modern discussion and problems involved in biblical theology is found in A. H. J. Gunneweg, *Understanding the Old Testament* (Westminster Press, 1978).

17. For example, the *Journal of Biblical Literature,* the organ of the Society of Biblical Literature, celebrating its one hundredth birthday in 1980, and founded by Protestant scholars to disseminate the research papers read at the annual meeting of the group. For many years the magazine has been a meeting place of Protestant, Catholic and Jewish scholars on even ground.

18. A case in point was the First Annual Jewish-Christian Theological Dialogue, sponsored by the Washington Theological Union, The Hebrew Union College, the Anti-Defamation League and the Catholic-Jewish Relations Office of the United States Catholic Conference, held in Washington, March 19–20, 1979, on the subject of *Mission.*

19. Most of the important recent studies are listed in the bibliographical essay, "Judaism on Christianity: Christianity on Judaism," in F. E. Talmage, *Dis-*

putation and Dialogue: Readings in the Jewish Christian Encounter (Ktav/Anti-Defamation League, 1975) 361–390.

20. See the brief survey of the problem in Eugene Fisher, *Faith without Prejudice* (Paulist Press, 1977) 124–140, and in John Pawlikowski, *Catechetics and Prejudice* (Paulist Press, 1973), both of which investigate the teaching materials used in Catholic religious education.

21. Many seminaries already have initiated such programs. Among Catholic seminaries, one can point to Immaculate Conception Seminary of the Archdiocese of Newark and the Catholic Theological Union in Chicago.

22. Jacob Neusner of Brown University has contributed much in this area already with his numerous studies on the form critical and transmission questions of the Talmudic materials. See, in particular, his massive twenty-two-volume study on the Laws of Purity issued between 1974–1977, *A History of the Mishnaic Laws of Purity* (Brill, 1974–1977), and his more recent, *Method and Meaning in Ancient Judaism* (Brown Judaic Studies, 10: Scholars Press, 1979).

23. See in particular the articles of Joseph Blenkinsopp and André Lacocque below, which both treat of the hermeneutical problems between Christian and Jewish interpreters. Also useful is Daniel Patte, *Early Jewish Hermeneutic in Palestine* (SBL Dissertation Series 22, 1975).

24. See the article by Leonard Kravitz below and the chapter by John Pawlikowski, "Jewish Views of Christianity," in his *What Are They Saying About Christian-Jewish Relations?* (Paulist Press, 1979) 69–92.

25. See the article by Monika Hellwig below, and the short survey in Michael McGarry, C.S.P. *Christology after Auschwitz* (Paulist Press, 1977) 56–96.

26. Witness the 2nd Annual Jewish-Christian Dialogue on the subject of "Creation" sponsored by the Washington Theological Union and Hebrew Union College, with the Anti-Defamation League and Catholic-Jewish Relations Office of the United States Catholic Conference, held in New York, May 15, 1980.

27. An excellent presentation of the issues of mission and witness from the Jewish perspective is now found in Helga Croner and Leon Klenicki, eds., *Issues in the Jewish-Christian Dialogue: Jewish Perspectives on Covenant, Mission and Witness*, Stimulus Book (Paulist Press, 1979).

28. A recent attempt to outline an interfaith program of dialogue which places high priority on discussion of biblical problems is Eugene Fisher, "Future Agenda for Catholic-Jewish Relations," *Origins,* Volume 7, #47 (May 11, 1978) 737–743.

PART I
TRENDS IN BIBLICAL RESEARCH

Judaism and
Modern Biblical Research

S. David Sperling

I

Muhammad has the distinction of referring to the Jews as the People of the Book, the book being the Hebrew Bible. Yet, even in the seventh century CE most Jews did not live by that book but rather by the complex of law and tradition which we know as rabbinic Judaism. Though the Bible had ultimately generated that complex, it was by Muhammad's day far more limited in application and scope than the more proximate and living tradition. The very name Torah which originally referred to the Pentateuch had been extended to include Mishna, Talmud, Midrash and even the teachings and exempla of contemporary masters. To "study Torah" meant, more often than not, to study rabbinic literature.

True, Jewish intellectual effort continued to be directed toward the Bible, though it was often motivated by extra-biblical needs. Chief among these were justification of legal rulings, derivation of homiletic, and moral lessons and source material for poets and philosopher-theologians. Nor could Jews ignore the application of Scripture to polemic within and without. Christianity had centuries earlier claimed the Hebrew Bible as its own. In its Greek and Latin garbs, the Hebrew Bible had become the Old Testament of Christendom. Islam assailed the imperfection of the Jewish (and Christian) Scriptures to which it opposed the Koran, revered as God's original revelation. In spite of the continued preoccupation of the Jews with the Hebrew Bible, the medieval period saw the rise of rabbinic

19

study to a higher status. Talmud, especially, appeared to the student to require greater ingenuity than Bible and at the same time to allow for greater flexibility in interpretation. Study of Talmud was also of greater relevance, for it approximated more the socio-political realities of medievalism than did the Bible whose legal material sometimes reached far back into the Bronze Age. Biblical interpretation itself could not ignore rabbinic tradition. Those medieval scholars who insisted on explicating the plain sense of the text were careful to add that their interpretations in no way undermined the authority of the Talmud.

Jewish study of rabbinics maintained its priority for centuries and, within some circles, continues to do so to this day. In traditional religious schools, *yeshivot,* Bible study is generally limited to the youngest students and to penitents (*baale teshuvah*) who are expected rapidly to graduate to Talmud. Outside of these groups however, serious Jewish study of the Bible has emerged as a significant enterprise and is clearly a distinguishing feature of modern Judaism.

Critical study of the Bible is itself a modern phenomenon. Though not without antecedents, modern biblical study came into its own in the early nineteenth century. The pioneering work was done by Christian students of the New Testament, some of whom began to apply scientific method to the study of the Hebrew Bible. Jews only came into contact with this branch of scholarship when they began to attend German universities. Men like Heinrich Graetz who is primarily remembered as an historian, Samuel D. Luzzato, a fine philologist, and Zacharias Frankel and Abraham Geiger, who pioneered in Septuagint studies, were among those to show the results of this renewed Jewish interest. Yet it must be noted that the movement of the *Wissenschaft des Judentums* (Science of Judaism) paid relatively little attention to the Bible and was far more concerned with historiography. Motivated as were these Jews to be regarded as citizens of their own countries, they were more concerned with the history of the Jews in the Gentile world than in the biblical period. Internally as well, each of the ideological factions in nineteenth-century Judaism attempted to demonstrate that its approach was sanctioned by earlier historical trends within Judaism. There was also the matter of availability of research materials. The European libraries contained innumerable hitherto unpublished manuscripts whose very existence had been unknown to Jews. Most of this material was relevant to the study of medievalism and classical rabbinics.

Of no little relevance to the Jewish attitude toward modern biblical studies were the conclusions drawn by its leading exponents. The nineteenth century witnessed the consistent application to the Bible of the techniques of lower and higher criticism. Broadly speaking, lower criticism deals with the establishment of correct texts, higher criticism with literary and historical problems. Jews had traditionally been more comfortable with the first. We may even say that Jewish lower biblical criticism had begun with the promulgation of the Torah in the fifth century BCE.

Ezra was himself the ready scribe of the Torah, most likely influenced by the critical methods of the hallowed Babylonian scribal art. Indeed the many references to scribes in New Testament and early rabbinic sources point to a high degree of concern with textual reliability. Jewish law regulates closely the types of material employed in writing biblical books and even the size and shape of letters. The Middle Ages saw the flowering of Hebrew philological studies particularly in those countries in which the dominant culture was Muslim. The Karaites who denied the authority and accuracy of rabbinic tradition devoted themselves with great zeal to textual and grammatical study of the Bible and may have been among the first Masoretes or "transmitters." Within rabbinism, Jonah ibn Janah (about 995–1050) emended and transposed biblical verses. More guardedly, David Kimhi (about 1110–1170) and Abraham ibn Ezra (1080–1164) also took liberties with the authorized texts, as did Rashi (1040–1105), the most famous of the medieval Jewish exegetes.

Higher criticism was generally avoided. It may be said safely that the founders of rabbinic Judaism recognized scores of higher critical problems, but, like their contemporaries the Church Fathers, they deal with them in a different context. To cite a parade example, the rabbis noted the different divine appellatives in the creation tales of Genesis but interpreted these as references to different attributes of God rather than to distinct literary sources. An exception to this Jewish tendency, though not the only one, was Abraham ibn Ezra who suggested that numerous parts of the Bible could not have been written by Moses.

The first Jewish scholar to attempt a systematic higher criticism of the Bible was the Dutch philosopher Baruch (Benedict) Spinoza (1632–1677). In his *Tractatus Theologico-Politicus,* Spinoza outlined a method of biblical interpretation with the goal of deducing the authors of the various books and the identification and period of their work. He attributed the authorship of the Pentateuch to Ezra and dated the origin of the Canon to work of Pharisees in Hasmonean times. The *Tractatus* had been written in Latin however, and Spinoza died excommunicate. Accordingly, his work did not influence Jewish scholars in his own time nor for generations afterward. The most important modern higher criticism is based on the work of Christian scholars and chiefly on that of Wellhausen.

Julius Wellhausen (1844–1918) did not originate the documentary hypothesis which is associated with his name. He himself acknowledged Wilhelm M. L. de Wette, Leopold George, Wilhelm Vatker, Eduard Reuss and Karl Heinrich Graf as predecessors. It was Wellhausen's synthesis, however, which proved to be the most persuasive and influential. Briefly, the Wellhausen analysis identified four major literary sources in the Pentateuch, none of which is extant in isolation, but which can be distinguished by the literary critic drawing attention to style, vocabulary and preoccupation as well as theological outlook. These are labeled J, E, D and P. The J document used the tetragammaton (German: Jahwe) for God, beginning with the primeval history and referring to God's holy mountain as Sinai. J portrayed God in very anthropomorphic terms. Wellhausen considered the J source to be the most primitive, to be dated to the ninth pre-Christian century. The E document, written about a century later, preferred to designate God as Elohim until Moses learned the name Yahweh and assigned to the holy mountain the name Horeb. Wellhausen felt that E was more spiritualized than J. The D source was to be found almost exclusively in Deuteronomy and consisted mostly of farewell sermons delivered by Moses before his death. The D legislation was clearly aware of the laws of J and E but added the requirement that all cultic observance must be restricted to the Lord's chosen city. Wellhausen followed Graf and de Wette in associating D with Josiah's reform of 621 BCE (2 Kgs 22–23; 2 Chr 34–35). The P document was concerned with worship and the cult and was therefore a Priestly source. Lists of tribes, chronologies and genealogies were basic to P. For Wellhausen P was the latest source, to be dated after the return from the Babylonian exile about 450 BCE. The various sources were combined by different redactors. First the J and E sources were united; later D was added to these. Finally, about 400 BCE, the Pentateuch was completed.

Wellhausen's source analysis has in essentials stood the test of time, in the opinion of this writer. Moreover, it does not contain anything offensive to anyone who does not hold Mosaic authorship of the Pentateuch as an article of religious faith. The great rabbinic scholar David Hoffmann (1843–1921), for example, wrote a two-volume work against Wellhausen's hypothesis, as well as German commentaries on Genesis, Leviticus and Deuteronomy, because he found it necessary to oppose any attempt to undermine the sanctity of the Torah. (It is of interest to note that he applied to his talmudic researches the literary-critical methods which he rejected in biblical criticism.) Yet even non-fundamentalists among early twentieth-century Jewish scholars were cool to the Wellhausen hypothesis because of the history of Israelite religion and Judaism which derived from it.

Wellhausen had utilized his source analysis to reconstruct the religious development described in the Bible. An evolutionist, he concluded that ethical monotheism had evolved gradually out of the animism of the "patriarchal" period, passing on the way through polytheism and henotheism, until it was given its distinctive character under the influence of the prophetic movement. The Pentateuchal sources reflected this movement in which monotheism slowly asserted itself, accompanied by an increasing formalism and legalism. P was the most formal and therefore the latest stage. Indeed, the increased cultic regulations of P were opposed to the "uncommon freshness and naturalness"[1] of early Israelite religion. It was under the influence of P that the three earlier sources were combined with it to form the Torah.

The Pentateuch was thus not "the starting point for the history of ancient Israel"[2] but the end of it. Prophecy belonged to the religion of Israel while the Law belonged to Judaism, "the religious communion which survived the destruction of the nation by the Assyrians and Chaldeans."[3] Wellhausen characterized the Law as

> that artificial product the sacred constitution of Judaism (in which) worship no longer springs from an inner impulse; it has come to be an exercise of religiosity . . . it is a dead work.[4]

The Torah as a canonical book was a product of the legalism of the post-exilic Jewish "church"[5] which was centered around the cult of the second temple. Jewish legalism was contrasted by Wellhausen with the person of Jesus for whom "love is the means, and the community of love the end."[6]

Leaving aside the fact that this picture hardly did justice to the historical Jesus and the early Church, it can easily be read as a frontal attack on Judaism and its practitioners. Not atypical was the reaction of Solomon Schechter, at that time President of the Jewish Theological Seminary in New York and regarded as the major architect of Conservative Judaism, who referred to the higher criticism as the higher antisemitism. Schechter died in 1915, and Pentateuch criticism was not taught at his seminary until more than fifty years after his death.

II

Nonetheless, Jewish scholarship could not ignore higher criticism. Certain Jewish scholars were quite articulate in attempting to reclaim the Hebrew Bible as an object of serious critical study by Jews. Perhaps the most interesting and certainly the most poignant author was Arnold B. Ehrlich whose three-volume commentary appeared between 1899 and 1901.[7] Harry M. Orlinsky has aptly characterized Ehrlich as "an utterly egocentric personality."[8] A recluse who signed his Hebrew name "ibn Boded" (the loner), Ehrlich was a brilliant and highly intuitive linguist who approached his subject with almost missionary zeal.

Such a zeal was not accidental. Ehrlich was well acquainted with the Christian world because for a time he had been a convert to Christianity and an instructor in Franz Delitzsch's missionary Institutum Judaicum, where he had aided Delitzsch in the publication of a Hebrew New Testament. Though Ehrlich's Commentary was dedicated to Delitzsch, "his unforgettable fatherly friend,"[9] it was written in Hebrew "for the sake of my brethren and my people who know only Hebrew, who began as I did."[10] The work, published in New York, often attacked Jewish scholarship as parochial and unenlightened. Nonetheless, Ehrlich's defense of the Jews comes through in his spirited championship of Jewish exegesis of many passages, at the expense of Christian exegesis.

Even while praising Christian scholarship, beginning with Johann Reuchlin, he comments that had it not been true that the Old Testament was revered in the New, "our scriptures would be reviled as we ourselves are."[11] Though Ehrlich's work is essentially a textual commentary, it contains numerous higher critical statements. In the introduction he wrote:

> My brethren hesitate to approach this task. . . . O my brethren, do not sin mortally. The earlier generations were not angels. . . . The *Torah* was given (sic!) in sections. Nay more, there were many years between those sections, sometimes as many as two hundred years.[12]

As pointed out by reviewers, Ehrlich refused to be chronologically precise and often contented himself with describing passages as "early," "very early" or "late." Non-Jewish scholars are better acquainted with Ehrlich's seven-volume German commentary which appeared between 1908 and 1914.[13]

Ehrlich had seen himself as a solitary laborer and had contrasted his efforts in biblical studies both with the old-style rabbinic scholars and the medievalists of *Wissenschaft des Judentums* "who waste their days in discussing worthless poems and poets."[14] Fortunately, Ehrlich's perception was not an accurate description of reality. In 1904 Abraham Kahana initiated a project which lasted over a quarter of a century and resulted in a series which remains the only Hebrew multi-volume critical commentary as of this writing.[15] Though never completed, the many volumes published made thorough use of the ancient versions, of ancient Near Eastern sources, of comparative Semitic as it was practiced early in this century, and of the documentary hypothesis. The list of contributors to this series is extremely impressive, especially considering the youthfulness of some of the participants. We may mention Samuel Kraus, Hirsch Perez Chajes and Felix Perles. The young Moses Hirsch Segal was later to be a professor of Bible at the Hebrew University of Jerusalem. Yet another commentator was Max Margolis, perhaps the most eminent American Bible scholar of the early twentieth century and the editor-in-chief of the 1917 Jewish Publication Society's translation of the Bible.

The generation which came to maturity at the beginning of the twentieth century may be considered the first one of serious modern Jewish Bible scholars. We may single out three of its representatives, all of whom were European-trained but reached prominence in Israel. Naphtali Herz Tur-Sinai (Harry Torczyner, 1886–1975) was an ingenious and sometimes overly ingenious linguist who published extensively in German, Hebrew and English. He rejected the Wellhausen documentary hypothesis in favor of a more radical one of his own. Tur-Sinai posited an ancient historical framework, no longer extant, which provided a narrative setting for books which no longer have one. Thus Psalms, for example, allegedly belonged to the narrative biography of David and Proverbs to that of Solomon. Any serious scholar must take Tur-Sinai's researches into account, up to a point. Perhaps most convincing are his several books on Job in Hebrew, English and German.

Another prominent member of this first generation was Umberto M. D. Cassuto (1883–1957), scion of an old Italian-Jewish family and a product of both the University of Florence and the rabbinical seminary of that city. Most of his early scholarly activity was in the field of Italian Jewish history. From the age of forty, however, he devoted himself almost exclusively to the Bible and the ancient Near East. Cassuto loved Dante and bel canto. This appreciation of lyricism and poetic style led him to reject many of the rigid canons of the documentary hypothesis. Though personally an observant Jew, he was not a fundamentalist. Rather, he made provision for the operation of oral tradition in ancient Israelite literary transmission and argued that many of the surviving biblical prose texts had been composed originally as poetic epics. Cassuto convincingly reconstructed the ancient Hebrew combat myth which dealt with the conflict between the Creator and the chaotic sea god. By utilizing Ugaritic poems of ancient Syria, biblical poetry and rabbinic legend, he was able to demonstrate the survival of this myth over a two thousand year period. Extremely provocative in its implications was Cassuto's hypothesization of a grand early Israelite epic which was closer in its religious world view to Canaanite paganism than is the literature of the Hebrew Bible. Such a source could account for the strong similarities between the myths of ancient Canaan and the writings of those biblical authors, such as Jeremiah, who are most inimical to the vestiges of the pre-Israelite heritage.

Perhaps the most influential scholar of the period under discussion was Yehezkel Kaufmann (1889–1963). Born in the Ukraine, Kaufmann studied in *yeshivah* in Odessa, earned a Ph.D. at the University of Berne and lived for some ten years afterward in Berlin, emigrating to Palestine in 1928. Among his voluminous writings we must mention his eight-volume history.[16] In that work, he accepted the basic source division which Wellhausen had advocated but took issue with its chronology and, more significantly, with the reconstruction of Israelite religious development which Wellhausen had advanced. Kaufmann attempted to show that the Priestly source (P) was actually older than the Deuteronomic one (D), and that it could serve as a useful tool in describing pre-exilic Israelite religion. Furthermore, Kaufmann advanced the daring theory that Israelite religion had been monotheistic from the time of Moses and that the masses in ancient Israel had understood it as such. What, then, was the meaning of all the prophetic fulminations against idolatry which to Wellhausen had indicated that vast abyss between the popular religion and the ethical monotheism of the prophets? In Kaufmann's view, the prophets were attacking not idolatry but a vestigial fetishism which their idealism could not tolerate. Indeed, ancient Israel no longer understood true idolatry and its rich mythology and cult. Consequently, the prophets denounced not the gods but only "stick and stone."

The reader will perceive immediately that both Wellhausen and Kaufmann greatly overstated their cases. The great German critic of unquestioned genius had approached his material with an evolutionary scheme not at all derived from the documents. Kaufmann for his part committed the methodological error of denying the explicit witness of the very documents on which he attempted to base his reconstruction of the history of Israelite religion. Nor was each man totally disinterested. It is clear from his writings that Wellhausen had little sympathy for Judaism. Kaufmann in contrast was a strong believer in the Jewish sense of mission and in the relevance of the prophetic message for all time. His strong sense of Jewish nationalism comes through elsewhere, in his commentaries to the biblical books of Joshua and Judges. What both men shared to a fault was a tendency to deal overly with Israel in isolation and to limit their researches too much to the Bible. To put the matter a bit differently, it is always possible that, even in the most successful literary criticism, one considers only the growth and production of a written composition rather than the events described in that composition. Neither Wellhausen nor Kaufmann dealt sufficiently with the evidence of Near Eastern archaeology, which has come into its own in the twentieth century.

III

Archaeology serves as a useful counterpoint to the conclusions of biblical criticism because it enables us to go beyond the limits of the Bible itself. Many books and articles refer to "Old Testament times," "the biblical period," "biblical archaeology," and the like. Though of value, such terminology may mislead the uninitiated into ignoring the basic question about the importance of the Bible during the period in which its major documents were composed: Were these documents of sufficient importance to characterize their period of composition by their name, or does their viewpoint reflect that of a small though clearly articulate minority? It would appear from application of literary criticism that the components of the Hebrew Bible played little prescriptive part in Israelite life during the first half of the first millennium BCE and became "holy scripture" only during the Second Commonwealth. Accordingly, we require more direct evidence from that period and earlier in order to reconstruct extrabiblical reality.

By archaeology we mean the study of artifacts or material remains of the past. These fall broadly into two groups, written and non-written remains. In general, archaeologists of the later twentieth century deal with the non-written material, leaving epigraphers and philologists to study the written. Art historians, ancient historians and comparative religionists as well as biblical scholars evaluate the finds within the context of their own disciplines. Needless to say, there is much overlap in the above areas.

All too rarely do we encounter the ideal archaeological situation in which an artifact is accompanied by sufficient literary and/or pictorial data to render its identification and significance certain beyond all doubt. Scholars are therefore often dependent on the Bible, at least as a point of reference. To take one example, excavations at Lachish revealed that one stratum of occupation had been destroyed in the mid-thirteenth century BCE. No Israelite victory stele has been found there, yet the event is plausibly connected with the Bible's conquest-traditions in the Book of Joshua, especially since comparative analysis of stratification in the excavated sites of Bethel and Hazor, which appear in the same Joshua conquest-traditions, reveals that these cities were also destroyed within the same period. Similarly, excavators at Samaria were aided by the biblical reference that the city was first established as the Northern royal capital by King Omri in the seventh year of his reign, as well as by notices in the annals of the kings of Assyria.

In some cases archaeological evidence can answer historical questions raised by the biblical narrative. That King Sennacherib failed to take Jerusalem is maintained by the Bible and admitted guardedly by the Assyrian himself in the account of his third campaign. In contrast, we know that if "Daniel" was thrown into a den of lions it was surely by no "Darius the Mede," who turns out to be imaginary. At other times, archaeological evidence is more indirect but nonetheless useful, by providing a corrective to the Bible's often cavalier treatment of problems that may be most interesting to moderns. Thus the Book of Kings may dismiss a long and successful royal reign by saying that King so-and-so did evil in the sight of the Lord and directing us to the now lost alleged royal archives of ancient Israel for detailed information. The same book may, in contrast, dwell at great length on the incredible feats of men of God who brought rain, revived the dead and split the sea. The great classical prophets Isaiah and Jeremiah do not concern themselves with the geopolitical and economic considerations which brought Babylonians and Assyrians to invade Israel. For them it was sufficient that Israel had sinned and that invaders were the instruments of divine reprisal. In like manner, the Bible has little positive to say of the rich civilizations and cultural achievements of ancient Canaan, Syria, Egypt and Asia Minor.

Naturally, the application of archaeology to biblical problems has severe limitations. In some cases this is due to the concern of biblical narrative with individuals or tiny groups. There is the further complication of the country's checkered military history. Perhaps the most severe limitation of archaeology and modern critical method in general is the inability to deal with the crucial questions of faith on which the biblical worldview is predicated. That Moses was an historical character is a probability.

That Isaiah lived is a virtual certainty. That the first saw God face to face and the second only his train filling the temple is a matter of faith or the lack thereof.

This recognition should not deter us from utilizing archaeology to answer questions about the beliefs and practices of ancient Israel. In Wellhausen's view we could have no genuine reminiscences of the pre-monarchic period, for literacy was itself an innovation in that time. By the end of the decade following the publication of Wellhausen's *Prolegomena,* the Amarna letters had been discovered in Egypt. Nearly three hundred of these letters had been written in what are now Israel, Lebanon and Syria, about half in Israel proper. The area has since revealed the existence of five alphabets known prior to the Israelite settlement. One of these, the Ugaritic, was utilized to write religious texts in northern Syria as early as 1500 BCE. It is from Ugarit that we learn of the *rb khnm,* "chief priest," whose office prior to 1800 undermines seriously Wellhausen's contention that the analogous Israelite office of "high priest" was a post-exilic innovation retrojected anachronistically to the pre-exilic period. In fact, the elaborate character of the Old Babylonian sacerdotal structure centuries prior to the Israelite period should warn us against construing such institutions simply as products of theocratic legalism. To take another case, the P source devotes much space to a tabernacle which allegedly accompanied the biblical wilderness wanderings under Moses. Wellhausen maintained that the tabernacle in actuality represented the central sanctuary demanded by Josiah's reform of the late seventh century BCE and was implemented successfully only in the post-exilic centuries. Kaufmann argued that the biblical tabernacle might be a *bamah* or "high place," a type of cultic installation outlawed by the Deuteronomic reform of Josiah. The discovery in the Negev of the temple which stood on the northwest corner of the Israelite citadel of Arad has substantiated Kaufmann's theory. The excavations of Yohanan Aharoni have shown that the Arad temple may have been constructed as early as the eleventh century BCE and that its altar corresponds exactly to the measurements of the wilderness tabernacle. Ostraca discovered at the site bear the names of priestly families known from the Bible. The temple was destroyed in the late seventh century BCE, almost certainly in connection with the Josianic reform. We may then suppose that if the wilderness sanctuary of P was an anachronistic retrojection, it was a retrojection of an early settlement or monarchic institution rather than of a post-exilic one. Furthermore, Arad may clinch Kaufmann's argument for the antiquity of P. It may demonstrate that D required the destruction of that very type of sanctuary to which P ascribed

Mosaic origin. It may even be ventured that since the Arad temple is an original Israelite construction distinct from Canaanite culture, its origins might be of pre-settlement times.

By the time of Wellhausen's death in 1918, so much of the ancient Near East had been revealed that the Wellhausen school should have modified its hypothesis concerning the primitive origins and linear evolution of Israelite religion.

For his part, though, Kaufmann had less justification for ignoring, or failing to take into serious account, data which undermined his argumentation. Yet he continued to maintain that Israelite apostolic prophecy was an entirely unique phenomenon, in the face of the formally similar phenomenon known among the Western Semites of Mari in Eastern Syria in the eighteenth century BCE. Furthermore, our greater knowledge of Near Eastern religions has enabled scholars to explain numerous biblical passages as mythological allusions. This presents a serious challenge to Kaufmann's contention that Israel was ignorant of the rich mythology of its surroundings. Similarly, Kaufmann had attempted to dismiss the cult of the queen of heaven, known from the Book of Jeremiah, as a rather homespun affair. Yet the very features which he singled out have been shown by the Israeli scholar Moshe Weinfeld to characterize the cult of the queen of heaven throughout the Aramaeo-Assyrian world. In light of the above facts the numerous mother goddess figures which have been found in Israelite areas may be more than the simple charms of the superstitious. It may be interjected, though, that the widespread Israelite-Canaanite religious syncretism subscribed to by some scholars is supported by neither literary criticism nor archaeology.

IV

Form criticism, associated with the name of its founder Hermann Gunkel (1862–1932), is, like source criticism, a method of literary analysis. In form criticism, though, an attempt is made to go beyond the written texts to any earlier oral stage which might be related to a life-event. Gunkel realized that it was necessary to examine biblical texts in the light of literary productions of the ancient Near East. In so doing he was able to demonstrate that certain genres revealed literary patterns characteristic of the life-situation which had generated them. Among the types he identified were community hymns, community laments, cult songs, imprecatory psalms, prophetic sayings, and so on. Each of these types has its own structure, though mixed types are found as well. Thus funeral hymns would have a different structure than wedding songs, but one might more reasonably expect crossover between individual and community laments. Gunkel compared cultic and mythological motifs in Israel with those in Egypt and Mesopotamia in order to outline the similarities and differences between Israelite and non-Israelite culture. Carefully applied, form-criticism yields illuminating results and has shown itself particularly effective in dealing with the smaller units characteristic of oral tradition such as the prayers in the Book of Psalms.

The obvious advantage of form-criticism is that it permits a synthesis of literary and cultic data. Furthermore, in drawing upon Near Eastern literature outside of the Bible the results are less subjective. In Mesopotamian prayer literature, for example, the types or *Gattungen* are often marked as "prayers of lifting the hand," "incantation," "prayer of appeasing the heart," "prayer to avert portended evil," "incantation hymn," and the like. Israelite literature is generally not so marked but similarities in structure and phraseology to undisputed Mesopotamian literary types can help to isolate particular Israelite genres.

Form-criticism is not without its pitfalls. It may first be noted that it tends to minimize the role of individual literary creativity. Secondly, in drawing evidence cross-culturally one may make unwarranted inferences with regard to one or the other. A particular pattern may indicate one type of life-event in Mesopotamia and a completely different one in Israel. Perhaps the weakest link in the chain has been the highly imaginative reconstruction of the Israelite ritual calendar with the hypothesization of festivals whose existence can scarcely be demonstrated. In general, contemporary Jewish scholars have availed themselves of form-critical techniques to identify literary genres but have been conservative in their attempts to reconstruct the cultic occasions which produced them. A notable example of this tendency is Weinfeld's work[17] which disproves Gerhard von Rad's contention that the arrangement of much of the Book of Deuteronomy reflects

> a liturgical ceremony, the framework of a religious celebration in the center of which was the proclamation of commandments and the commitment of Israel to the intent of Yahweh's law.[18]

By careful attention to form-critical technique, Weinfeld demonstrated that the book emanates from a scribal circle within the Israelite court.

All too often form-critics have ignored the caveat of Theodore H. Gaster. In his study of Psalm 29, Gaster identified the work as a

> form of the laudation of the victorious god which formed part of the seasonal pantomime of the New Year Festival. . . . This in no way implies that the seasonal pantomime actually obtained in Israelite cultus as has been so frequently supposed. All we are suggesting is that certain hymnodic patterns derived from the earlier usages survived in literary convention.[19]

V

Philology and text interpretation have perhaps been the areas in which Jewish biblical scholarship has excelled. This has been true both of scholars for whom the Bible has been the primary concern as well as of those who have researched in comparative Semitics and Near Eastern languages and cultures and then applied the results of some of those labors to the Hebrew Bible.

In the first category we may single out two individuals who could be viewed as the elder statesmen of American Jewish Bible scholarship, both of whom are Canadians by birth, Harry M. Orlinsky and Harold L. Ginsberg. An outstanding philologist, Orlinsky has made enormous contributions to the study of the Septuagint and the Masoretic text. He has always been a scholarly individualist. Thus he was able to demonstrate the textual unreliability of the St. Mark's Isaiah Scroll which had been all but universally hailed as a source of precious Hebrew variants to the received text of Isaiah. In like manner, he has repeatedly pointed out the severe shortcomings of the text-critical apparatus of the *Biblia Hebraica*,[20] a standard scholarly tool in most circles. Orlinsky's independence made him an early critic of the "amphictyony theory" of the German scholars Albrecht Alt and Martin Noth. An ingenious attempt to explain early Israelite tribal organization, the theory was for a time accepted as virtual fact. Orlinsky proved that it had no basis. He has also maintained that the famous "Suffering Servant" passages in Isaiah have been generally misinterpreted. Of special significance is the fact that Orlinsky's work has been made available to non-specialists. He was the only Jewish scholar to serve on the Protestant committee which produced the Revised Standard Version of the Old Testament. Subsequently, he served as editor-in-chief of the Jewish Publication Society's translation of the Torah (1962, revised 1965) and co-editor of the recently published second volume of that translation of the prophets (1978).

H. L. Ginsberg (as he prefers to sign) has published extensively on biblical subjects, Aramaic, Phoenician, Ugaritic, and comparative Semitics. His penetration of texts goes beyond the words to content and meaning. It is difficult to approach Isaiah, Job, Daniel, Ecclesiastes or Hosea without referring to Ginsberg's articles, monographs and special studies devoted to those books. One is always struck by his common sense as well. Thus he accounts for the Aramaisms in the Book of Job by the simple and convincing observation that the characters are "Easterners," and we know from Genesis that "Easterners" speak Aramaic. Job is, then, a dialect story. Much of Ginsberg's research has come before a wide reading public. Editor of the Bible division of *Encyclopaedia Judaica,* he served with Orlinsky on the Jewish Publication Society's Torah translation and was editor-in-chief of the volume on the prophets. Ginsberg is also the author of the introduction to the Society's edition of *The Five Megilloth and Jonah* (1969) and *Isaiah* (1973).

A prominent scholar in the second category was Ephraim A. Speiser (1902–1965) who pioneered in the archaeology of Iraq. He brought the Hurrians, a forgotten people, back into history. Though most of his work dealt with the languages and cultures of Mesopotamia, he seldom lost sight of the Hebrew Bible. His commentary on Genesis synthesized literary criticism and the results of his own researches and those of others in ancient Near East studies. Along with Orlinsky and Ginsberg, Speiser was a contributor to the Jewish Publication Society's Torah. In addition, he was editor of the first volume of the *The World History of the Jewish People.*

VI

An extremely important role has been played by the discovery of written archaeological sources bearing on the Bible. In 1918, the year of Wellhausen's death, no one could have suspected the existence of Ugaritic. But nine years later, following a chance discovery by a Syrian farmer, French archaeologists unearthed the ancient city of Ugarit. Inhabited by a Semitic population as early as 2050 BCE, the city was destroyed about eight hundred years later. Thus, its history ended just about the time that datable Israelite history began. Situated far in the North, on approximately the same latitude as Cyprus, Ugarit was a rich port city with a diverse population. In addition to the local Ugaritic language, scribes wrote in Akkadian, Sumerian and Hurrian. Relations with the Hittites, Egyptians and Aegean islanders are well documented. The decipherment of Ugaritic has proved of extreme value to biblical scholarship. Ugaritic is sometimes strikingly similar to Hebrew and Phoenician. More striking, however, is the poetic technique employed by the ancient Syrian bards which, like biblical Hebrew, relies heavily on synonymous parallelism. Indeed, as shown by Umberto Cassuto and Moshe Held, the very pairs of words used in synonymous parallelism are often the same in Ugaritic and Hebrew, a sure indication of cultural continuity between Israelite creativity and its predecessors. This is especially interesting because of the great distance between Northern Syria and the Israelite heartland. We thus have evidence for a certain uniformity of literary culture in the entire area occupied by the modern states of Israel, Lebanon and Syria.

In addition to the literary material, scholars have studied cultic terminology at Ugarit, much of which is reflected in the biblical sacrificial practice underlining its genuinely antique character. Ugaritic legal texts, mostly in the Akkadian language, have provided the background for understanding some biblical institutions, notably land tenure and the monarchy.

Perhaps most important to us is the information concerning Ugaritic religion, from which we can derive the Canaanite point of view. In the texts and artistic representations we find the heroes of the Canaanites, who for the Bible are villains. Baal appears as powerful and valiant. His rain and thunder provide prosperity to the masses. Asherah and Astarte are powerful goddesses reflecting the female aspects of divinity. An examination of the Ugaritic texts shows that El, head of the pantheon, had both his name and his reputation for beneficence and wise counsel usurped by the God of Israel. Yahweh usurped many of Baal's attributes as well. Baal was a god of thunder and fertility, elements which would not have been very important in the Israelite pre-settlement cult but became increasingly so under the monarchy. Yahweh even took over from Baal the epithet "cloud-rider." It was H. L. Ginsberg who demonstrated that Psalm 29 preserves an ancient Baal storm-theophany reworked to serve the needs of Israelite cult.[21]

It may be noted that Jewish scholars have been in the forefront of Ugaritic studies. Ginsberg's *Ugaritic Writings,* published in Hebrew in 1936, was a pioneering breakthrough in Ugaritic grammar and text explication. His two translations of the Keret legend remain unsurpassed. The standard Ugaritic textbook was written by Cyrus Gordon. Umberto Cassuto, Moshe Held and Samuel Lowenstamm have made highly significant contributions to Ugaritic lexicography, grammar, and text explication and have illumined many a biblical obscurity by recourse to relevant Ugaritic parallels.

Another source of written archaeological material with great relevance to the Bible is Tel Hariri, known anciently as Mari, situated some fifteen miles north of the modern border between Iraq and Syria. This Syrian site was founded at the end of the fourth millennium BCE and was ruled by west-Semitic dynasties from the last quarter of the nineteenth century through the first half of the eighteenth. The names of individuals mentioned in the thousands of Mari documents composed in Akkadian are often very similar to biblical name types, especially those which the Bible associates with the patriarchal and pre-monarchic periods. Though this in no way demonstrates the historicity of these biblical traditions, it may indicate their great antiquity.

Some specific Mari institutions merit special mention. The method of concluding a covenant known from Genesis 15 and Jeremiah 34 is paralleled closely by a Mari practice. As in other early west-Semitic sources, the notion of "the God of the fathers," a divinity to whom offspring refer, usually anonymously, occurs at Mari. This usage is also attested in the Hebrew Bible in documents describing the pre-settlement period. Of major importance is the phenomenon of apostolic prophecy. The Mari letters have revealed the existence there of male and female ecstatics who delivered prophecies prefaced by the claim, "the god has sent me," much in the manner of the Israelite prophets. Thus far, none of the letters has told us of any individuals who might be compared to an Isaiah or a Jeremiah. Yet the presence of the institution at so early a date among an ethnically related people is surely of significance for the history of Israelite prophecy. To put the matter in perspective, it must be recalled that the great Hebrew classical prophets were not themselves representative of the prophetic profession, as may be seen clearly from the books of Jeremiah, Amos and Kings.

From Tel Atshana in Turkey come the documents of ancient Alalakh, written mostly in the eighteenth and fifteenth centuries BCE in the Akkadian language. Legal documents from Alalakh show that a father could ignore the natural birth sequence in determining filial succession, a situation which obtains in the narratives of Genesis but is outlawed by Deuteronomy. Of considerable interest is the inscription discovered on the statue of King Idrimi. Though written in Akkadian, it is a far cry from the literature of Mesopotamia, the home of the Akkadian language. Rather, its style and motifs resemble biblical writings. Scholars have noted the reunion motif which recalls the Joseph story, as well as the flight and return of the royal pretender which reminds the reader of David's exploits. Outside of the Bible it is rare in Near Eastern ancient literature to find as much attention paid to personality in narratives of royal accomplishment.

Mesopotamian civilization was the single most significant cultural influence in the ancient Near East. Most of its literary productions were composed in Akkadian, a Semitic language, itself strongly influenced by non-Semitic Sumerian. From its center in Iraq, Mesopotamia disseminated its scripts, languages, and literatures. Some of the best known older discoveries in Mesopotamia include the legal code of King Hammurapi of Babylon from the eighteenth century BCE with many parallels to biblical law, the Gilgamesh epic which includes a flood-story to which the biblical Noah tales are closely related, and the Babylonian creation story *Enuma Elish*. Less well known to non-specialists are more recent publications. We may mention the Sumerian law code of Lipit-Ishtar of Isin, a century earlier than Hammurapi, and the Akkadian laws from the city of Eshnunna. The Eshnunna laws are in some instances verbally so close to the covenant code of the Book of Exodus as to render the reader incredulous. A major contribution to the Mesopotamian background of the Bible was the publication in 1969 of the Atra-hasis epic. This Old Babylonian tale proceeded from the creation to the flood in the same manner as the Genesis narrative, indicating that the Bible preserved a much earlier literary tradition in which both motifs were joined.

The covenant theology of the Bible has received considerable attention in recent years. It is well known that the Bible conceives of the relationship between God and Israel as a covenant or treaty in which proper adherence is rewarded and violation severely punished. Wellhausen had maintained that our extant biblical covenants with their moral prescriptions could not antedate classical prophecy but depend upon its influence. This view can no longer be maintained. Political treaties emanating from the Hittite Empire no later than the thirteenth century BCE, composed in Turkey in Hittite and Akkadian, outline a pattern of suzerain-vassal relationships which many of the biblical covenants appear to follow. The publication of the vassal treaties of the Assyrian king Esarhaddon who lived in the seventh century BCE illustrated the continuity of covenant patterns and demonstrated the extent of late Assyrian influence on the scribal circles which produced Deuteronomy. More recently, Moshe Weinfeld proved that the biblical covenants of God with Abraham and David depend on Akkadian and Hittite covenants of grant.

Likewise within the Mesopotamian orbit, the excavations of Tel Mardikh, ancient Ebla, have been much in the news. Ebla was a Syrian city of great prominence in the late third millennium BCE. Most of the tablets are in Sumerian, though a very large number are written in a hitherto unknown Semitic language whose actual affinities have yet to be determined. As of this writing, the amount of published texts is very small and consists in the main of geographic and proper names. Some names contain the element *Ya* which some have connected with the divine name Yahweh. Still others have claimed that Ebla provides further background for the patriarchal narratives of Genesis. Further comment will have to await more detailed publications.

The eminent Egyptologist John Wilson once noted that the major influence of Egypt upon the Hebrews was negative. Nonetheless, Wilson and others have shown strong similarities between Hebrew and Egyptian wisdom-literature, as well as between Egyptian love-poetry and the Song of Songs. The heretic Pharaoh Akh-en-aton wrote a beautiful hymn to the sun-disc, remarkably similar to Psalm 104. The Egyptian creation by Ptah and his words cannot fail to remind any reader of the first chapter of Genesis.

From Egypt, too, come the archives from Elephantine dated in the fifth century BCE. Located near present-day Aswan, these documents in the Aramaic language have revealed the life of an early Jewish diaspora community, distant from Jerusalem but in contact with her ruling authorities. The Elephantine documents include the oldest Jewish marriage contracts (*ketubot*) as well as records of sales and transfers of property. Remarkably enough, the language of these documents employs terminology, much of it of Akkadian origin, which centuries later was to become common in the time of the Mishnah and Talmud, though unattested in the Hebrew Bible.

Of no small fascination is the religion of these early diaspora Jews. They maintained a temple which included animal sacrifices, either in ignorance or defiance of the Josianic reform, until its destruction by the rival Egyptian priesthood devoted to the god Khnub. Though the Elephantine Jews worshiped Yahu (short form for Yahweh), this did not prevent them from adoring other divinities, one an apparent combination of Yahu and the Canaanite goddess Anat.

An extremely interesting literary find at Elephantine was the oldest extant version of *The Words of Ahiqar.* The book contains two parts: the life of the wise Ahiqar, vizier to high Assyrian kings, followed by sayings or epigrams reminiscent of the Book of Proverbs and of ancient Near East wisdom literature in general. In the life-section, the reader finds a tale of a betrayed, loving stepfather and his ruthless stepson who will do anything to rise to power in the court. In the end, justice triumphs and we may discern echoes of the Joseph tale and of the later Book of Esther and even the Arabian Nights. The Jews of Elephantine, who were well acquainted with political intrigue, had good reason to enjoy this book despite its clear pagan features. Indeed, the Jews of Elephantine left no Pentateuch fragments. We may note further that Passover, alone among all the Israelite festivals, was observed in this colony. Elephantine Jews intermarried with non-Jews. In at least one case, however, the offspring of such a marriage have names witnessing to Yahweh worship.

The perceptive reader will note that most of the written material mentioned thus far has been found outside the very area which produced the Hebrew Bible. Indeed, relatively few written archaeological remains have survived the centuries, owing to a number of factors. Most important have been the relative poverty and backwardness of ancient Israel, the fragile nature of the writing materials, and the climate. The student who includes Bible within his purview of the ancient Near East must draw on material often distant chronologically and geographically. Accordingly almost any written document from the Syria-Jordan-Lebanon-Israel area of the late second or first millennium BCE, coming as it does from the same ethnolinguistic area as the Bible, may be expected to advance our understanding. We may mention the numerous Phoenician inscriptions, the ninth-century Moabite stone, the Lachish letters, the Gezer calendar, the Siloam inscription and the Arad letters. Among the most famous finds from the Israel-Jordan area are the scrolls from the area of the Dead Sea. Most of these documents are of considerable importance for the study of Palestinian Judaism and the pre-history of Christianity in the Hellenistic Roman period. For the student of Hebrew Bible, however, they provide our earliest examples of pre-Christian biblical texts. These include a Psalm scroll, a complete Isaiah scroll, part of Leviticus in the paleo-Hebrew script, part of Ezekiel and fragments of every biblical Hebrew book but Esther. Important Septuagint finds have been made there, in addition to a targum of Job and a free Aramaic paraphrase of Genesis. There are also portions of apocryphal works which did not become part of the Hebrew Bible. Among these are parts of a Hebrew Book of Jubilees and an Aramaic Enoch.

Having surveyed the more important methods and tools in contemporary biblical research and drawn attention to the work of some of the leading Jewish scholars, we may now outline some traits which may be said to characterize Jewish biblical scholarship.

VII

The very involvement of Jewish scholars in Bible scholarship is significant, for, as we have seen, biblical studies in the modern period began as a Christian enterprise. In some circles biblical scholarship is still considered a mark of heterodoxy. In the United States, biblical criticism is taught as a matter of course only at the Conservative, Reform and Reconstructionist seminaries, while Pentateuch criticism was avoided for most of the history of the Jewish Theological Seminary. The Orthodox Jewish seminaries do not teach biblical criticism at all. In general, Orthodox Jews in America, Israel and elsewhere have remained on the periphery of biblical scholarship. Somewhat encouraging is the on-going publication of a Hebrew Bible commentary, sponsored by the Orthodox Rabbi Kook Institute in Israel, which draws on the disciplines of archaeology, philology and history, to the extent that these do not oppose the Jewish tradition.

For Israeli scholars in particular, the reclaiming of the Bible is related to the reclamation of Jewish nationhood. For an earlier generation the results of higher criticism were often viewed as a means of undermining the struggle for Jewish legitimacy in a Christian world. The political reality of the State of Israel has given a greater sense of personal security to Jews in all parts of the world. For many, the land of Israel has become a fulfillment of Judaism's traditional expectations. It is not surprising, then, that contemporary Israeli scholarship excels, in addition to archaeology, in geography, the study of flora and fauna, and military history.

Contemporary Jewish Bible scholarship, as distinct from Christian, is generally more concerned with its antecedents. Characteristically, articles by Jewish scholars in a 1978 Festschrift for H. L. Ginsberg extensively cited Rashi, Abravanel, and ibn Ezra, as well as talmudic and midrashic sources, though these were cited as resources rather than authorities.

Jewish scholarship is also quite conscious of the contributions to philology offered by later dialects of Hebrew. It is now undisputed that the Hebrew of the Mishnah and early Midrash was not an artificial academic dialect but a later development of classical Hebrew. Rabbinic sources have thus been rendered philologically more legitimate. In this vein it may be remarked that the revival of Hebrew as a spoken and written language in the contemporary world has made easier and more natural the acquisition of biblical Hebrew.

An important trend in contemporary Jewish biblical scholarship is the concentration on the structure of the individual literary units, i.e., the books of the Bible. Given the accepted results of the literary-critical method, scholars are asking increasingly about the principles which determined a book's final form. Some remarks by Moshe Greenberg, with due credit to his predecessors may serve as a programmatic statement. Greenberg defines a book as

> an organization of literary units meant to convey a complex ideational message. . . . By ideational message we do not mean the mind of the author—his ideology, his world view, or even his intention, but only what is found in the components of the book and implied by the manner of their disposition. While extrinsic information may bear on the message, and the ideology or historical background of the author may offer clues to the meaning of elements in the book, the primary object of understanding is the book's own message, and that must be gathered in the final analysis from the book itself.[22]

Greenberg notes further that since the recognition of the composite nature of the Pentateuch,

> attention has been diverted from the textual entity transmitted by tradition to its newly analyzed hypothetically attested datum. . . . It alone is the undoubted product of Israelite creativity.[23]

The phrase "Israelite creativity" would appear to be a deliberate rejoinder to Wellhausen and his spiritual successors who viewed negatively the work of redaction, considering it the labor of second-class minds.

The approach described by Greenberg is most hospitable to Jewish scholarship because it facilitates the synthesis of traditional Jewish exegesis and modern critical method. The rabbis from the first century onward were for the most part believers in the unity of Scripture as a whole and in the literary integrity of material to which tradition had long ascribed single authorship. Working from this belief, these scholars sought to establish literary and associative connections with the several books and among them.

Naturally, the rabbinic connections were often far-fetched. Nonetheless, scholars familiar with the associative approach may employ them as a corrective to the atomistic approach of literary-critical analysis. Rabbinic commentary on the Bible is useful for another reason. The rabbis were not unaware of inconsistencies and contradictions inhering in the Bible. Often they employ these difficulties in the service of their homilies and legal rulings. The perceptive modern scholar may often find that the rabbinic comments draw attention to difficulties which he might otherwise have overlooked. Furthermore the rabbis cited in Talmud and Midrash appear to have committed most of Scripture to memory. They often associated verses widely separated in the written texts. On occasion these associations prove most illuminating for critical biblical research.

The ability to recognize the integrity of the biblical books has far-reaching ramifications in contemporary Jewish-Christian dialogue. The canonical books of the New Testament reflect varied Christian viewpoints in the early Church. Yet, they agree on the basic premise that in the person of Jesus Christ the Old Testament has been fulfilled. With the suppression of the Gnostics, the Church was able to contain the Old Testament by interpreting it in the light of the New. The Jews for their part disregarded the advice of Eusebius to burn their own Scriptures but sought instead to find in them the underpinnings for rabbinic Judaism. The second-century martyr Rabbi Akiba had dismissed the older view that two Torahs, a written and an oral, had been given to Israel. He argued, rather, that the oral was to be derived from the written. Needless to say, the Synagogue had at least one advantage: though Christians had taken Hebrew Scripture as their own, the Jews had not reciprocated by taking the Christian. Jews, generally, did not read the New Testament.

VIII

Perhaps the greatest recognition brought about by contemporary biblical scholarship is the realization that the bulk of the Hebrew Bible, with the exception of the latest books, reflects a religious viewpoint which is not Jewish, as Wellhausen claimed—echoing in an ironic way the rabbinic viewpoint—nor is it Christian, as the New Testament would have it. The biblical books, rather, reflect certain tendencies in that Near Eastern religion which is conventionally termed "Israelite." By examining the biblical books with attention to their integrity, we may outline some of the major principles of "biblical religion" within the "Israelite" tradition.

The major object of worship in biblical religion is Yahweh, usually translated as "Lord" but meaning originally "Creator." He is known by other names as well, such as El, Shaddai, Elohim, Adonai and numerous epithets, some of which belonged originally to other divinities. Though all of the biblical books agree that Yahweh alone is to be worshiped by Israelites, they disagree on the question of his unique divine existence. Indeed, some biblical sources require the existence of other divinities conquered by Yahweh or otherwise subservient to him. The Book of Deuteronomy credits Yahweh with instituting astral worship for the benefit of the Gentiles (4:19).

Religious authority in biblical religion is vested in particular individuals. Our sources identify different classes of priests, all male, and prophets male and female. Affiliation with the priesthood required some claim to particular ancestry, though the sources differ with regard to particulars. As far as we can tell, personality was not a consideration. In contrast the prophetic calling depended more on personality than on lineage. We do not know of a single case in which a prophetic parent was succeeded by a child similarly endowed. The Bible vilifies the sons of Samuel and tells us no more of the children of Isaiah and Moses than their names.

The practice of biblical religion was geographically limited. Land outside of Israel was considered impure. The worship of Yahweh was not only a requirement for an Israelite but a privileged link to his tenure in the promised land. Exile from the land was exile from the divine presence.

The moral canvas was limited as well. Reward and punishment were promised by the Bible, but all such recompense was limited to this world. With the exception of the concept of the Day of the Lord, which would be either darkness or light, depending on whether we believe Amos and Malachi or their detractors, biblical religion taught that the righteous would benefit by longevity, fecundity, material prosperity, tenure in the promised land together with their brethren, and the respect of their fellows. The wicked would die barren, early and despised.

Classical Judaism emerged slowly after the fall of Jerusalem in 586 BCE. Yet, within the varieties of practice and belief held by those who called themselves Jews, there was a remarkable degree of consensus. The Bible had demanded Yahweh's exclusive worship, revealing at the same time that its demand had been honored as much in the breach as in the practice. Post-exilic Jews held that Yahweh was the sole God; not even Gentiles were permitted to worship another. Even the less subtle forms of polytheism and dualism had to masquerade as monotheism. Divinities of sea, storm and death became now "princes" of these domains, subservient to the one and only "King of the kings of kings."

Religious authority moved from people to Scripture. Priests and prophets remained, but their authority was limited by the written word, the Torah. Some groups claimed authority for traditions handed down by their fathers, but even these could not ignore the primacy of God's revelation in the written word. If living in accordance with that word required that recalcitrants be threatened into compliance by a Persian or Seleucid king, that only showed that God's way was recognized even by these.

Just as Yahweh's dominion knew no bounds, neither did the habitation of his people. Some even worshiped him in temples remarkably similar to the one in Jerusalem. These worshipers were no longer ethnically homogeneous. If polytheism was illegitimate, then even the Gentile must turn or be turned to the God of Israel. The Jew was to worship his God in the land previously deemed impure and to bring his neighbors into the cult with him.

Finally, ever larger groups of Jews began to feel the severe deficiencies of a moral teaching which no longer reflected reality. The authors of Job and Ecclesiastes had argued that God's recompense was faulty at best. Not content with this negative conclusion, many Jews became receptive to those ideas characteristic of the newer religions of later antiquity and yearned for a super-mundane salvation. Some believed in an ideal king, others in a resurrection, still others in an afterlife, and probably most in a confused amalgam of these.

The basic premises of post-exilic Judaism took on different forms and shapes over the course of centuries, crystalizing ultimately in the varieties of rabbinic Judaism and Christianity. Modern biblical scholarship has amply demonstrated that both Judaism and Christianity are far removed from the religion of the Hebrew Bible. Just how far biblical religion was itself removed from the actual situation which prevailed in ancient Israel remains a matter of scholarly controversy. Still, it is clear that Judaism and Christianity are eisegetical variations on the themes of the Hebrew Bible rather than plain sense interpretations. Jews and Christians alike must reckon with the theological fact that our religious traditions would have made little sense to Isaiah, Jeremiah, Ahab, Elijah or Moses.

A remarkable talmudic anecdote describes how Moses was once transported in a vision to the second-century academy of Rabbi Akiba, where he was unable to follow some of the more complex arguments. To Moses' amazement he heard Akiba credit him with the authorship of one of these, and his mind was set at ease.[24] This story may serve as an illustration of the tensions within contemporary religious Judaism with regard to the Hebrew Bible. In theory the Hebrew Bible was never superseded. Yet the early rabbis of the Talmud were well aware that Moses would have been an inferior student in the school of Rabbi Akiba.

The more conservative Jewish circles choose to take seriously Akiba's affirmation that he and Moses were in full agreement. The more liberal elements choose to give more weight to the recognition of Moses that much had changed in 1,400 years. For the liberals, among whom the author of this essay may be counted, Judaism is a developing religious tradition, the study of whose past may serve as a guide to its future. In this study an understanding of the Hebrew Bible and the world which produced it is crucial. Jewish and Christian scholars share the common task of recovering the biblical world. Though perhaps the biblical authors would not understand us and our quests, we may imagine that our attempts to understand them might set their minds at ease.

NOTES

1. Julius Wellhausen, *Prolegomena to the History of Ancient Israel,* with a reprint of the article "Israel" from the *Encyclopaedia Britannica* (New York, 1957), p. 412.

2. *Ibid.,* p. 1

3. *Ibid.*

4. *Ibid.,* pp. 421, 424, 425.

5. *Ibid.,* p. 422.

6. *Ibid.,* p. 510.

7. Arnold B. Ehrlich, *Mikra Ki-Peshuto, The Bible According to Its Literal Meaning,* prolegomenon by Harry M. Orlinsky, 3 vols. (New York, 1969).

8. *Ibid.,* p. ix.

9. *Ibid.,* following title page.

10. *Ibid.,* p. xxxvii.

11. *Ibid.,* p. xxxvi.

12. *Ibid.,* pp. xxxvi–xxxvii.

13. Arnold B. Ehrlich, *Randglossen zur hebraeischen Bibel,* 1908–1914.

14. Arnold B. Ehrlich (cf. n. 7), p. xxxvii.

15. Abraham Kahana, *Tanakh'im Perush Mada'i* (*The Bible with a Critical Commentary*).

16. Yehezkel Kaufmann, *The Religion of Israel* (Chicago, 1960), translated and abridged edition of *The History of the Israelite Religion.*

17. Moshe Weinfeld, *Deuteronomy and the Deuteronomic School* (Oxford, 1972).

18. Gerhard von Rad, "Deuteronomy," in *The Interpreter's Dictionary of the Bible* I (New York, 1962), pp. 831–838.

19. Theodore H. Gaster, "Psalm 29," in *The Jewish Quarterly Review* 37 (1946/7), pp. 55–65; quote on p. 64.

20. Rudolf Kittel, ed., *Biblia Hebraica* (Stuttgart, 1954).

21. Harry M. Orlinsky, *Essays in Biblical Culture and Bible Translation* (New York, 1974).

22. Moshe Greenberg, *Understanding Exodus* (New York, 1969), p. 1.

23. *Ibid.,* pp. 4–5.

24. TB *Menahoth* 29b.

A Christian View
of Bible Interpretation

Jorge Mejia

I

It may be overstating the case if we say that we live in a time of crisis with regard to Bible interpretation. The word crisis has become fashionable in the last thirty or forty years, a word easy to apply to any particular field of human endeavor, whether secular or religious. Certain signs, however, point in the direction of at least a widespread dissatisfaction with present methods and procedures of so-called scholarly Bible interpretation.

Having behind me a rather long career as professor of Bible at an important theological school in Latin America, I have perceived students pass from a non-reflexive acceptance of critico-historical methods to a much more articulate desire to "read" the Bible in a way relevant to their lives, in actual religious and pastoral, at times even political context. One pressing question in study groups, seminars and private conversations used to be: "What has source-critique or *Formgeschichte* or structural analysis to do with the hearing, preaching and 'actualization' of the word of God?" Actualization used to be a central topic of discussions, not necessarily in the meaning of a slogan. Other Bible teachers in other places may have had the same experience. Criticism is voiced against certain leading centers of Bible learning because students, especially those from the so-called third world, do not seem to find in the courses offered what they are seeking and what in their opinion might be useful for their future ministry of teaching in their countries.

Some might think that such trends are only one more instance of a periodic upsurge of fundamentalism, not to say obscurantism, to which some churches or religions are prone. Certain groups within the Roman Catholic Church experienced such temptation fifteen to twenty years ago, before and during the Second Vatican Council where this question was one of the major issues within and without the conciliar aula and finally became the Dogmatic Constitution on Divine Revelation, *Dei Verbum.*[1] I would hesitate, however, to subsume the present situation, or what I perceive as the present situation, in an unqualified way under the same categories.

It is undeniable that there always is a trend of fundamentalism. It would indeed be realistic, I believe, to consider for the benefit of those now engaged in scholarly Bible work how many among their own religious community as well as in others have never been won over to the scientific view of Scripture and never will be. One only has to look at some of the larger Christian churches and movements and to the Jewish orthodox tradition to become doubtful if it can be ascertained to any reliable degree which is the majority or minority view. That does not solve any problems, of course, but it might give all of us who are convinced of the real value of the historico-critical method a more sobering view regarding the acceptance of such method.

There seem to be various reasons for such dissatisfaction with critical study and reading of the Bible. One that is of real pastoral importance within the Church and Judaism is the challenge posed by some of the results of such studies to traditional affirmations of either the Christian or the Jewish faith. To quote some relevant examples taken from the Christian faith: Is Christ's death to be considered redemptive or sacrificial in any true sense in the teaching of the more ancient layers of Gospel tradition?[2] Is the Church as a post-resurrectional institution connected in some way with the historical Jesus, and, if so, how?[3] What about Christ's divinity?[4] Regarding the Jewish faith—without in any way ignoring the fact that the Jewish and Christian faith are not parallel at all[5]—one could enumerate almost all the commonly accepted conclusions of critical literary analysis: non-Mosaic authorship of the Pentateuch, non-Isaiah authorship of the second and third part of Isaiah, the documentary theory of the composition of the Pentateuch, traditio-historical conclusions regarding for example the history of the Levitic priesthood, and so on.

Uncertainty about what we used to call "accepted" scientific conclusions of critical Bible study could easily be another reason for dissatisfaction. Some of the examples given above indicate conclusions which seemed to be certain and more or less beyond all discussion. Within the documentary theory of the Pentateuch, one of the pillars of the whole construction since the times of Karl Heinrich Graf was the special position of P (the Priestly source) at the end of the whole development. While later studies had contributed to a modification of this conclusion—to the extent that not necessarily everything contained in P was to be considered the end product of a rectilinear evolution—very seldom had the conclusion itself been questioned or denied.[6] Yet, since the work of Yehezkel Kaufmann and others,[7] the conclusions about the place of P have become subject to doubt, if only because in the opinion of several authors P can no longer be considered as a unit, with the same date for all its parts.[8] This in turn means a re-elaboration of what could be called the "classical" view of the composition of the Pentateuch.

In the New Testament field, certainty has not been achieved in the all-important question of the composition of the Synoptic Gospels, parallel in a sense to the question of Pentateuch authorship. Priority of Matthew is still being defended rather emphatically by scientifically-minded individuals and groups.[9] The other "classical" position is perhaps able to answer the objections, but it is a moot question whether it can prove beyond doubt its main affirmations.

It could well be that lessened confidence in science as such helps toward a detachment from what has been held as assured "scientific" acquisitions in critical Bible study. Whatever one may think, it seems clear that present and future Bible scholars will have to be more careful in advancing conclusions based on foundations which are no longer quite safe—and probably never were.

On a deeper level still, a more general question could be and, I believe, is being asked. There seems to be a gap between the scientific approach and its current means of expression and dissemination (magazine articles, introductions, scientific commentaries) on the one hand, and the pastoral and spiritual use of the selfsame Bible in the daily life of the Christian churches and the Jewish religion on the other.[10] The gap is most visible when priests or ministers or rabbis propose in their homilies what could be called scientific views and conclusions which radically differ from what their listeners hold as revealed truth.[11] The gap is also evident when Bible commentaries, intended, it is to be supposed, for the formation of pastors and other interested persons, follow a path which is in itself strictly faithful to scientific methods and so far valid, but alien to quite an extent to what our communities believe and celebrate and, most probably, will go on believing and celebrating in the foreseeable future.[12]

I would venture to say that one of the problems of biblical theology lies precisely in this: What is biblical theology, as distinct from the history of the Hebrew or primitive Christian religion, good for if it does not profit the reader or enable him to communicate to others the richness of the word of God, if it does not provide a real means of success to the religious message contained in the Bible? One wonders whether this is not the case with the more renowned and most widely used treatises on biblical theology.[13] Does not true religious insight into the message of the Bible ask for a commitment of the same kind on the part of the scholar? Science and faith must, indeed, not be confused with one another, but are they to be kept apart? Does this in any way benefit the faithful for whom in the last analysis scientific work ought to be intended? It is rather easy, indeed too easy, to criticize the biblical writings of the Church Fathers from the vantage point of present scientific achievement. It should be recognized at the very least that, with all their limitations, they went far along the path of making the Bible accessible to the common people, in a way that stands forever as a model to all of us. Something similar could justifiably be said of the ancient and later midrashim in the Jewish tradition. It is only fair to state that scientific biblical scholarship stands on the shoulders of both these traditions, much to its good. The present lack of a comparable association of sound biblical scholarship with deep personal and pastoral commitment to the Book is all the more deplorable. It goes without saying that the same personal and pastoral commitment is required in relation to people—of our own or another religious persuasion and those who have none at all—for whom ultimately the message of the Book is intended.

In the framework of the situation here summarized, it would not be too much to affirm that at present several types of Bible reading and interpretation exist side by side. This particular fact can be explained as a result of pluralism, and there is indeed a trend toward the justification of pluralism in religious thinking and living. This may be true to some extent, but it goes far to prove that so-called scientific Bible interpretation has not yet won the field. It poses a serious question, indeed, about the absolute or relative value of scientific Bible reading as ultimate key to biblical understanding.

This is not the proper place to list, much less to comment on, all the present forms of Bible interpretation. They range from the mere pietistic through the Freudian to the political, which indeed is mostly Marxist. If we leave aside the first, dismissing it as simply fundamentalistic (which, however, would be rather a rash thing to do), we cannot ignore that the other two, and particularly the political approach, are quite widespread, even attempting to find for itself what could be called some scholarly status.[14] If this last phenomenon remains rather isolated, it is not infrequent on the other hand that books on political theology and, to some extent, on liberation theology[15] contain whole chapters on a "class" reading of the Bible, or a "reappropriation" of the Bible by the "poor," to whom it rightly belongs.[16] The "political" reinterpretations of the Exodus in a Marxist key are, I believe, well known.[17] It goes similarly with the life and death of Jesus, which necessarily includes a project for reinterpretation of the Gospels.[18] This particular instance sometimes uses, rather uncritically it seems, conclusions of uncertain scientific interpretation.[19] In such a way, the problems at the level of traditional teaching of the faith referred to above combine with new problems posed by the trend toward "political" reading of the Bible.[20] In the main, however, it could be said that representatives of what is called a "committed" (*engagé, comprometida*) interpretation could not be or should not be comfortable with scientific interpretation and its more or less "neutral" character.[21] Pure science does not by itself espouse the cause of the proletarian.

While this last type of Bible reading and exegesis has originally been connected with Latin America, it is by no means limited to that part of the world, as the books quoted in the Notes indicate. In fact, what is called "third world" theology stands rather close to this kind of interpretation.[22] To some extent, such trends could be taken to represent different, sometimes rather wild, efforts to make the Bible relevant to the present plight of human life, personal and social, that which indeed scientific exegesis seemed not to be able to do. One wonders, therefore, whether, even in these more extreme forms of reading, interpreting and of course translating the Bible into concrete human situations, some kind of challenge is not posed to the assumptions of scientific interpretation.

Thus, from two different and even opposite aspects of the spectrum, similar or parallel objections are raised against that kind of interpretation. Pastoral and spiritual reading and preaching of the Bible does not always seem to find in the scholarly approach the solid doctrinal and religious nourishment needed for the life of the faithful in Church and Synagogue alike. Social and more specifically political commitment is now trying to find its own way toward a reading and interpretation more directly in line with change and revolution. While in this last instance it can be argued that a real danger exists of merely "using" the Bible for aims alien to its original inspiration and message, the question remains open for the true need of a reading of the sacred books that can inspire the kind of action called for from believers, in the present situation of man and society.

A new dimension still has been added to the already complicated problem of Bible exegesis by the present trend toward dialogue among the Churches and/or between the Churches and Judaism. Regarding the first kind of dialogue, it has been said—and rightly so, I believe—that common faith in the word of God as contained in the books of the Bible is the same or almost the same for all Christian churches, and it is and remains a powerful bond and a solid basis on which to build the desired edifice of definitive and even organic unity.[23] It is usually held furthermore that a certain acceptance of the selfsame methods of biblical research created within a number of churches, or at least on the scholarly level of these churches, weaves new bonds of unity, mainly because like methods should bring about like results.[24] One difficulty still to be solved in this respect is the fact that the churches do not base their dogmatic affirmations mainly on the results of scientific exegesis, however much attention they are likely to pay to such results. Nor should it be forgotten, as was previously mentioned, that neither all the churches nor all levels within the churches are inclined to accept scientific methods.

The Jewish-Christian dialogue, on the other hand, has created a completely new situation in the field of Bible reading and interpretation. The Hebrew and the Christian Bible are, of course, not identical, and the methods of access to the biblical message for Jews and Christians are not the same. I would venture to say this applies even when scholarly and scientific methods are employed on either side. Nevertheless, the fact that, to some extent at least, such methods are used in the Jewish and Christian academic milieu cannot fail to reinforce and strengthen existing foundations for interrelatedness and convergence. For, as it must be said again and again, whatever the real differences between the two Bibles, the Christian one simply cannot exist without the Hebrew.

This "dialogical" aspect of Bible interpretation, whether in its intra-Christian or Jewish-Christian dimension, must not be lost sight of by exegetes, preachers and catechists alike, although admittedly it adds a new challenge and particular difficulties to present Bible work and Bible use.

II

The *status questionis* thus imperfectly described most certainly does not serve to discredit scientific methods, nor should it be a proposal for their dismissal. But it leads to a relativization of their value and a reconsideration of their application. It may be worthwhile to dedicate some paragraphs to both aspects of the question.

The history of employing scientific methods to Bible study has not been without its difficulties nor has it developed in a straight line. We will not here relate it in its entirety.[25] It will suffice to recall that it was originally connected with illuminism, rationalism and the affirmation of the scientific way of thinking, which goes a long way toward explaining why the churches were not at all happy with this development. On the one hand it did not seem adequate to submit the books containing the word of God to the same methods of research as the classical authors; such efforts had a certain ring of desecration. On the other, the first results collided directly with what had for centuries been held as sacred teaching, for example the Mosaic authorship of the Pentateuch. This in turn seemed to pose insoluble problems to the principle of Bible inspiration and inerrancy. Although a tradition of biblical learning and even biblical scholarship had always existed in the Church from at least the remote days of Origen, such independent methods were altogether new, unexpected and troublesome. The churches as well as Judaism, at least mainline Judaism, shrank from such dangerous novelties.

It must in all honesty be said that some efforts toward reconciling the Church, specifically the Roman Catholic Church, with the developing biblical science were quite unfortunate. Alfred Loisy is a case in point. He was a young Bible professor at the Institut Catholique in Paris when he discovered the new critical methods as they were then, in the last decades of the nineteenth century, applied to the study of Scripture, mainly in Germany. Loisy began to publish learned articles and books in which he tried to apply those new methods to the solution of old and difficult problems like the origin and formation of the Canon. The project in itself seemed unexceptionable. But Loisy must have perceived quite soon that the question was not only one of methodology but a philosophical and theological one as well.

At the time, the rediscovery of antiquity—brought about by the first archaeological excavations in the Middle East—and the conclusions of physical and biological sciences (evolutionism, in the first place) and their philosophical interpretation (the theory of progress) served to create an intense ferment within the churches, most especially in the Roman Catholic. Thus, in Loisy's case it never was a question of pure and, so to speak, aseptic critical methods applied to the study of the Bible; he rather presented a typical example for the connection of such methods in the mind of their proponents with the new philosophical and theological ideas. He was, as such, intimately convinced of the difficulties of reconciling such ideas with the official teaching of his own Church. This is why almost from the beginning of his career he used abundantly the disconcerting procedure of anonymity or pseudonymity, signing his articles with different names or none at all. The whole problem exploded with the publication in 1902, this time under his own name, of the so-called "petit livre rouge" (because of the color of its covers), *L'Evangile et l'Eglise,* which was soon condemned.

Loisy's case was not an isolated phenomenon but part of a larger movement of thought, known by the rather vague designation of "modernism." The condemnation of the book just mentioned, together with other condemnations, brought about before long the publication of an encyclical by Pope Pius X, *Pascendi Dominici gregis* (September 8, 1907), which tried to present in some kind of organic way all the philosophical and theological ideas deemed incompatible with the official teaching of the Church. Other measures, doctrinal and disciplinary, then ensued.

One may think that the manner of dealing with Alfred Loisy was inspired by obscurantism, even a certain amount of personal animosity. There seems to be some measure of truth in such affirmations.[26] But it cannot be denied that Loisy did not strike, even in his first critical writings, a careful balance between the requirements of scientific method and those of the faith to which he was committed. His late and last writings sadly manifest how far he had drifted from recognizable Christianity, not to speak of Roman Catholicism.

At the same time, it is easier to admit now that the methods then in use almost exclusively were rather limited and one-sided. They mostly consisted of *Literarkritik* and *Quellenkritik* which came dangerously close to being considered absolute criteria as true keys to the secrets of Scripture. One has only to recall the boast by Julius Wellhausen when he turned to New Testament studies because, he stated, there was nothing more to be said of the Old.[27] There also exist examples of the extreme application of such literary methods which tended to explain the composition of the biblical books, or at least some of them, with the help of a scissors and paste procedure. Such efforts are now viewed as curiosities, but there is reason to believe that even today these methods are sometimes employed in a similar way. In short, a certain horizontality or bi-dimensionality of *Literarkritik* can be self-defeating, whatever its merits.[28]

It appears understandable to a certain extent, therefore, that the Roman Catholic Church did react, through its newly created Pontifical Biblical Commission, with utmost energy and sometimes a painful lack of discernment, to the application of those methods and what looked like their theological consequences.[29] Undeniably, such measures and their even more rigid translation into practice created in our Church a widespread diffidence for *Literarkritik* and critical methodology in general. One has only to recall what happened to Fr. Marie-Joseph Lagrange, founder and rector of the Ecole Biblique in Jerusalem,[30] in spite of the extreme prudence and care of his exegetical teaching, written and oral. It cannot be denied, though, that to some people, and in certain contexts of the Catholic academic world, the use of critical methods was tantamount to advancing unacceptable theological and philosophical views.

Literarkritik was soon to pass through a thoroughly purifying crisis from which it would emerge not only substantially changed but also demoted from its royal place as the only "higher critique" (*Hochkritik*). Without entering into much detail because the story has been told many times over,[31] it will suffice here to mention two factors which greatly contributed to such change and, indirectly, to a freer acceptance of critical methods by the Church, specifically the Roman Catholic Church. These factors have something in common, in that both are grounded in the discovery that literary products have a historical dimension, either at the level of the literary creation itself or of the culture, people, facts and, in general, *realia* of which they are the expression.

Thus, *Formgeschichte* and the *formgeschichtliche Methode* try to explore the "birthplace" (*Sitz im Leben*), history and development of the literary genres of various literary units in the Bible. Many scholars changed the object of analysis in their biblical research work. The question became mainly who, what, and which circumstances were responsible for the forms of expression identified in biblical writings. A substantial effort was thereby undertaken to overcome the limitations of the strict application of the source-method.

Archaeology was the other great factor of change. Two discoveries were made which, though connected, are progressively in need of being carefully distinguished from one another. The first one concerned the great, prestigious civilizations of the ancient Near East, Mesopotamia (Assyria, then Sumer), Egypt, Syria, Hatti, Crete, Cyprus. The other centered on the more modest material and artistic achievements of Retenu/Canaan/Israel. The temptation was great, in view of this cultural gap, to explain the chief product of Hebrew civilization, namely the Bible, as a by-product of the greater neighbors, particularly Mesopotamia. The *Bibel-Babel* debate will be remembered in this context.

Friedrich Delitzsch (1850–1922), a famous German orientalist and biblical scholar, notably in the field of textual studies, is linked with this debate because of the famous lecture he gave on the subject at the *Deutsche Orient-Gesellschaft* on January 13, 1902, stating in a very clear way the so-called "Pan-Babylonian" position. But the question had already been posed before this lecture. It was, in fact, a consequence of the first attempts at the study and translation of the cuneiform documents (mainly Assyrian), then recently discovered in what is now Iraq, mostly in Nebi Yunus (ancient Nineveh). They consisted of a whole collection of tablets, soon identified with the library of King Assurbanipal of Assyria (circa 669–630 BCE). One of these documents happened to be what is now known as the eleventh tablet of the Gilgamesh Epic, where the Mesopotamian Noe (Utanapishtim, in Akkadian) tells the visiting Gilgamesh the story of the Flood. The parallels with the biblical narrative in Genesis, chapters six to nine, seemed evident, while the differences were not so carefully assessed. Other documents also seemed to confirm the picture. Hence, a rather simple theory was proposed to the effect that biblical literature and biblical religious teaching was not an isolated phenomenon dependent on divine revelation but mostly a local, poorer version of writings and ideas current in the Middle East, well before the time of the biblical authors. They were as such scarcely original and had, indeed, no real value for Christians. In the slogan-like German formula which circulated in public—not without, as must be painfully recognized, a clear antisemitic ring—*Bibel* depended on *Babel,* according to the proponents of that theory. Similar temptations have assailed Bible scholars ever since. Ugarit and the Dead Sea Scrolls are two instances of such a tendency. One may wonder whether Ebla is going to become a third.

At the same time, however, a sound and sober trend of biblical or Palestinian archaeology was constantly progressing, ever more conscious of the need for refining methods, carefully assessing results and refraining from another, more subtle temptation, to "prove" the truth of the Bible.[32] This attitude did much to digest the results of Near Eastern archaeology and thus providing a needed background, historical as well as cultural and religious, to the biblical writings including the New Testament, while simultaneously helping to perceive their originality precisely against such background. The work is going on and will probably never be finished.

Archaeology has the remarkable merit of giving to the Bible as a religious literary product of antiquity true historical depth, while *Literarkritik* tended very much to reduce change and development to ideological schemata, with scarcely any connection to real life. Even *Formgeschichte,* with all its concern for *Leben,* can and should benefit from sound archaeology, considering that it may also become entangled in exclusive, literary history.

Judaism and the Church have always had a deep commitment to history. It is thus quite understandable that, when the road to *Hochkritik* seemed closed, scientific energy reoriented itself toward archaeological research. The Jerusalem school officially calls itself now Ecole Biblique et Archaeologique. The amount of work done by the different archaeological institutes in the Holy Land is simply enormous. We need mention only the (then) American School, the British School, the Studium Biblicum Franciscanum and many others; soon the Jews and the Israelis joined in the venture. The results are there for anybody to assess, grounded in constantly refined and more sophisticated methods.[33]

Yet archaeology is not all, and soon problems on the methodology of applying archaeological results to biblical research began to appear. It could be said, somewhat rashly, that archaeology has created as many problems as it has offered solutions. To quote but one famous example: the rather negative results of the Kenyon excavations in Jericho.

Miss Kenyon, working with new and more refined methods of digging and interpreting, disproved in her own excavations (1952–1958) the conclusions of the former Garstang excavations (1929–1936). Garstang believed that he had discovered the remains of the walls which collapsed at the sound of Joshua's trumpets (cf. Jos 6), that is, the walls of the Late Bronze II city. Miss Kenyon, however, identified very few remains of that period (an oven and some remains of a house), while Garstang's walls were pushed back in time almost one thousand years, to the Early Bronze Age. Jericho seemed, strangely enough, to have been almost a desert or at least to have been very sparsely inhabited at the supposed time of the Israelite conquest. This is not the only case in which conclusions regarding that particular period of history had to be modified or at least carefully reconsidered. It is sufficient proof for the extreme care with which archaeological arguments must be handled.

If by now it is sufficiently clear to all but the most fundamentalist scholars that archaeology is not the key proof for the historicity of the Bible, the exact place of that discipline in exegesis is still quite open to debate.[34] It must also be admitted that, for all its undeniable achievements, a widespread mistrust of many trends in present-day exegesis about arriving at really solid "historical" results has not been dispelled. Martin Noth was not convinced that we could replace Moses in his proper historical context while affirming the fact of his historical existence.[35] The tradition about him seems to lead us back only to his tomb.[36] One is immediately reminded of similarly cautious, reticent conclusions regarding important religious affirmations of the traditional Christian faith and their grounding in the New Testament.[37]

Thus it is rather easy to see how different methods, springing from different schools and different ideological contexts, follow parallel paths. *Traditionsgeschichte* is closely connected with *Formgeschichte* and also tends to overcome the iron-clad two-dimensional limits of traditional *Quellenkritik,* going even beyond the strictly literary field and trying to rejoin "reality." But does it? The basis which supports its mostly negative conclusions seems to be so very narrow at times. It cannot be denied, on the other hand, that *Traditionsgeschichte* has sometimes lent a certain depth to the merely literary analysis and thereby helped to place the problems of historicity on a new and sounder foundation. Yet the religious, not necessarily "dogmatic" reader of the Bible would soon feel frustrated, were he to follow this path exclusively. The alternative is certainly not a blind jump into the so-called irrationality of faith; it is rather the discovery of a methodology which gives us a means for bridging the gap between the history of tradition and archaeological research.

Redaktionsgeschichte is still another welcome correction of the absolute rule of *Quellenkritik,* but in a new direction. Religious and theological teaching was not a secondary, more or less casual result of the combination of sources but the advised intention of writers, authors and redactors of the biblical books. While dealing with any particular text, exegesis has to take this overall perspective into account. Additional problems, however, tend to remain unsolved, such as the relation between the authors themselves and either the Abrahamic/Mosaic or the Jesus revelation. The danger of perceiving the Bible, Jewish or Christian, as a mere *ens per accidens,* wherefrom almost any doctrine can be legitimately derived, is not thus dispelled. On the contrary, sometimes as a result of the application of such methods, it is held as guiding principle.

Thus far, we have been moving in the field of diachronic analysis, an analysis in which the succession in time, or the time factor, is well-nigh indispensable. The main point is to learn how the literary end-product in the Bible came into being. To some extent, it is the search for an "historical" explanation, however obscure the connection with the *was* (what) of history might be or be held to be impossible to discern. Nevertheless, the preoccupation with what belongs to the original is present, as a pointer toward authenticity.[38]

More recently, a trend toward synchronic analysis developed. The focus no longer is on how the literary work came into being but what it is as such, in its own distinctive reality as such a work. This trend in itself is pluralistic, at times more given to aesthetic analysis, at others to the use of strictly comparative literary methods, at still other times to so-called structural analysis in relation to the philosophy or philosophies of language. The last method and to some extent the comparative-literary one tend to set aside the question of, indeed the quest for, meaning. In other words, the "structure" has a meaning of its own, independent of the author's intention. It is easy to see that this amounts to a Copernican revolution of traditional exegesis whose main question is: *Quid senserit auctor?* Though many books and articles have been written on structural analysis[39] it is not as yet altogether clear how this new method and its application will be combined with others, if at all.

This last point introduces the question of meaning. What is to be considered, in the final analysis, the true meaning of Scripture, indeed of any piece of writing? Is it really what careful exegetes—working with scientific, objective, so-called historico-critical methods—try to arrive at, by reconstructing the "mind" of the author(s), *mens auctoris?* Or is it what the text says to me, to us, in any given situation with all its historic and subjective conditioning? If so, what are we supposed to do with the results of scientific exegesis? These questions and many others are raised by the contemporary debate on hermeneutics.[40] Such discussions seem to be very fashionable, though not necessarily in connection with the proposals of structuralism. More truly, the conflict exists from the very moment when "independent" exegetical methods are applied to a book which is considered the faith-deposit of a religious community and of millions of religiously committed people who read that book in the perspective of their faith and celebrate it in their words and institutions. One wonders if structuralism and the philosophies of meaning have not simply brought to a head a previously existing conflict that had already produced less scholarly manifestations. We might here ask if the initial opposition by the Church to the application, or a certain kind of application, of critical methods does not amount to an expression of this same conflict, though proposed in apparently different terms? I would personally affirm this view.

As a consequence of all this—the multiplication of scientific methods, mutually corrective of each other, and the present crisis in the question of meaning or the true interpretation of Scripture—a thorough reassessment of the whole problem seems to be called for. That will take time and the contribution of many converging efforts. In the meantime and quite unavoidably, many paths will be followed that lead strictly nowhere, as more or less we can see round about us right now. From the point of view of a Catholic exegete, however, it seems possible to offer some leads toward a solution.[41]

III

Among the scholarly community, scientific methods in the study of the Bible are almost universally accepted. The exceptions are so isolated and extreme that they remain virtually alone. This would be true of many if not most of the Christian scholarly bodies and to a lesser extent perhaps of Judaism.

It is well known that, slowly and carefully, the Roman Catholic Church lifted the ban (so to speak) on the use of scientific methods and therefore accepted to live with the conclusions flowing therefrom, without necessarily adopting any of them and affirming herself free to refuse whatever might appear in opposition to her official teaching. The relevant steps are not to be recounted here. One could say, however, that the high-water mark was reached with *Divino Afflante Spiritu,* Pius XII's famous encyclical on biblical studies, of September 29, 1943.[42] Whatever come afterward are applications of the principles there affirmed, whether it is the letter, so impressive in its time, by the then Secretary of the Pontifical Biblical Commission to the Cardinal Archbishop of Paris,[43] or the so-called Instruction by the same Commission, *Sancta Mater Ecclesia,* of April 21, 1964 on the "historical truth of the Gospels,"[44] or even the relevant chapters of *Dei Verbum,* the Second Vatican Council's Dogmatic Constitution on Divine Revelation.[45] The last document, of course, gives to the whole development the consecrating seal of conciliar authority, at a moment when this was very much needed. Given the peculiar structure of the Roman Catholic Church, however, all this carries substantial weight, even though the structure may today be under discussion. Other churches have found other solutions and so has Judaism, always indeed short of official sanction.

But the Roman Catholic Church has never lost sight of the limitations of scientific methods, extrinsic and intrinsic. Pius XII, while promoting their application, quite clearly stated that the Catholic exegete should not forget the divine character of the word he was called to comment upon, and that he should also take into account the Church's magisterium, the teaching of the Church Fathers, even the *analogia fidei,*[46] that is, the orientation which the content of faith can offer as a guide to interpreting difficult passages. Still more directly, the Pope insists that the exegete should not limit his work to that which the application of historico-critical methods would reveal, but should look for the theological teaching of books and individual texts, not only for the enlightenment of theologians but also for the sake of the life and work of priests and laymen.[47] Critical methods are thus set in the wider context of the service of faith and the Christian community. In the selfsame process of the exegetical task there are criteria of an altogether different order which are to be taken into account (*diligenter rationem habeant*). Science was not to have the last word, however necessary its methods were taken to be.

Sancta Mater Ecclesia, in the midst of the debate referred to above, spoke of using "with dedication" (*sollerter*) the "new exegetical aids" (*nova exegeseos adiumenta*), explicitly naming for the first time the method of the "history of (literary) forms."[48] At the same time it said that the "norms of rational and catholic exegesis should be carefully observed"[49] and it advised the exegete to be prudent (*circumspecte se gerat*) because, mingled with the method were often "philosophical and theological principles which could not be approved" (*haud probanda*) and which frequently (*non raro*) "pervert" (*depravant*) "the method itself and its conclusions."[50] The document goes on to illustrate what is meant by such general affirmations. The aim of the exegetical task in this particular field was defined as "to shed full light on the perennial truth and authority of the Gospels."[51] A pre-scientific or ultra-scientific criterion is thus indicated.

Vatican Council II has given ample evidence of deep appreciation for the conclusions of scientific exegesis, especially in its contribution to better understanding of the theological teaching of Scripture. Let us only point to the first chapter of *Lumen Gentium* and its biblical presentation of the Church.[52] Several other instances could be mentioned, easily illustrated now that the publication of the *Acta Concilii* has been completed.[53] The Council, on the other hand, does not leave any doubt about the existence and application of other criteria in discerning the truth of Scripture which, if connected with the former, are not in any way reducible to them. Thus, the Council states in the third paragraph of n. 12 of *Dei Verbum* that Scripture should be read and interpreted in the same Spirit through which it was written.[54] It goes on to affirm that

ad recte sacrorum textuum sensum eruendum, non minus diligenter respiciendum est ad contentum et unitatem totius Scripturae, ratione habita vivae totius Ecclesiae Traditionis et analogiae fidei ("Rightly to understand the meaning of the sacred texts . . . no less attention must be devoted to the content and unity of the whole of Scripture, taking into account the tradition of the entire Church and the analogy of faith").

Here, then, we have a set of hermeneutical rules which go well beyond the boundaries of scientific exegesis and belong to another register. That the same Council has itself applied such rules is easy to see. In the same section of *Dei Verbum* where reference is made to critical conclusions regarding the origin and redaction process of the Gospels, in the wake of the then recent Instruction by the Pontifical Biblical Commission,[56] the first affirmation contains a principle which, however it may be borne out by scientific exegesis, is here grounded on another level of certainty:

> Sancta Mater Ecclesia firmiter et constantissime tenuit ac tenet quattuor recensita Evangelia, quorum historicitatem incunctanter affirmat, fideliter tradere quae Iesus Dei Filius . . . ad aeternam (hominum) salutem reapse fecit ac docuit ("The Church is convinced, and so she teaches, that the four Gospels are historical and that they faithfully reflect what Jesus, the Son of God . . . did and taught, for the eternal salvation [of man]").

It seems abundantly clear that any scientific conclusion regarding the Gospels, if it comes from a Catholic exegete, should take careful note of such affirmation. The latter can and should be interpreted, but it cannot be lightly dismissed.

Something similar happens, to offer another important example, when the Declaration *Nostra Aetate* n. 4 states that

> quae in passione eius [Christi] perpetrata sunt nec omnibus indistincte Iudaeis tunc viventibus, nec Iudaeis hodiernis imputari possunt (" . . . what happened in his passion cannot be charged against all the Jews, without distinction, then alive, nor against the Jews of today").[57]

This, of course, is founded on sound exegesis, as has by now been made quite clear. But once the affirmation is thus made by an official organ of the Church's magisterium, it becomes normative and gives the right clue for the interpretation of difficult passages like 1 Thes 2:14–16 and others.[58] Further examples could easily be given.

While affirming the value of scientific methods of exegesis, the Catholic Church, then, simultaneously proclaims a theological status of Scripture, the immediate consequence of which is the need for and affirmation of additional hermeneutical principles. Such a theological status would also be affirmed—within the characteristics of each tradition—by the other Christian churches and, in its own way, by Judaism. Scientific methods, therefore, have no absolute value in the doctrine and practice of the two great biblical religions.

IV

If one now were to ask what exactly is the meaning of this theological status and how can it combine with the requirements of scientific methods, an answer can be provided along the following lines, the perspective being mainly that of the Church to which the author belongs:

Scripture is unlike any other book. Books in general are, admittedly, more than the limited product of a particular person's imagination; to some extent they have a meaning of their own. Beyond that, however, Scripture is truly the word of God. The whole mystery of who is the beginning and end of all lies hidden among its lines and pages, and this word is not passive, being the same word which created the universe (cf. Is 55:10–11). It is self-revealing and challenging and eternally valid and meaningful for all generations. No time and no man can exhaust its meaning. At the same time, it is conditioned at the human level because it was originally given to a people and to a set of men who belonged to a particular culture. This applies even to the New Testament where, however, a new dimension of content and new transmitters have left their traces; yet the latter point does not cancel the former.

Without espousing any particular theory of inspiration, anyone who happens to believe that in the particular book of Scripture which he approaches something more and radically different from a mere word of man is offered—however much such word is present and necessary—will easily understand that strictly human resources fall short of that book's requirements. Such book of itself has dimensions which *per se* lie beyond the pale of human analysis. Prophecy is one, typology is another; both belong to the mysterious reality of the word of God. To reduce one or the other, more or less systematically, to *ex eventu* or *post factum* would simply ignore what Scripture really is. There is a mystery in Scripture, or, rather, Scripture itself is a mystery despite its very human means of expression. To be able to perceive it, one has to hear through the human voice another voice which is not human, somehow like Elijah on Mount Horeb (cf. 1 Kgs 19:12). It means that, to be adequately understood, Scripture must be received and read in faith. Outside of faith, something essential within Scripture will remain hidden. Christians would even go a considerable step further and say that the Book is opened only by the Lamb, dead and alive (cf. Rev 5:1–14).

That is why Scripture is being read and interpreted by a praying and celebrating community which, in the first place, is a believing community. The relationship between Scripture and liturgy is not accidental. It is in the celebration of the mysteries that Scripture's mystery is approached. Thus, liturgy in itself is an interpretation of Scripture which the reader or, for that matter, the scholar cannot afford to ignore. The more-than-human voice is best perceived in such a context.

This brings us to a further point. Scripture is always read, and therefore interpreted, within a tradition. People and Book go together, as closely as Book and liturgy. Jews are very much aware of this and so should Christians be, particularly Catholics who could learn from Jews in this regard.[59] Exegesis is not performed in a vacuum. Yet scholars tend very much to relate only to their own scholarly community, which, however, crosses denominational lines, and that is good. Still, scholars are frequently quite oblivious to what the faith-community discovers and teaches about the Bible, admittedly with pre-scientific methods. But the believing community may have heard the voice of God and entered into the mystery of Scripture. The gap between scientific exegesis, and, say, the Fathers of the Church is now rather wide. One wonders whether Rashi is not much more alive in Judaism than Augustine or Origen in the Christian churches. Besides, tradition lies not only in the past but in the present, and scientific exegesis should be prepared to receive as much as it is prepared to give, with regard to those whom in the final analysis it is supposed to serve.

One could even go a step further and suggest that if the Bible really is the word of God who talks to man and particularly to his people, then whoever wishes to hear and receive his message should be personally attuned to him. A personal relationship to God would then be a prerequisite for the attainment of meaning, or one of the meanings, of Scripture. This does not signify that he who is a sinner, or an unbeliever, or more or less indifferent to the Person revealed in Scripture, is bound to be wrong in his exegetical efforts. If there is a measure of truth, however, in the ancient axiom recently repeated by the Vatican Council,[60] that Scripture be read and interpreted in the same Spirit through which it was written, then such need for personal religious commitment to the God of Scripture should be taken seriously. Saints or future saints are certainly not excused from studying, but their reading, understanding and putting into practice the meaning of Scripture, while helped by rational endeavor, derives from another source. We could also quite appropriately ask what a science of Scripture is good for unless it transform the lives of those who study it and of the community around them.

In the Roman Catholic Church and in different ways also in other churches, there arises the question of official teaching, normative tradition or magisterium. That aspect is not greatly cherished in our time. Ordinary people, and biblical scientists, in particular, do not understand very well, if at all, how authority and science can be combined. A certain amount of exaggeration in the exercise of authority in this particular field has of course not helped to solve the problem. It is also common knowledge that "there are but few texts whose sense has been defined by the authority of the Church, nor are those more numerous about which the teaching of the Holy Fathers is unanimous" (*pauca tantum esse . . . neque plura ea esse, de quibus unanimis Sanctorum Patrum sit sententia*).[61] But there are indeed some, and that suffices to set a limit for the Catholic exegete. The mere existence of such limits, then, implies as previously mentioned that the true meaning of Scripture is not solely "scientific" but is attained by other criteria as well, unless of course the whole idea of authoritative interpretation is simply rejected.

Yet, even with regard to the great many passages and books where the exegete is free to discover his own solution and, indeed, to apply scientific methods, the Catholic scholar (and not only he) cannot forget in his exegetical work that he is a believer and a member of a believing community. This is where "the analogy of faith"[62] comes in, serving as guide and help more than as a limiting factor. One does not or should not interpret the Bible outside of or against the faith-conviction of the community to which one belongs by professing that faith.

Along with *analogia fidei* goes another hermeneutical principle which is not much in favor today, challenged as it is by scientific exegetical conclusions, to wit, the unity of the Bible.[63] Again, this seems to be a textbook case of conflict between scientific exegesis and the theological status of Scripture, as we called it. Who can maintain that Scripture is one, when even the New Testament—centered as it is in the self-revelation of Christ—recognizes such qualitative differences as the theology of Mark, Proto-Mark, Luke, Proto-Luke, Paul, Deutero-Paul, James, and John, with their various sources and the like? The Old Testament certainly looks to many people like the end-product of a very casual compilation, indeed in two versions, the "Alexandrian" canon and the Hebrew Scriptures, not to mention Qumran which, as far as it is a collection complete in itself, lies somewhere between the two.[64] Judaism and Christianity, again, would differ quite deeply on the precise formulation of the principle of scriptural unity, Judaism finding complete unity in the Hebrew Scriptures, while Christianity would affirm that the New Testament necessarily belongs within such unity, to the extent that each Testament requires the other for proper understanding.

The criterion for the affirmation of unity, whether in the Jewish or Christian sense, is not in the first place critical exegesis, however much such exegesis properly applied can contribute to the illumination of the principle. It is the theological conception that in Scripture there is more deposited than a casual accumulation, through accidents of religious history, of many books and writings of the most diverse origin, although more or less in the stream of either Jewish or Christian faith, rather loosely interpreted. There is a divine purpose and the intention to communicate through history and men in history the revelation of God, centered in Christ for Christians (and thus progressive), and in the Torah (with its oral complement) for Jews. The unity, then, if it also demonstrably exists at the level of the human writers,[65] is ultimately due to the unity of divine purpose and thus, again, to the fact that Scripture is the word of God.[66]

Having arrived at this point, two problems cannot possibly be evaded: on one hand, the introduction of theological elements into the assessment of the Bible, with the attribution to them of a certain normative value, and, on the other, the apparent anomaly of affirming simultaneously the hermeneutical validity of such theological elements and of scientific methods. Let us deal with them one after the other, in proper awareness of their interconnectedness.

To begin with, I am tempted to say that the introduction of theological elements should not call for an apology. Long before it became an object of modern science, the Bible had been an object of faith, and it has never ceased to be that. Such a conviction of course may be dismissed as illusory, as incompatible with present scientific standards, or, at least, as subject to the conclusions of scientific analysis in the sense that what we should or should not believe about Scripture is in the first place determined by science. I shall come back to this last point when answering the second question. The main problem is whether the believing exegete can be satisfied with such statements or whether he should not loyally try— while maintaining intact the content of his faith in Scripture as God-given and God-filled, and the required hermeneutical consequences—to face up to the challenge of modern exegetical methods. This may, admittedly, induce him to redefine or reformulate some of his conceptions but never to reject them, being as they are of a higher order of truth. The rationale for this procedure is simply that of faith, that is, the rationale of convictions not merely grounded in rational evidence.

Regarding the second question, the easy way out (and the one quite frequently followed) is, as just mentioned, the reduction of the content of faith-deposit in Scripture to whatever conclusions scientific methods arrive at. Thus, if according to scientific analysis and from the literary and historical point of view, Christ's pre-existence is considered but a late development of New Testament christology—quite different from the presentation of Jesus which the earlier strata of the Synoptic Gospels seem to offer—then the conclusion seems to be that although within some circles in a later period he was held to have been pre-existent, in fact he was not. Again, if God's revelation of himself and his acting in man's history, even by miraculous interventions (*pelé*), are held to be merely one way among others of writing history, without necessarily corresponding to anything real but only to some sort of religious conception of God and his deeds, then very little remains of either Jewish or Christian faith, both of which are founded upon God's communicating himself to man and intervening in man's personal and collective life by saving deeds.

I venture to submit here that if one order of convictions is to give way to the other, it should not be that faith surrender to the results of scientific analysis but vice versa. Perhaps this is posing the problem too crudely. It could be rephrased, stating that the challenge should be accepted at the same level of the scientific process without any fear that the true content of faith will be endangered. This, however, requires certain *Vorverständnisse* (accepted premises), namely that those propositions coming from the faith to which Scripture itself gives witness are accepted as such instead of being swept under the rug. This, in turn, means that the process of scientific analysis itself can and possibly will be modified, without losing its scientific character. In other words, some guidance (to use this word) of the scientific *démarche* by higher convictions should be admitted, much as Jacques Maritain proposed in his conception of "philosophie chrétienne." That is, I believe, what the Church means when she advises the Christian exegete to resort to hermeneutical principles which are explicitly Christian. Similarly, in the well-known Jewish orthodox diffidence about modern exegetical methods a negative expression of the same basic conviction seems to be at work. However that may be, it can be confidently submitted that the times of "absolute autonomy" for science (including exegetical science) are past.

A further conclusion may be drawn at this point, without going here

into details. A very urgent problem at this stage of Bible study and interpretation most certainly is: What is the aim of such study? Or, what do
we study and interpret the Bible for? Is it merely, as would seem from
many if not most commentaries, for the intellectual pleasure of arriving at
some satisfactory rational explanation of all the peculiarities, literary, historical and religious, of the books and sections of books that are part of
the Bible? That such exegetical aim would be justified by itself might seem
above question. Still, the problem is whether in this way we really attain
the true meaning of the Bible, that is, the message which the Bible was
meant to convey in the first place, or whether, instead, we only pave the
way for such real and meaningful understanding—if in fact we do. This
is where the modern distinction between *sens* (meaning) and *signification*
(import) may have an important application.[67] But what is *sens* without
signification? The Christian and Jewish traditions have always held,
though in different ways, that there exists a "spiritual," "religious," "theological," or "deeper" meaning of Scripture which is attainable only by
methods which in all probability would not qualify today as "scientific,"
whatever their degree of "rationality" might be. Midrash attempts to discover this meaning, as does typology and, generally speaking, that very
traditional method of reading and interpreting Scripture which is expressed in a medieval Latin distich; the latter forms the point of departure
for Henri de Lubac's famous book on the four meanings of Scripture.[68]
There is, admittedly, no need to insist on the four meanings as such nor,
for that matter, on any particular midrashic tradition. It would, however,
be extremely unwise to dismiss offhand the quest for meaning to which
such methods are witness, even if only time-conditioned witness. Such a
quest looks for something in Scripture which goes beyond the conclusions
of scholarly exegetical analysis without necessarily denying its useful-
ness—something which really helps to discover the message of the Bible
so as to become true spiritual nourishment for the reader in the context
of contemporary life.

The problem of actualization should be mentioned at this point. The
bridge over the cultural and historical chasm between texts written in an
ancient Jewish or Hellenistic-Jewish cultural context and the requirements
of contemporary man, without dismissing any part of the Bible as useless,
can be built only upon such foundations.[69] There is an "eternal" meaning
to the Bible which, properly understood, speaks to all generations. This is
why the Bible was written or, if you wish, was inspired. And this is what
the exegete should look for if he chooses to adhere to something more than
a rather recent scholarly tradition.

I would finally like to refer in passing to another and more complicated question, unavoidably raised I believe by the present situation of the exegetical discipline: the question, namely, of the philosophical presuppositions of Bible interpretation. Is not a philosophical position of some kind at least implicit in any exegetical endeavor? And if so, would any one philosophical conception be as good as any other in such an endeavor? Bultmann comes immediately to mind with his commitment to a particular brand of existentialist philosophy. Admittedly, because of its many implications, the question is extremely difficult and delicate to raise. But since exegesis today demands such deep awareness of its own problematical situation, it may be worse not to face the question squarely.

V

At the beginning of this article, I tried to convey some of the malaise which we now experience at different levels and for different reasons vis-à-vis our very much sophisticated contemporary exegetical methods and their application, or certain forms of application. Nothing could be worse at this point than to reject the use of such methods and seek refuge in some new fundamentalism, of which there are some signs. The situation here described is meant to recall to all of us who hold the Bible as our normative reference, and as the vehicle for God's definitive revelation, what the Bible really is and according to what criteria it should be read if it is to be properly understood and believed in, not just "explained," even in the era of scientific exegetical methods. This is what I have tried to do in these pages. The development of a solution is far from complete. This article is at most an attempt at stating the terms of the problem. I am convinced, though, that if the Bible is to continue to serve as source of faith and of life, for Jew and Christian alike, that is, as the medium for an encounter with the living God while at the same time being subject to the strictures of scientific analysis, a path similar to what is here indicated should be followed. The Book which comes from God and leads to God can be read, understood, and preached, only in the light of God himself.

NOTES

1. References to the origin of such a debate can be found in L. Alonso Schoekel, "Dove va l'esegesi cattolica?" in *La Civiltà Cattolica* 3 (1960) 449–460. The question was taken up by A. Romeo, "Divino afflante Spiritu e le Opiniones

Novae," in *Divinitas* 4 (1960) 387–456, in what was exactly the *oppositum per diametrum*. Thus, the stage was set for a painful conflict in which personal integrity, respect for the other's intentions and elementary justice, not to mention charity, were not always honored.

2. This is not the place to introduce such a debate in detail. May it suffice to quote one major piece of the discussion: H. Schuermann, *Jesu ureigener Tod* (Freiburg: Herder, 1975).

3. Another debate into which we should not enter here. The general impression is that most exegetes solve the question negatively.

4. Cf. the position taken by Raymond E. Brown, *Jesus God and Man* (Milwaukee: Bruce, 1968).

5. A comparison was drawn by Martin Buber, *Two Types of Faith* (New York: Harper, 1961). We do not wish to enter here on a discussion of the adequacy of Buber's description of Christian faith.

6. A. Soggin, *Introduzione all' Antico Testamento* (Brescia: Paideia Editrice, 1979³), pp. 203f, mentions the objection by A. Jepsen in an article, "Zur Chronologie des Priesterkodex," in *Zeitschrift fuer die Alttestamentliche Wissenschaft* 47 (1929) 251–255.

7. *Ibid.,* pp. 201ff.

8. *Ibid.,* pp. 205–212.

9. E.g., B. Orchard, *The Griesbach Solution to the Synoptic Question* (Manchester: Koinonia, 1976), Vol. I. To some scholars in Israel (Lindsey, Flusser) Luke would be the first Gospel.

10. This does not intend to deny at all the efforts on various sides, especially in the Christian churches, to close the gap, but the gap is still there.

11. Some of the examples given in previous paragraphs could aptly illustrate that situation.

12. I tried to present this problem in a recent article, "Los Evangelios de la Infancia en un libro reciente," in *Documentación CELAM* 3 (1977) 235–246, esp. 241f. The book referred to in that article is Raymond E. Brown, *The Birth of the Messiah* (Garden City, N.Y.: Doubleday, 1977). I would like to reaffirm here what I think is already clear from that article: Brown's book is not in any way the best example for the problem described.

13. The question would be precisely this: Does the "scholarly" aspect of such works always support the religious quest and does it introduce readers to the mystery of the word of God? I do not intend to say that the one never helps the other. Admittedly the balance is extremely difficult to strike. The whole matter depends on the general orientation.

14. Some books could here be mentioned, e.g., J. P. Miranda, *Marx y la Biblia* (Salamanca: Sígueme, 1972); F. Belo, *Lecture matérialiste de l'Evangile de Marc* (Paris: Cerf, 1974).

15. Cf., e.g., G. Girardi, *Christiani per il socialismo, perchè?* (Assisi: Citadella Editrice, 1975).

16. *Ibid.,* pp. 35, 59, 77.

17. The latest treatment of the subject is S. Sabugal, *Liberación y Secularización?* (Barcelona: Herder, 1978), pp. 48–97. I myself wrote on this question on the occasion of the CELAM symposium on liberation theology in 1973, "La Liberación. Aspectos bíblicos," in *La Liberación, Diálogos en el CELAM* (Bogota: CE-LAM, 1974) 271–307, also published in *Teología* (Buenos Aires) 10 (1972/73) 25–61. The bibliography is more fully discussed in the thesis by M. Hofmann, *Identifikation mit dem Anderen, Theologische Themen und ihr hermeneutischer Ort bei lateinamerikanischen Theologen der Befreiung* (Stockholm: Verbum, 1978), pp. 226–251.

18. Cf. Sabugal, *op. cit.,* pp. 146–223, and my article quoted in note 17.

19. J. Sobrino, *Christología desde América Latina, Esbozo a partir del seguimiento de Jesús histórico* (Mexico: Ediciones CRT, 1976), and L. Boff, *Paixâo do Christo, Paixâo do Mundo* (Petropolis: Vozes, 1977), belong in this context. On the first, I expressed my opinion in "Una nueva Cristología 'latinoamericana,' " in *Documentación CELAM* 2 (1977) 1383–1396. I referred to the second in "La Cristología en el Documento de Puebla," in *Lateranum,* NS 45 (1979) 130–57, esp. 133–135. Both authors, however, avoid carefully the crass socio-political interpretation of the Gospels, which is evident in other writings.

20. This is particularly the case in the interpretation of the death of Jesus, its motivation and its "horizon."

21. This is where Latin American and, generally speaking, third world political theology dissociates itself from European theology of the same kind and criticizes the latter; cf. G. Gutierrez on Johannes B. Metz.

22. Two meetings of so-called third world theologians have taken place, the last one in Nairobi in January 1979. I am not conversant with the Bible reading of black theologians.

23. Cf. Austin P. Flannery, ed., *Documents of Vatican II* (Grand Rapids: Eerdmans, 1975), "Decree on Ecumenism," pp. 452–560, no. 21, where this point is mentioned in a very balanced way.

24. Two rather remarkable instances of such an achievement are the fruits of the Lutheran/Roman Catholic official dialogue in the United States. Cf. Raymond E. Brown, K. P. Donfried, J. Reumann, eds., *Peter in the New Testament* (New York: Paulist Press; Minneapolis: Augsburg Publ., 1973); also Raymond E. Brown, K. P. Donfried, J. Reumann, J. A. Fitzmyer, *Mary in the New Testament* (New York: Paulist Press; Philadelphia: Fortress Press, 1978). The exegetical conclusions of both books are open to criticism and are, indeed, so intended.

25. The main study on the subject still seems to be Hans J. Kraus, *Geschichte der historisch-kritischen Erforschung des Alten Testaments von der Reformation bis zur Gegenwart* (Neukirchen: Neukirchner Vlg., 1956), at least for that part of the Bible.

26. Cf. E. Poulat, *Histoire, dogme et critique dans la crise moderniste* (Paris-Tournai: Casterman, 1962); *idem, Intégrisme et catholicisme intégral* (Paris-Tour-

nai: Casterman, 1969). See also the review article by R. Aubert in *Concilium* 17 (1966) pp. 91–108.

27. I am unable to ascertain the authenticity of such a dictum. It might well be the expression of animosity toward a much discussed figure; cf. Hans J. Kraus, *op. cit.*, p. 237: "Ich habe das Alte Testament etwas satt bekommen."

28. The validity of *Literarkritik* has been carefully defended by Roland de Vaux against the traditio-historical school of some Scandinavians (Engnell in the first place) which accused the method of being "interpretatio europeica moderna." Cf. "A propos du 2ème centenaire d'Astruc; réflexions sur l'état actuel de la critique du Pentateuque," in *Vetus Testamentum* Suppl. 1 (1953) 182–198. But de Vaux applied the method in a very nuanced way.

29. Reference is here made to the relevant decrees by the Pontifical Biblical Commission; cf. *Enchiridion Biblicum* 1961[4], nos. 324–339, 383–413. The interpretation of such decrees is now governed by the unofficial but meaningful article by the then secretary of the Commission, A. Miller, "Das neue biblische Handbuch," in *Benediktinische Monatsschrift* 31 (1955) 49f. The under-secretary, A. Kleinhans, published an article along the same lines; cf. *Antonianum* 30 (1955) 63–65. Then, J. Dupont commented upon both in *Revue Biblique* 72 (1955) 414–419.

30. In its general outline, the story was told by F. M. Braun, *L'oeuvre du Père Lagrange, étude et bibliographie* (Fribourg: Imprimerie St. Paul, 1943).

31. Cf. Hans J. Kraus, *op. cit.*, pp. 265–334.

32. The names and feats of biblical archaeology are by now part of the history of biblical exegesis during the last fifty years. Cf. especially W. F. Albright, *The Archaeology of Palestine* (London: Pelican, 1949); also G. E. Wright, *Biblical Archaeology* (Philadelphia: Westminster Press, 1957[1]). Books such as C. Marston, *The Bible Comes Alive* (London: Eyre & Spottiswood, 1937), and W. Keller, *Und die Bibel hat doch Recht* (Duesseldorf, 1956) are now mostly considered curiosities but did enjoy real popularity in their day, even among pastors and religion teachers.

33. Cf., e.g., D. W. Thomas, *Archaeology and Old Testament Study* (London, 1967).

34. This seems to be the gist of the debate in the 1950's between W. F. Albright and Martin Noth. Cf. Martin Noth, "Der Beitrag der Archaeologie zur Geschichte Israels," in *Vetus Testamentum,* Suppl. 7 (1960) 262–282.

35. Cf. Martin Noth, *Ueberlieferungsgeschichte des Pentateuch* (Stuttgart: Kohlhammer, 1948), pp. 184f. How far the pendulum has swung may be gauged by the recent book by Henri Cazelles, *A la Recherche de Moïse* (Paris: Cerf, 1979).

36. Cf. Martin Noth, *op. cit.*, p. 186: "So kaemen wir schliesslich auf die Mosegrabtradition als das ... urspruenglichste noch erhaltene Element der Moseueberlieferung hinaus." Henri Cazelles, *op. cit.*, p. 8: "Pour M. Noth, Moïse ne serait guère qu'une sépulture sur le Mont Nébo."

37. One example in point is the current discussion on the historicity of the

affirmation of the virginal conception of Jesus; cf. Raymond E. Brown, *The Birth of the Messiah,* appendix IV, pp. 517–531.

38. As if the more ancient layer attainable were closer to the truth, a presupposition which seems to forget the concept of tradition.

39. Cf., among many others, P. Ricoeur, *Ermeneutica filosofica ed ermeneutica biblica* (Brescia: Paideia Editrice, 1977), originally published in 1975 but part of a series of lectures given by many scholars in the field, at some theological faculties in Switzerland in 1972/3. Ricoeur follows his own path.

40. Cf., e.g., P. Grech, "La nuova ermeneutica biblica: Fuchs e Ebeling," in *Atti della Settimana Biblica Italiana* 21 (1972) 71–90.

41. It goes without saying that I am here speaking strictly for myself.

42. Cf. the official Latin text in *Enchiridion Biblicum,* nos. 538–569.

43. Instruction of the Pontifical Biblical Commission, "The Historical Truth of the Gospels," translated in *Theological Studies* 25 (1964) 386–408.

44. Official Latin text in *Acta Apostolicae Sedis* 56 (1964) 712–718.

45. Cf. Austin P. Flannery, *op. cit.,* pp. 750–765.

46. *Enchiridion Biblicum,* no. 551.

47. *Ibid.*

48. *Acta Apostolicae Sedis* 56 (1964) 713.

49. *Ibid.*

50. *Ibid.*

51. "Ut (the Catholic exegete) Evangeliorum perennem veritatem et auctoritatem in plena luce collocet"—*ibid.*

52. Austin P. Flannery, *op. cit.,* pp. 350–358, nos. 3ff.

53. *Acta Synodalia Sacr. Conc. Oec. Vaticani II* (Typis Polyglottis Vaticanis, 1970ff.), four volumes in several parts.

54. "Sacra Scriptura eodem Spiritu quo scripta est etiam legenda et interpretanda (est)": a most traditional affirmation the history of which would be useful to follow.

55. The "non minus" refers to the previous paragraph where abundant reference is made to some scientific methods of exegesis (*genera literaria*).

56. *Acta Apostolicae Sedis* 56 (1964) 715. Cf. *Dei Verbum* in Austin Flannery, *op. cit.,* p. 761, no. 19.

57. Cf. Helga Croner, comp., *Stepping Stones to Further Jewish-Christian Relations,* an unabridged collection of Christian documents (New York: Stimulus Books, 1977), p. 2.

58. The same applies to the following affirmation, not easy for many people to swallow: Iudaei tamen neque ut a Deo reprobati neque ut maledicti exhibeantur, quasi hoc ex Sacris Litteris sequatur ("The Jews should not be presented as rejected or accursed by God, as if this followed from the Holy Scriptures"); cf. Helga Croner, *op. cit.,* p. 2.

59. I would like to quote here from a remarkable article by J. M. Dubois, O.P.

of Jerusalem, "Ce qu'un chrétien peut attendre d'une lecture juive de la Bible," in *SIDIC* 10 (1977) no. 2, 22: "De même en effet que la sagesse philosophique trouve sa santé dans un consentement à l'être et au vrai antérieur à toute attitude critique, de même la sagesse de la Foi et de l'existence chrétienne repose sur une lecture candide de la Parole confirmée par la Tradition, c'est-à-dire en définitive par la vie de la communauté ecclésiale et par l'existence des saints." And further on: "Les méthodes d'analyse et d'exégèse peuvent certes critiquer les conditions de cette lecture, elles ne pourront jamais la supprimer car elle leur est antérieure." I would gladly devote my whole paper to nothing but commentary on these two sentences.

60. Cf. *Dei Verbum,* in Austin P. Flannery, *op. cit.,* p. 757, no. 12.

61. Pope Pius XII, encyclical letter on *Promotion of Biblical Studies* #47 (U.S.C.C., 1944), translated from the Latin, *Divino Afflante Spiritu* (*Enchiridion Biblicum,* #505)

62. Cf. Austin P. Flannery, *op. cit.,* p. 757, no. 12. It would be interesting to follow this theme (*analogia fidei*) in the theological tradition.

63. Cf. *ibid.:* ". . . no less attention must be devoted to the content and unity of the whole of Scripture. . . ." This also is a theme to be carefully studied, particularly in the context of present biblical scholarship.

64. The Siracide seems to be admitted but not Maccabees nor the Greek versions of Esther and Daniel.

65. Cf. the articles by F. Dreyfus, "Exégèse en Sorbonne, exégèse en Eglise," in *Revue Biblique* 82 (1975) 321–359; "Actualisation à l'intérieur de la Bible," in *Revue Biblique* 83 (1976) 161–202—this last one still unfinished.

66. The question of the Canon should come in at this point but cannot now be dealt with adequately. It will suffice to say that I would maintain that the Canon is not a product of chance either, however long the time-process to acknowledge its proper limits has taken.

67. J. M. Dubois, *Lettres aux Amis* (of St. Isaiah House, Jerusalem) 51/52 (1978) 18, applies the distinction to precisely this problem.

68. Henri de Lubac, *Exégèse mediévale, les quatre sens de l'Ecriture* (Paris: Aubier-Montaigne, 1959–1969). The Latin distich reads, in one of its many versions:

Littera gesta docet, quid credas allegoria,
Moralis quid agas, quo tendas anagogia.

It is contained already in the *Postillae* by Nicolas of Lyra (ab. 1330).

69. Bultmann's attempt should be mentioned here, but it includes setting the Old Testament aside, more or less, and choosing the *was* (what) over against the *dass* (that, ought), but the latter also belongs to the Bible.

PART II
THE RELATIONSHIP
OF HEBREW BIBLE
AND NEW TESTAMENT

A Jewish Reading
of the New Testament

Leonard S. Kravitz

I

A Jewish reading of the New Testament presents a number of problems. What kind of Jewish reader is involved? If we mean a Jew associated with the religious traditions of Judaism, it must be stated that there are Jews whose understanding of their own tradition precludes their delving into any other. These Jews would feel, moreover, that the very fact that Christianity, whose source is in the New Testament, split off from Judaism makes the reading of that book anathema. On the other hand, there are Jews who have no association with their own religious tradition and who would feel that the reading of a source book of another religion would make as little sense in their life as a perusal of their own.

To the Jew who associates with his own religious tradition and yet is comfortable with the reading of another tradition's source book, reading the New Testament would present the same conceptual problems as reading the Koran would to a Christian, or reading the Book of Mormon to either a Christian or a Muslim. It implies that a particular conceptual claim is made for a book which ostensibly supplants or completes one's own tradition. As far as he remains true to his own tradition, the reader is constrained to deny the claims of the book which he now undertakes to read. To the level that he hears the Divine speaking to him from the pages of his own religious texts, he will feel unable to hear the Divine in the text which he is now going to peruse. To the level that he feels an exclusivity in his own tradition, to that level he may feel that another religious tradition cannot reveal the Divine, either to him or to anybody else. Simply put, he may feel that another claim to religious truth is a claim which is in error. He may consider, however, that the Divine may speak to him through the pages of his own tradition while speaking to others through their own tradition. In sum, reading another's sacred literature raises the question: Why mine against theirs? Or: Why mine among theirs? And to which of any or all shall the tag "sacred" be applied?

Religious traditions make competing claims. How those claims are adjudicated will depend on the particular understanding of one's own religious tradition. Hence, before coming to read a particular religious text, a *Tendenz* is operative which must be attended to. Another's religious tradition is always read from the "outside." It is read through the lenses of assumptions, conscious and unconscious, of one's own tradition. The reader carries within him the baggage of understanding that he applies to his own tradition. If he is aware that his own tradition came into being after a period of reflection on certain events, he will not be surprised to see a similar development having occurred in the literature he is now about to read. If he perceives strata within the written documents of his own tradition, he will look out for such strata within the tradition he now faces. In fact, he may more easily see the strata, the retelling, the contradictions and contrasting elements, precisely because he looks at the new literature from the "outside."

Why would anyone read another's religious literature? Why particularly would a Jew read the New Testament? He would not read it as his sacred literature but as that of another; more precisely, he would read it as *literature*. More than that, he would read the New Testament as the source book of his neighbor's religion, the base of belief of a vast number of people throughout the world, the text which depicts the emergence of Christianity from the parent-religion of Judaism, to which he himself is committed. This reading of the New Testament, then, will not be *the* but *a* Jewish reading of the New Testament by one who is not a New Testament scholar but who is fairly knowledgeable about his Jewish sources. This reading will not be objective, as has been said, but will attempt to be sympathetic. It may open a window for him on the rabbinic period of Jewish history, about which he knows something and would like to know more, realizing that in principle the fact of separation of the Christian group from the Jewish will create in the Christian literature a particular *Tendenz* itself.

Before even approaching the first page of the New Testament, the reader knows that Christianity began among Jews; yet, all the Jews then and all Jews now did not and do not accept its beliefs. That fact tells him that the Jewish Christians, to the extent that they were Jews, had accepted Jewish elements of identity formation, namely a literature and a pattern of life: the Hebrew Scriptures and the enactments of the Torah, the institutions of the Temple and Synagogue, the leadership of priests and scribes, and all others associated with the Jewish polity. He knows also that the polity existed under the hegemony of the Roman Empire, as administered by Herod, a king chosen by Rome. Hence, the Jewish reader may assume that an emerging group will argue for its position from within the textual system held in common. The method of argumentation will be that used by the Jewish group, though the conclusions will differ. Had they remained the same, the Jewish Christians would have remained Jews. Had the methods been different, the Jewish Christians would not have been Jews in the first place, nor would they have been able to argue with other Jews. To argue from a text, one must share it as well as a method of arguing from that text; to arrive at a different conclusion, one must apply the method already agreed upon, in a different manner.

Differences in interpretation, of necessity, would come to challenge authority, for in any textual system that has a method of interpretation, there must exist an authoritative interpretation, lest the society based upon those interpretations collapse. Knowing the history of Judaism, the reader is aware that the conflicts of Jewish life have arisen precisely over the matter of "proper" interpretation, as have indeed the conflicts in the subsequent history of the Christian faith. To differ over interpretation means to differ with those whose positions are based on particular interpretations. Thus forewarned, the Jewish reader will anticipate that the New Testament, presenting a different interpretation of passages in the Hebrew Scriptures, will contain the presentation of conflicts with authority figures of the Jewish group. He will not be surprised that "scribes, elders . . . and chief priests" (Mk 8:31) or Pharisees and Sadducees (Mk 8:11) are negatively described. Such attacks are entailed in the notion of differences in interpretation. Once one assumes attacks upon authority figures, one may even expect the pattern of such attacks. In religious conflicts dealing with that which is treasured and held with affection, one rarely finds a balanced and fair presentation of the other's side. The Jewish reader reflecting on the language used by the Rabbanites against the Karaites or by the Jewish philosophers against some of the rabbinic authorities of their time, or on the mutual incriminations of the Hasidim and Mitnagdim, would expect the New Testament to paint the "other side" in the darkest colors, their virtues proclaimed not to be virtues at all, their failings presented in the vilest form. To assume otherwise, and, indeed, to find anything else, would make the New Testament a truly super-human book.

The separation of religious groups, moving from schism to heresy to different religious status, is always a painful process. A Christian reflecting upon the separation of Protestant Christianity from Catholic Christianity or a Jew pondering any controversy in Jewish history knows that there is to be found, to say the least, intemperate language. Words, alas, can wound, and at times will even kill.

What is at stake is the meaning of words in the Scriptures held in common; what will separate the emerging Church from the Synagogue is the meaning of some definite words. Who interprets and how the process of interpretation is carried out is what the separation of mother and daughter faiths is all about.

II

Armed with such an understanding, a Jew comes to the reading of the New Testament. What does he find? The first thing he notes is that the book was originally written in Greek, *koine* Greek, the Greek of the marketplace, but Greek nonetheless. If a Jew thinks of that literature supposedly contemporaneous with the New Testament, i.e., rabbinic literature, he thinks of literature written in Hebrew. He knows that the spoken language of the Jews was Aramaic, while the written, at least as presented in the Midrashim and the Mishnah, was Hebrew. He knows that Greek was prevalent in Jewish Palestine,[1] but such usage entered a Hebrew corpus and constituted simply elements scattered throughout a larger whole. That such usage should occur is obvious, since the Jewish people lived within Roman Palestine whose cultural overlay was Greek. The struggle over Hellenistic culture was the essence of the Maccabean wars. True, the Hebrew Scriptures had been translated into Greek; yes, as a later midrash would put it, the words of Yaphet might be within the tents of Shem;[2] still, no book in Greek served as an operative element within rabbinic Judaism. Here, now, a whole series of books which comprise the New Testament is entirely in Greek. (I do not enter here into the question whether or not the New Testament was a translation from the Aramaic.) It assumed *ipso facto* a different audience, one that could read Greek and would be more open to those elements which derived from Hellenistic culture in general.

A difference in schooling is implicit in the fact that the New Testament was written in Greek. By virtue of that fact, the entire school system created by the rabbis to train Jews to study their own literature (at five, to study Scripture; at ten, to study Mishnah; at thirteen, to understand enough to follow the Commandments; at fifteen, to study the Talmud[3]) is here set aside by the requirement to know Greek sufficiently well to read the New (in yet another sense of the word) Testament.

That ideas originating in Greek culture could easily enter the New Testament becomes evident in the opening verses of the Gospel of John. Indeed, that a Greek audience was addressed is attested by Paul's statement that the meaning of the Christ is problematic not only for Jews but for Greeks as well (1 Cor 1:22ff).

The language and some of the concepts of the Graeco-Roman world employed in the New Testament suggest that the audience addressed was no longer the Jewish group from whom the emerging Church separated itself. What we have in the books of the New Testament is the resultant of a certain period of time, namely from the emergence of the Jewish-Christian groups to the time of the writing down of a new gospel directed to a wider world. One may suspect that the very movement toward that wider world was partly the result of a lack of acceptance of that literature by the parent Jewish group. Had the Jewish group accepted the New Testament as "gospel," one would assume that the book of the origins of the Christian faith had been written in the language of the Jews, either in Hebrew or at the very least in Aramaic.

The language employed in writing down the events surrounding a man and his followers in Palestine, a man who spoke Aramaic and read Hebrew, who read the Torah and preached in synagogues and differed with the authorized interpretations in that preaching, strongly suggests the separation of the two groups and a movement away from the attempt by the followers of the daughter religion to convince those of the mother religion.

A Jewish reader now notes that the first books of the New Testament consist of four gospels, three of which seem to retell the identical story and a fourth which rather reflects on it. What immediately strikes the Jewish reader is that a claim is made about the main character in those gospels, Jesus of Nazareth. He is called the Christ, which is Greek for Messiah, the Anointed. Now, hope for the Messiah can be found in biblical and rabbinic literature as well. The word itself, in that context, means one anointed as king. In later biblical literature, after the Jewish people had lost their political independence, there evolved the hope that once again there would be a king over Israel, which is to say that the people of Israel would once again be independent. More than that, in the manner of kings of the ancient world, he would exert his dominion over other nations. Hence, the psalmist hopes that God will soon say:

> I have appointed my king over Zion,
> my holy mountain.
> I will announce the decree.
> The Lord hath said to me:
> "My son art thou. . . .
> I will give thee nations for an inheritance,
> and for thy possession the uttermost ends of the earth.
> Thou shalt break them with a rod of iron;
> like a potter's vessel shalt thou dash them into pieces" (Ps 2:6–9).

The hoped for restoration was yet expanded beyond the control over nations to a control over nature itself, as we read in the words of that unknown prophet who writes in the Book of Isaiah:

> And there shall come forth a shoot out of the house of Jesse
> and a twig shall grow forth out of his roots.
> And the spirit of the Lord shall rest upon him,
> the spirit of wisdom and understanding,
> the spirit of counsel and might,
> the spirit of knowledge and the fear of the Lord.
> And his delight shall be in the fear of the Lord.
> He shall not judge after the sight of his eyes,
> neither decide after the hearing of his ears.
> With righteousness he shall judge the poor,
> and with equity decide for the meek of the land.
> And righteousness shall be the girdle of his loins
> and faithfulness shall be the girdle of his reins. And the wolf
> shall dwell with the lamb
> and the leopard shall lie down with the kid,
> and the calf and the young lion and the fatling together, and
> a little child to lead them.
> They shall not hurt nor destroy in all my holy mountain,
> for the earth shall be full of the knowledge of the Lord
> as the waters cover the sea (Is 11:1–9).

These verses will play their part in "proving" that Jesus is, indeed, the expected Messiah. It should be obvious from the foregoing why this must be so.

National restoration and cosmic change would later on alternate in their application to the meaning of the Messiah. As the Jewish people suffered more and more under Roman control, one or the other theme would take on greater importance; yet in both themes there was agreement that whatever the messianic advent might mean, it would at the least bring deliverance of the Jewish people from Roman control. Whether initiated from on high or acted on from below, the coming of the Messiah would mean that the Jewish people would achieve their political independence.

Jews prayed for this event, as evinced in the prayer text of the Eighteen Benedictions which seems to have been accepted about 90 CE. And for this the Jews revolted a second time against Roman rule, in the Bar Kokhba insurrection of 132–135. Rabbi Akiba, the leading authority of that time, considered Simon Bar Kokhba the Messiah; however, the revolt failed and Akiba was martyred. Yet, the yearning for the Messiah continued. In opposition to the more extreme forms of such yearnings, Samuel, a sage of the third century, declared:

> The Messianic age differs from the present in nothing except that Israel will throw off the yoke of the nations and regain its political independence.[4]

Still, the cosmic theme was not to be suppressed, and again and again it showed up in Jewish history. The more rational the mode of Jewish thinking, the greater the emphasis on national revival. Thus, Maimonides (1135–1204) stressed the saying of Samuel,[5] while Abraham ben David of Posquières (1125–1198), a somewhat mystical commentator, emphasized the more cosmic nature of the advent of the awaited Messiah.[6] Yet all Jews within the religious tradition recited, and recite to this day, the statement in the Creed composed by Maimonides:

> I believe with perfect faith in the coming of the Messiah,
> and, though he tarry I will wait daily for his coming.[7]

Jews have waited. And as verses held to be messianic promises, such as "Nation shall not lift up sword against nation nor learn war any more" (Is 2:4; Mi 4:3), have not been fulfilled, and as so many tragic events culminating in the Holocaust of our own time have occurred in Jewish history, Jews still wait.

Thus when a Jew reads the first verse of the New Testament and sees there the claim that Jesus is the Messiah, he tells himself that it cannot be so. The promises are yet unfulfilled; the pain of our people is still too great; suffering abounds in the world as well. Whatever Jesus was, whatever the meaning and significance of his life, he could not be the Messiah, at least as Jews understand the term.

To read the New Testament in which the word "Christ" is applied to Jesus suggests to the Jewish reader who knows that Christ and Messiah both mean "the Anointed" that it is the difference in interpretation of commonly held words which separates Judaism from Christianity. Had the interpretation remained the same, there would have been no divorcement.

Reading the New Testament with Jewish eyes, one may surmise that the meaning of the term Messiah/Christ was in question at the very origins of the Church and in the earliest strata of its literature. "Who do men say that I am?" is the question which Jesus puts to his disciples (Mt 16:13; Mk 8:27; Lk 9:18). Their answer is most interesting: "Some say John the Baptist, some say Elijah, and still others one of the prophets" (Matthew adds, "Jeremiah"). All these worthies were dead; for Jesus to have been any one of them, resurrection had to have taken place already. If therefore the resurrection, a central event in the Christian faith, is the main proof of the validity of Jesus' role, then, as the New Testament presents the popular mind, it would have taken place toward the beginning of Jesus' ministry. It seems that we have here an anticipatory anachronism. Either the people took resurrection as a not uncommon event touching one, John, who had been killed in Jesus' lifetime, or one, Elijah, who in the folk mind had not died but been taken up to heaven (2 Kgs 2:11) (and whom later Jewish tradition would see as a kind of emissary between heaven and earth, visiting the Jewish people on significant occasions such as at every Seder, and who would precede the messianic advent), or one, a prophet such as Jeremiah, who was separated in time from Jesus by some five hundred to six hundred years, at which point the resurrection of Jesus after the crucifixion loses its unique quality—or the question recorded in the three Synoptic Gospels read resurrection back into time.

When Jesus pressed his disciples for their view, Peter responded, "You are the Christ, the son of the living God" (Mt 16:16; cf. Jn 6:69), which seems to be an allusion to Ps 2:7. The meaning of the term Christ or Messiah, is the crux of the different views of the Synagogue and the emerging Church. For the Jews, the minimal meaning of the messianic coming was freedom from Roman domination. When therefore the "Pharisees and Herodians" asked Jesus about the payment of tribute to Caesar (Mt 22:18; Mk 12:14), they were doing more than attempting to set a trap for Jesus, as the text and some Christian commentators[8] suggest. They were asking whether he claimed to be the Messiah, a claim which, if fulfilled, would free them from paying that tribute.

The Jewish meaning of Messiah underlies the first question put by the apostles to the risen Jesus: "Lord, wilt thou at this time restore again the kingdom to Israel?" (Acts 1:6). They, too, expected the Messiah to be he who restores political independence.

The change in expectations associated with the Messiah and the shift in meaning of the term are the burden of much of the New Testament. The Jewish reader might add that such changes and shifts were required by the events of the history subsequent to the life of Jesus. Roman domination did not immediately end; political independence did not come to the Jewish people, to say nothing of a change in nature: any lamb lying down with a lion would do so at its peril. Jesus could not have been the Messiah as Jews understood the meaning of the term; hence, a Jew might say, the meaning of the term had to be changed.

A shift in usage symbolizes the shift in meaning. A Christian speaks of the *Christ* not merely because the New Testament is written in Greek but because the *Messiah* no longer applies. One could argue that the New Testament was written in Greek precisely because a shift in meaning had occurred. Had Jesus been the Messiah expected by the Jews, either all texts would have been written in Hebrew or none would have been required.

What the Christ now has come to mean is that he is the one who changes the world within but not that without. That change requires an altered attitude, not a change in acts. Hence, the entire *mitzvah* system of the Synagogue[9] would gradually be seen as irrelevant to Christian religious life. This message is not immediately presented and its ramifications are not fully grasped; the question of faith versus works, therefore, is being debated within the New Testament (cf. Rom 4:4f; Jas 2:21ff) and in later Christian tradition.

III

What is taught is that the law is not enough; a change in attitude is also required. Jesus tells his followers, therefore, that merely observing the prohibition against murder does not suffice; hostility which might engender murder must also be curbed (Mt 5:21f). Merely avoiding adultery is not enough; lust which might entice one to such a sin must also be controlled (Mt 5:31f). To argue that these and similar statements have parallels in rabbinic literature would miss the point. What is at stake is the authority of Jesus, not his exegesis.

The problem of authority is related to the question of who Jesus was, and what was the new meaning of the Messiah. If he was merely, as those in his hometown synagogue of Nazareth saw him, "a carpenter, the son of Mary, the brother of James and Joseph and Judas and Simon" (Mt 13:54ff; cf. Mk 6:3; Lk 4:23), then he has no authority. Concerning his teachings, they may well ask, "From whence hath this man these things?" (Mt 13:56; cf. Lk 4:22; Mk 6:2) and be offended at him.

If Jesus, however, is one who during his life was able to work miracles (Mt 14:13ff; Mk 6:41ff), drive out demons (Mk 1:24ff), forgive sin (Mk 2:6; Lk 5:32), heal the sick (Mk 2:3ff) and raise the dead (Mk 5:36ff) and by his sacrificial death bring about remission of sins (Rom 3:35)—in short, if he is the *Christ*—then it is clear that at the beginning of his career already he will speak with authority (Mk 1:22) because that authority is greater than that of Moses, in the same manner that the authority of a son is greater than that of a servant (Heb 3:5f).

If Jesus' authority is greater than that of Moses, it is obvious that he can come to "fulfill the law" (Mt 5:17). Entailed in that very notion is a challenge to those who hold fast to the Law of Moses, particularly to those whose authority in the Jewish polity is based on that law. We should not be surprised, moreover, to find certain attacks upon the Jewish leadership. For example, if one claims authority on the basis of that which is now superseded, one may be viewed as a hypocrite; therefore, reading the charge that "the scribes and Pharisees" are hypocrites does not surprise the Jewish reader. He understands that such a charge is structurally required, and he will see no need to defend the Pharisees or any other Jewish leaders of the time.

The charge of hypocrisy also contains a message within a message: Not only do the Jewish leaders teach that which they themselves do not observe, but that which they teach should not be observed because it has been superseded.

An attack on law, then, was an attack on authority, and vice versa. This may be observed in the scene wherein Jesus contends with the Pharisees with regard to the laws of ritual cleanliness (Mt 15; Mk 7). He does not observe those laws and calls them the tradition of men. For the Pharisees, these laws were part of what is termed Oral Law, given at Sinai together with the Written. To suggest that any part of the Oral Law was merely the tradition of men was to challenge their belief that the Oral Law was Divine in origin. Since the Pharisees had contended with the Sadducees precisely on the nature of the Oral Law, and since they based their authority upon it, Jesus' suggestion that any part of it was merely the tradition of men was to challenge their authority as well.

The attack upon the Oral Law also carried with it an attack upon the Written. First, because a written law needs interpretation—and to challenge the authoritative interpreter is to challenge the law itself. Second, because the new claim of authority made in Jesus' name carried with it the possibility of changing or supplanting the Written Law. That becomes evident in the discussion of divorce. When the Pharisees are portrayed as asking Jesus whether it is lawful for a man to put away his wife (Mk 10:2), the gospel writer cannot possibly assume that the Pharisees were ignorant of Deuteronomy 24. Rather, he anticipates the supplanting of the Written Law as a demonstration of the higher authority residing in Jesus. He will determine what the law is.

The structuring of that discussion serves to disparage the authority of the Written Law. To the question,

> "Is it lawful for a man to divorce his wife?" Jesus responded, "What did Moses command you?" The Pharisees answered, "Write a bill of divorcement and . . . put her away." Jesus replied, "For the hardness of your heart he wrote you this precept. . . . What God hath joined together let no man put asunder" (Mk 10:2–8).

This suggests that it was Moses who wrote the precept on divorce, without Divine revelation. No Jewish leader of the time, whether Pharisee or Sadducee, would agree with that; none would say that Moses was the source of the Law but that God was its source. To suggest that the Law originated with Moses, a mere mortal, ultimately threatens the authority of both Sadducee and Pharisee as teachers of the perfect Law of the Lord.

The discussion about what is permissible on the Sabbath (Lk 13:14–16) contains an attack upon law and authority as well. Not only does Jesus heal a chronic condition on the Sabbath, which contravenes Pharisaic teaching that only when there is danger to life may healing be done on the Sabbath day; Jesus also allows the plucking of corn on that day. To the Pharisaic mind, such activity went against both Written and Oral Law. By what authority could Jesus so teach? A later retelling of the event makes that clear. As the gospel of John presents the story (5:2–17), the Jews say that Jesus by breaking the Sabbath made himself equal to God (Jn 5:18). Jesus' reply suggests something of that equality: "The Son can do nothing of himself, but what he seeth the Father do" (Jn 5:17). There is a further statement, "All men should honor the Son, even as they honor the Father"

(Jn 5:23). In this context it becomes evident once more that to adduce rabbinic parallels to "The Sabbath is given to man and not man to the Sabbath" (Mk 2:27)[10] is to miss the point; again, the issue is authority. This is made manifest in the statement, "Therefore the Son of man is Lord also of the Sabbath" (Mk 2:28).

Once it is understood that authority is the issue and it is therefore important who wields it, the advice given to Jesus' followers not to pray in the synagogue (Mt 6:6) and not to use the prayer texts of the synagogues but rather one of Jesus' making (Mt 6:9ff) takes on a new dimension. To pray in the synagogues is to pray under authority of those who teach that which is superseded. Central to the synagogue service, moreover, is the reading of the Torah on sabbaths and festivals and at least twice during the week. That very reading is inimical to the religious life; it is a veil over the heart (2 Cor 3:15). To hear the words of the Law and listen to its specifications is to be tempted; as Paul put it, "I have not known sin, but for the Law" (Rom 7:7). Such a law is not directed toward a person who is saved by following the authority of the Christ but is at best intended for one who is "lawless and disobedient" (1 Tim 1:9), somebody tainted by the worst and most unredeemable of sins.

To the Jewish reader accustomed to the formula of benediction in Jewish worship, ". . . Who has sanctified us by His commandments . . .", the words of Paul seem most strange. How does one live without law? How does one approach God without Torah? Yes, he understands that to the Christian, faith in Christ makes him a new creature (2 Cor 5:17). Yet the Jewish reader of the New Testament notes that the old problems have not disappeared. Fornication remains a temptation (1 Cor 5:1f; 1 Thess 4:3). Family life still needs to be properly structured (Eph 5:2ff). Even children, of whom Jesus had said "Such is the kingdom of heaven" (Mt 19:14; Mk 10:14), had to be reminded of the Decalogue's command to honor their parents (Eph 6:1; Col 3:20). Even though all the law is to be fulfilled in the love of God, as Dt 6:4 would have it, one has the feeling that the love of God has not in itself been efficacious in making for the love of one's fellowman (1 Jn 4:20).

The Jewish reader putting forward this comment does not do so in order to gain a point. It is rather to share with the Christian peruser of the New Testament the insights of Jewish tradition: if virtue with the law is difficult, virtue without it is all the more so. This insight seems to be echoed by the writer of the Letter of James (2:21ff) who comments on the verse, "Abraham believed God and it was counted unto him for righteousness" (Gn 15:6), in a manner different from Paul (Rom 4:4ff). Paul argued that the verse proved that faith was all. James asserts that it was Abraham's act of offering his son Isaac as sacrifice that imputed righteousness to him and entitled him to the encomium of being called "friend of God" (Jas 2:23). James' concluding statement of the discussion rings a responsive chord in the Jewish heart:

> For as the body without the spirit is dead, so faith without works is dead also (Jas 2:26).

The issue of authority resonates in the New Testament, particularly in the gospels, in still another way. The Jewish society of the time of Jesus is represented by its various leaders, priests, Pharisees, elders, scribes, Sadducees, and heads of synagogues. What of the people over whom they exercised authority? Do they accept that authority? This is a crucial question in that the success of the Christian position depended upon the people's ceasing to follow the Jewish leaders and beginning to accept the authority of the Christian leaders.

The gospels suggest a very tenuous relationship between the leaders and the led. Jesus is shown to make immediate inroads upon the loyalty of the people by his miraculous acts of healing, even though those acts are associated with tests of authority. Jesus not only heals, he heals by forgiving sin, thought by the Pharisees and the scribes to be a prerogative of God (Mk 2:6; Lk 5:21ff). His fame spreads, and wherever Jesus goes, he is followed by the masses. He is a popular hero in all places save his hometown of Nazareth, as we have seen.

Jesus' authority is a challenge to the religious authorities of his period. They attempt to harm him without at the same time antagonizing the people (Lk 20:19f). Their fear of the people is also the reason for the religious leaders' inability to challenge Jesus' authority in debate. When Jesus asks them how they would deal with the authority of John the Baptist, whether deriving from heaven or from men, "the chief priests, the scribes, and the elders," even in Jerusalem, their seat of power, are shown to be constrained by their perception of the beliefs of the multitudes; "they feared the people" (Mk 11:32f; Mt 21:26ff; Lk 20:1–6).

The Jewish reader may feel that this presentation of the pusillanimous quality of the Jewish leadership in the time of Jesus is yet another aspect of the structurally mandated hypocritical nature of that leadership. Not only are these leaders untruthful to what they pretend to believe about the Law, they are also deceitful in regard to what they believe about Jesus. We are given a double-bind argument: if they are sincere about what they believe concerning Jesus, they must try to kill him; if they refrain from killing him, they are not sincere.

The people and their leaders seem to become unified only at the time of Jesus' public trial. When given the choice between Jesus and Barabbas, the people and their leaders (Lk 23:13), indeed "all the people" (Mt 27:25), opt for the life of Barabbas and the death of Jesus. Writing at a later time, John has "the Jews" say: "Away with him! Away with him! Crucify him" (Jn 19:15). To the Jewish mind, that statement seems to reflect the separation between the Jewish and Christian groups. Such a separation would explain the rather positive description of the Roman Pilate as unwilling executor of the Jewish will who acts upon the threat of being charged with disloyalty to the emperor (Jn 19:12). One wonders how such cowardly Jewish leaders and such a weak Roman procurator were able to exercise control, each in his own way. However that may be, the Jewish reader will reflect ruefully how the phrase put into the mouths of the people, "His blood be upon us" (Mt 27:25), has resonated down the dark and bloody corridors of Jewish history.

If the New Testament account is taken as it stands, then the people's participation in the death of Jesus indicates that what had restrained the leadership, i.e., the people's belief that Jesus was a prophet (Mt 21:46), no longer obtained. The Jewish group no longer took Jesus for a prophet; he no longer held for them, if indeed he ever did, any authority at all.

For those who still believed, Jesus' death proved, paradoxically speaking, his mission because he had predicted it; indeed, he had willingly accepted it. Though all his disciples had forsaken him, and though one of their number had betrayed him, Jesus by his death was to convince many more than just those who had followed him in his life. His death was interpreted as a new paschal offering; and just as the Passover sacrifice of the lamb was offered with unbroken bones, so the crucified Jesus' bones were not broken (Ex 12:46; Jn 19:36).

The connection of Jesus with the Passover could have been anticipated by the Jewish reader. He knows that there existed a rabbinic tradition arguing that just as the world had been created in the month of Nisan in which Passover occurs, so the Messiah would come in Nisan to inaugurate the end. This tradition was opposed by the view that later became dominant—that just as the world had been created in the month of Tishri, so the Messiah would come in Tishri.[11]

The resurrection is to the Christian the ultimate proof of Jesus' mission. According to the gospels, the resurrection convinced his despairing disciples. Their faith in his reappearance convinced them to "go unto all the world and preach the gospel to every creature" (Mk 16:15), though it is also recorded that some still doubted until he spoke to them (Mt 28:17), and Luke has it that some doubted until he showed them his hands and feet (Lk 24:39–41). They seemed completely convinced when he asked for food, and they gave him broiled fish and a honeycomb (Lk 24:42). John records a large dinner of one hundred and fifty-three fishes and bread, to which the resurrected Jesus invited his disciples: "Come and dine" (Jn 21:12).

To the Jewish reader, the resurrection of Jesus is an element of faith which he does not share. Were he to believe in it, then even as the synoptic gospels and John are structured, he would be brought to a belief in the mission of Jesus and the new meaning of Messiah, the Christ, which is the ultimate message of these books. The crucial question for him is not the person of Jesus but the state of the world. Though the religion founded in Jesus' name has done much to change the world, it remains a place, alas, where nation still lifts up sword against nation and war is yet learned every day. Not only do lambs not lie down with lions, but men and women cannot lie down in peace, and many there are who make them afraid.

IV

How, then, does the Jewish reader look at the Jesus revealed in the four gospels, granting that he does not accept the reports of miraculous events after Jesus' death nor those before his birth?

The gospels show Jesus as a Jewish teacher whose views gradually become at variance with those of the Jewish establishment of his time. At first, he preaches in synagogues in support of the Law. Gradually his doctrines are felt to be in opposition to the Law. He is reported to be a worker of miracles, able to heal those who are ill in body and mind. He can heal not only those in his presence but those at a distance (Mt 8:13ff). He can still a stormy sea and with two fishes and five loaves feed a multitude, the latter the only miracle reported in all four of the Gospels (Mt 14:13–21; Mk 6:30–44; Lk 9:12–17; Jn 6:1–12). Jesus also works at times in a "natural" manner, as when he eschews any attempt at a miracle and feeds his hungry disciples on the Sabbath by simply plucking ears of corn. Though he is able to wrestle with Satan in the Judean wilderness, he understandably departs for Galilee upon hearing that John the Baptist has been imprisoned (Mt 4:12). He is presented as a man evincing great love to all who meet him, one to whom the term "Prince of Peace" (Is 9:6) will be applied. Yet, he can say,

> I come not to send peace, but a sword. For I come to set a man at vari-
> ance against his father, and the daughter against her mother and the
> daughter-in-law against her mother-in-law. . . . He that loveth father or
> mother more than me is not worthy of me (Mt 10:34–37).

This ambivalent, even contradictory quality in the life of Jesus is evident even in the introductory genealogies; descent from David is established through his father Joseph who, it is made clear, is really not his father (Mt 1).

Reading the gospel accounts of Jesus' life is a difficult task for the Jewish reader. Since he is prepared to see Jesus only as a man like other men, the Jewish reader tends to see Jesus as a teacher like any other Jewish teacher, one moreover whose doctrine carried him away from the mainstream of Jewish teaching. That description, of course, is hardly that of the Church. To be fair, the Jewish reader must admit that there must have been something remarkable about the quality of Jesus' personality to elicit the devotion that he commanded. But it does not mean that the Jewish reader admits any aspect of Christian doctrine, for he would be constrained to say that the personality of Mohammed also must have been remarkable to elicit the devotion of his followers.

Christianity, the Jewish reader would say, begins with the life and death of Jesus of Nazareth but does not end there. The New Testament consists of more than the four gospels, though it would not exist without them. Christianity in its historical development would elaborate on the New Testament with an ever-expanding tradition. The Jewish reader would be prepared for such expansion since Judaism points up certain parallels. He knows that Judaism is more than the Hebrew Scriptures, encompassing as well Midrash and Mishnah, Gemarah and Responsa; he knows therefore that a text held to be sacred and passing through time is lovingly embroidered on by the generations who peruse that text to give meaning to their life.

It is the dimension of time and its effects which characterizes the remainder of the New Testament, particularly the Acts of the Apostles and the epistles. The disciples go out to preach their new understanding of God's relation to man through Jesus. They, too, work miracles and heal the sick (Acts 3:6). Like their Master, they attempt to convince their fellow Jews (Acts 3:12) and have to face the opposition of the Jewish authorities (Acts 5:17).

Saul of Tarsus was a leading figure among those opposed to the emerging Church. He is portrayed as having "made havoc of the Church" (Acts 8:3), approving the mob's stoning of Stephen (Acts 7:58) and cruelly persecuting the Church. Yet, from being a staunch opponent, Saul was to become the greatest spokesman for the new faith. His conversion experience on the road to Damascus (Acts 9:3–19) was to cause him to wander throughout Asia Minor, even to Rome, to preach not only to Jews but to the Gentile world as well. His personality dominates the rest of the New Testament, even as the personality of Jesus dominates the gospels.

Paul is to articulate what the Christ means, a meaning not to be apprehended by the mind but by the heart:

> For it was in the wisdom of God that the world by wisdom knew not God; it pleased God by the foolishness of preaching to save them that believe. For the Jews require a sign, and the Greeks seek after wisdom: But we preach Christ crucified, unto the Jews a stumbling block, and to the Greeks foolishness, but unto them which are called, both Jews and Greeks, Christ the power of God, and the wisdom of God. Because the foolishness of God is wiser than men; and the weakness of God is stronger than men (1 Cor 1:21–25).

It may well be that a conversion experience cannot be fully expressed. When Paul recounted his experience to King Agrippa, he added his own interpretation that such an experience was given to him that he might open the eyes of others and turn them from darkness to light (Acts 26:18). Yet it seems to the Jewish reader that Paul's proclaiming "Christ crucified, unto the Jews a stumbling block, and to the Greeks foolishness" is a call to a religious experience which may cast light for believers but leaves the unbeliever in darkness. To the believing Jew, the notion of a Messiah crucified while the world remains in sadness and pain is indeed something against which he must stumble.

There is a feeling which the Jewish reader gains from much of Paul's writing that the latter felt the end of time was at hand, for he said: "The time is short" (1 Cor 7:29). For that reason, he could say that it would be better if all were to remain celibate as he himself was. Such advice could be given if it is assumed that the human drama is coming to an end. Only within that context does Paul's insistence on justification by faith become intelligible to a Jewish reader (Rom 3:27). Faith may be important for an individual, but a society needs a law to function. For the Jews of Paul's time, the Law was not only God's gift but the structural backbone of Jewish society. The Law in its totality established the boundaries of the Jewish polity. To do away with it was to remove the separation between Jew and non-Jew, thereby dissolving the identity of the Jew. That was precisely what Paul intended when he said:

> There is neither Jew nor Greek, there is neither bond nor free, there is neither male nor female; for ye are all one in Christ Jesus (Gal 3:28).

This blurring of differences in faith, status and sex is intelligible to the Jewish reader only on the assumption that the end is imminent and that in the face of such an end differences no longer matter.

One may wait for the end which may come suddenly, like "a thief in the night" (1 Thess 5:2). Meanwhile, however, society must be maintained; wives must obey their husbands, servants their master (Col 3:18). The aforementioned equality of sex and status (Gal 3:28) is not to be acted on (cf. Eph 6:1–9).

As time has gone on, the temptations of life have remained. Paul must warn his readers against adultery, fornication, and uncleanness as well as hatred and murder (Gal 5:19ff). To the Jewish reader such warnings partake of the nature of law; they are injunctions to do or not to do. Paul's introductory motto for this passage, "I say then: Walk in the spirit" (Gal 5:16) suggests to the Jewish reader the very word for Jewish Law, *halakha,* a way to walk.

Time and the necessities of societal life seem to have caused even Paul to turn back to the Law. Now law, even Jewish law, contains a paradox: it assumes a freedom, the freedom to observe or not. In his attack on the efficacy of the Law, Paul had denied his own freedom. The Law was useless, he said, because he could not obey it. He was bound to sin, as he said:

> For that which I do, I allow not; for what I would, that I do not; but what I hate, that do I (Rom 7:15).

But in his call "to walk in the spirit" (Gal 5:25) by avoiding transgressions and follow "gentleness and goodness" (Gal 5:22), Paul assumes that his followers are able to observe his exhortations.

The Jewish reader will be reminded of yet another paradox of law when he reads Paul's words: "Stand fast therefore in the liberty wherewith Christ hath made us free" (Gal 5:1). Playing on the Hebrew word *harut* ("engraved"), as were the words of the Decalogue, the rabbis were wont to say that no man was free (*herut*) unless he "labored in the Law."[12] The Jewish reader might even note that Paul's summation of the Law, "Thou shalt love thy neighbor as thyself" (Gal 5:15), is the same as that of Rabbi Akiba.[13]

Time had brought law; it had also brought heresies (Gal 1:7; 5:19; Col 2:8). Those who would follow Paul as leaders would be concerned with the correct doctrine of the Church (1 Tim 4:1–6) and proper Church organization (1 Tim 3). The qualifications for a bishop are described, as are those for a deacon. They are to be husbands of but one wife, ruling their children and households well. Hence, marriage has now become an element for qualification, and to forbid marriage is heretical (1 Tim 4:3). Young women are to marry, bear children and guide the house (1 Tim 5:3).

Simple condemnation is not sufficient to stop heresy. A still later teacher speaks of "false prophets among the people and false teachers among you" (2 Pet 2:1). The Jewish reader reflecting upon his own religious history may note that heresy is more of a problem whenever it is a pattern of belief which holds a community together, rather than patterns of action.

Time plays yet another role in the last book of the New Testament, the Book of Revelation. To the Jewish reader the passage of time has affected the writings of Paul and the other epistles in making them more intelligible, more akin to Jewish sources. The Book of Revelation, dealing with the end of time, seems at first glance the least intelligible. Yet, on closer inspection he notes parallels to the biblical books of Zechariah and Daniel and echoes of the last chapter of Isaiah. Fornication still seems to be a problem among some early Christians (Rev 2:20ff); some of them are charged with belonging to a "synagogue of Satan" for claiming to be Jews while not really being so (Rev 3:9). The Jewish reader may wonder whether this refers to the appropriation of the term "Jew" or "Israel" by the Church. That the term "synagogue of Satan" would reappear in one of the sadder pages of Jewish history is known to the reader. In any case, he is puzzled by this Book.

V

Perhaps this note of puzzlement may well summarize the response of the Jewish reader to the New Testament as a whole. The "New Jerusalem" hoped for in the Book of Revelation (Rev 21:1) has not yet descended. As that New Testament writer looked toward the future fulfillment of what he felt to be God's promise, so does the present-day Christian look forward to a final fulfillment. And looking forward, he joins the Jew looking forward into time. In this as with regard to law, it seems to the Jewish reader that the Christian walks a path parallel to his own.

How, then, should the Jewish reader respond to the New Testament? Remembering that he reads the book as an outsider, the Jewish reader still finds great beauty in some passages and great problems in others. He sees evidence of what was the belief of the early Church, and what is the basis of belief for contemporary Christendom. As he knows that the Judaism of our time developed from rabbinic Judaism, so he surmises that present-day Christianity has evolved further, which is to say that it differs from early Christianity. He can see how the teaching of Jesus can serve as the core of Christian faith, even while he himself is not convinced by it. He can come to appreciate Paul's efforts in spreading Christianity beyond the confines of Palestine, though he as a Jew would not agree with many of Paul's statements.

In saying that, the Jewish reader does not intend to challenge the Christian's faith, for, in a sense, faith can never be challenged. Faith is, as Paul so beautifully put it, "the substance of things hoped for, the evidence of things not seen" (Heb 11:1). That which is hoped for cannot be contravened, and that which is not seen but yet believed cannot be disproven. As a Jew, he too hopes, and as a Jew, he too believes. Having read the New Testament, he now has a clearer idea of that which the Christian hopes for and that in which he believes.

NOTES

1. Saul Lieberman, "How Much Greek in Jewish Palestine?" *Biblical and Other Studies,* edited by A. Altman (Brandeis University Texts and Studies, Vol. 1; Harvard University Press, 1963) 123–141. Also Samuel Krauss, *Griechische und Lateinische Lehnwoerter im Talmud, Midrasch and Targum* (Georg Olms Verlagsbuchhandlung: Hildesheim, 1964).

2. T. B. *Megillah* 9b and *Bereshit Rabbah* 36:12 in *Midrash Rabbah,* translated into English by Dr. H. Freedman and Maurice Simon (London: Soncino Press, 1939) 294.

3. *Avot* 5:21.

4. T. B. *Berakoth* 34b, as quoted in Kaufmann Kohler, *Jewish Theology Systematically and Historically Considered* (New York: Ktav, 1968) 386.

5. Moses Maimonides, *Mishneh Torah,* "Book of Judges, Laws of Kings," chap. 12, nos. 1–2.

6. David of Posquières, commentary *ad locum,* quoted in Kaufmann Kohler, *op. cit.,* 387–388.

7. *Daily Prayer Book,* translated by Philip Birnbaum (New York: Hebrew Publishing Company, 1948) 90.

8. Cf., for example, C. E. B. Cranfield, *The Gospel According to St. Mark* (Cambridge Greek Testament Commentary series; Cambridge, 1963) 371.

9. See Leon Stitskin, "Witnessing and Personal Religious Existence," in Helga Croner, Leon Klenicki, eds., *Issues in the Jewish-Christian Dialogue: Jewish Perspectives on Covenant, Mission and Witness* (Stimulus Books; New York: Paulist Press, 1979) 118–125.

10. E.g., T. B. *Yoma* 85b.

11. T. B. *Rosh Hashanah* 11b.

12. T. B. *Erubin* 54a.

13. Found in the *Sifra* on Lev 19:18, and T. B. *Kedoshim,* ch. 4, no. 12. The statement also occurs in *Genesis Rabbah* 24:7.

Tanakh and the New Testament: A Christian Perspective

Joseph Blenkinsopp

I

The enterprise which, since the late eighteenth century, has gone under the name "theology of the Old Testament" is by definition a Christian phenomenon. In one way or another it represents an attempt to draw out the implications of the historical fact that early Christianity appropriated the Jewish Scriptures, made them its own and renamed them "the Old Testament." On closer inspection, however, this view of early Christianity taking over a distinct corpus of writings as a simple act of appropriation is not free of difficulties. It is questionable, to start with, whether such a *canonical* corpus existed at the time of primitive Christianity. The earliest lists of books contained in *Tanakh* derive from Christian sources of the second century, and for the definitive statement on content, order and authorship we have to wait for the publication of the Babylonian Talmud.[1] The Jewish leadership during the Yavnean period argued about the status of certain books considered problematic for one reason or another. Such discussions probably indicate a movement toward definition in the period between the destruction of Jerusalem and the Bar Kokhba revolt but they do not amount to proof that the canon was "fixed" even then, frequent statements to the contrary notwithstanding.[2]

A further relevant consideration is that early Christian teachers and preachers tended to favor the Greek translation or Septuagint which diverges from our Masoretic Bible in the number of books, their arrangement, the actual content of several of them (e.g., Jeremiah) and numerous points of detail. Here too we must take issue with a common misconception that this Greek version represents a kind of aberration from the *Hebraica veritas*. On the contrary, it contains much Palestinian textual tradition of greater antiquity than the Masoretic Bible. The latter, moreover, can be taken from one point of view as a polemical reaction to the Septuagint precisely by excluding what it had included. We must add that not just the content but the arrangement has a significance of its own. That the historical books in the Septuagint follow on without interruption after the Pentateuch may, for example, suggest that the latter was thought of primarily as narrative rather than law. That the prophets are placed last may have been intended to emphasize the predictive function of prophecy (since we then have an arrangement according to past, present and future) as well as locating the sapiential compositions at the center rather than the periphery—a position which they have generally had to accept in theologies of the Old Testament. This order, too, may represent a well-established and main-line option, since it seems to be presupposed in Sirach (39:1), though not in the prologue to his work.

It is true, of course, that early Christian writings contain references to "the law and the prophets" and in one instance to "the law of Moses, the prophets and the psalms" (Lk 24:44), and that such allusions to authoritative collections can be found at least two centuries earlier.[3] This, however, did not prevent certain groups within Palestinian Judaism from promulgating legal enactments deemed to have an authority equal to that of the laws in the Pentateuch. Both *Jubilees* and the recently published *Temple Scroll*, for instance, ascribe divine origin to prescriptions over and above those in Torah. We know of others who revised the laws, who accepted only those prior to the apostasy of the "golden calf," who put "the traditions of the elders" on the same footing as the written laws, and who rejected everything but the Pentateuch.[4] To be sure, we are speaking of groups, parties or movements within Judaism, but that such as we have mentioned, and no doubt others, existed and even flourished witnesses to a remarkable degree of tolerance and pluralism. The fixing of a canon in final, unalterable form is an act destined to promote or enforce religious uniformity. If it had been done any time prior to the fall of Jerusalem we can only wonder at its singular lack of effect. But in fact, as we have seen, there are no indications direct or indirect that this was the case.[5]

What for our present purpose it amounts to is this: that rather than viewing early Christianity as simply appropriating the canonical scriptures of Judaism we should see it as within a process which would eventuate in such decisions and definitions. In this respect it bears comparison with the Qumran community which also appended writings of its own to those— still inderterminate in number—which had at that time come to be endowed with a greater or lesser degree of authority.[6] Obvious as this point may be, it is not, I believe, unimportant for understanding what is involved in doing Old Testament theology. If it had been taken seriously from the outset it might have helped the practitioners bear in mind that the enterprise is best conducted in dialogue with Judaism and thus prevented it becoming another expression of Jewish-Christian alienation.

It would be widely agreed that the New Testament itself does not provide us with one hermeneutical key or one unambiguous approach to the Jewish Scriptures. Over a broad spectrum of theological inquiry—for example, the understanding of the nature of Church and its ministries—we are still coming to terms with the exegetical and historical fact of early Christian pluralism and polemic.[7] What is true of the New Testament in general will also necessarily be true of early Christian views of the person, mission and teaching of Jesus. Thus it would be convenient for one particular approach to our subject if it could be shown that according to the teaching of Jesus the ritual laws were now to be considered inoperative, leaving only the basic ethical content of Torah. A passage like Mk 7:14– 23 could be (and often has been) adduced as proof that Jesus abrogated the food laws and therefore the ritual law as a whole.[8] We cannot evade the question, however, whether this attribution does not represent one attempt to solve a problem debated vigorously in early Christian circles. And in fact the Sermon on the Mount takes us in quite a different direction with its statement, again attributed to Jesus, of the permanent validity of the entire law and its implied link between the ethical and the ritual.[9] It is difficult to see, then, how one approach to Torah or Tanakh as a whole to the exclusion of others can be authorized by reference to a mandatory starting point in the New Testament itself.

That the early Christian Church retained the Jewish Scriptures implies a refusal to identify itself as a new religion, and this in spite of the newness acknowledged in such terms as "the new covenant," "the third race," and "a new blood and spirit." In fact it was in reaction to Marcion's program in the second century of delineating a new spiritual religion over against the materialistic religion of Israel and Judaism that the Church defined its canon as the Jewish Scriptures with some writings of its own appended to them. Hence the view that it was merely a historical accident that Christianity arose out of Judaism, a view which found its most distinguished proponents in Schleiermacher and Harnack, is historically and theologically without foundation. In whatever form it is proposed, the idea that the Old Testament is expendable for the Christian fails to take account of two crucial facts. First is the Jewishness of Jesus and the consequent impossibility of severing him from the history and destiny of the Jewish people. Historically worthless and even bizarre as were the attempts, beginning with Friedrich Delitzsch, to depict an Aryan Jesus, they were at least logical in seeing the need to detach Jesus from Judaism. Just as decisive, however, is the early Church's understanding of itself as the definitive embodiment of the promises and purposes of the God proclaimed throughout the Hebrew Scriptures—as, in other words, the true "Israel of God" (Gal 6:16). And here too, we must add, the problem (in this case the identity of the true Israel) was at that time and indeed much earlier a problem internal to Judaism.[10]

Early Christian teachers and preachers tended to use the Scriptures as a depository of prophetic texts referring to Jesus and his community. In some instances such texts are brought to bear on specific events and circumstances of the life of Jesus and of the community in a patterned, formulaic and even learned way, as in Matthew's gospel or the use of psalms in the early chapters of Acts. In other cases the narrative or teaching has been shaped and given a certain resonance by allusion to biblical texts as, for example, Ps 22 in the passion story. Comparison of the former kind of usage with the Qumran *pesharim* is inevitable and useful, but it has to be noted that the latter are commentaries on prophetic books while the first generations of Christians did not, for whatever reasons, produce biblical commentaries. Typological interpretation is also attested, reflecting the conviction that the Scriptures foreshadow the events of the end-time realized in the history of the community. Both of these modes of relating the New to the Old Testament recur throughout Christian history, being especially prominent in Protestant Pietist circles and the older type of Roman Catholic apologetics and dogmatics.[11] It is hardly necessary to insist that they do not add up to an adequate method of doing biblical theology. Correspondences are established in a quite arbitrary and uncontrolled way, there is little or no sense of cohesion, organicity and development, and the science of the critical interpretation of texts counts for nothing. Less obviously, it dispenses one from the need to come to terms with the actual hermeneutics which shaped early Christianity in the context of Second Temple Judaism—a point to which we shall return.

II

It has become customary to trace the origins of biblical theology as a distinct discipline to the inaugural lecture of Johann Philipp Gabler delivered (in Latin) at the University of Altdorf on March 30, 1787.[12] As a child of his age, Gabler proposed to set up biblical theology independently of Church dogmatics on the basis of scientific, which meant in effect historical, principles. Since then no biblical theology worthy of the name has been able to evade the implications of the historical method, though a satisfactory way of combining the historical and systematic aspects of the discipline has proved remarkably elusive. In several instances what has emerged—in essence if not always in name—is simply a history of the religion of Israel. Others have elected to divide their work into an historical and systematic section but without always making clear the nature of the relationship between them. Others again have in effect dissolved that particular dichotomy by identifying history, or at least the biblical interpretation of history, as the locus of theology. But even those who, like Walther Eichrodt, aim at a genuinely systematic presentation presuppose a certain reconstruction and interpretation of the history. We shall go on to see that it is precisely in this matter of historical development and its interpretation that the relation between New and Old Testament has proved most problematic.

Perhaps the most common way of putting it is to speak of a continuous providential history which reaches its climax or goal in Christ and the Church. First proposed by Irenaeus, this deceptively simple view of the one *Heilsgeschichte* became the organizing principle of some of the most influential theologies of the Old Testament in the nineteenth century, most conspicuously that of J. C. K. Hofmann.[13] Needless to say, it is still with us today. It does not require a very profound analysis, however, to conclude that such a model can be construed in a variety of very different and mutually exclusive ways. If, for example, Christ the object of Christian faith is the goal of the history, does this imply that the historical process which led up to him is unintelligible and meaningless apart from Christian faith? Hermann Schultz, whose *Theology* will be discussed later on in this article, suggests that this is indeed the case when he states that "he who does not know the destination will fail to understand many a bend in the road."[14] Others have put it more explicitly and categorically.[15] Or again, is Christ the goal of the history in a way which allows the previous history of God's relations with his people to retain its validity or is it all superseded and invalidated? Or, finally, is there a pattern or progression detectable in the history of which Christ and the Church are in some way a part or do the latter, so to speak, stand outside the series?

A further problem which, though rather obvious, has been much neglected arises when we consider the actual shape and content of the historical narrative recorded in the Old Testament. The story-line begins with creation, records the archaic history of humanity, introduces the ancestors of the Israelite people, and details their oppression in Egypt, deliverance, wanderings in the wilderness and occupation of the land of Canaan. After the heroic age there is the passage to monarchy, the rise and fall of the two kingdoms and the exile in Babylon. If we include the Chronicler the story is taken down to the re-establishment of the community in and around Jerusalem, but that is as far as it goes. Other discrete bits of narrative found here and there in the Hebrew Bible fit in at different points of this sequential and cumulative narrative.[16] Thus, Job is placed at the time of the ancestors and Ruth in the days of the judges. Interestingly enough, none of the historical psalms goes down beyond the time of David.[17] If, then, early Christianity is somehow part of a history of divine deeds and disclosures, what are we to do with the period of the Second Commonwealth to which, as a historical fact, early Christianity belongs?

I believe it can be shown that failure to provide a satisfactory answer to this question has been a major factor in producing the impasse in which Old Testament theology now finds itself. As an historical phenomenon, early Christianity can be understood only within the history of Second Temple Judaism, and it is at least arguable that such historical understanding is a prerequisite for writing an Old Testament theology. The force of this observation cannot be blunted by countering that early Christianity is based not so much on these historical continuities as on the interpretation of Old Testament texts, since early Christian interpretation is also part of that history. It is arguable, therefore, that neglect of this period—which is as long as the period from the judges to the exile—or, even worse, a false evaluation of it will to a greater or lesser extent vitiate any attempt to write an Old Testament theology.

Perhaps the best way to substantiate this argument is to survey how the authors of Old Testament theologies over the last two centuries have actually handled the dimension of history and this segment of the history in particular.[18] The period from Gabler to the present falls conveniently into two equal parts, the watershed being the appearance of Wellhausen's *Prolegomena to the History of Ancient Israel* in 1878.[19] The choice of this particular point in time is not arbitrary, since, if the Vatke-Reuss-Graf-Wellhausen hypothesis about the chronological order of the Pentateuchal sources is correct, as current scholarship still by and large assumes it to be, earlier historical reconstructions will be outmoded. This will be the case even with those essays which in other respects can still be read with profit. The *Theology of the Old Testament* of Gustav Friedrich Oehler, for example, appeared in a second edition (posthumously) after Wellhausen's *Prolegomena* but was completely unaffected by what we can call the Wellhausen revolution.[20] In other respects, however, it was up with the times theologically in its insistence on treating the history developmentally and organically. In this respect both Oehler and Wellhausen reflected the pervasive influence of both German Romanticism and Hegel's philosophy of history but with widely different results. Oehler divided his work into three sections: Mosaism, prophetism and wisdom. The time-span corresponding to the first division goes from creation to the occupation of the land while the second takes us from the judges to Ezra, Nehemiah and the end of prophecy. The third, by far the shortest, has no corresponding historical epoch. It is set out so as to end with a discussion of Qoheleth, since this book exemplifies the failure of Israelite wisdom to solve the riddle of life, thereby setting the stage for the new covenant. His last sentence runs as follows:

> For from a persuasion of the vanity of all earthly good arises the longing after the eternal and saving blessings of the New Testament, and the desire for the coming of that immutable kingdom of God announced by prophecy, in which the inquiries of Old Testament and all other wisdom have found their enduring object.[21]

Without for a moment wishing to demean or write off Oehler's effort at synthesis, it has to be said that the unscientific and—in the last section—even bizarre arrangement of the material serves to set out in clearer relief a thesis which would dominate Old Testament theology down to the very recent past: that the historical development, after reaching its apex in prophecy, ended in spiritual failure and thus prepared for the advent of Christianity. The discovery that the laws, and especially the ritual laws, stand at the origins not of Israel but of Judaism, together with the rediscovery of prophecy as a distinct form of religious individualism, seemed to offer the possibility of supporting this thesis with better exegetical arguments and putting it in sharper focus. But the impetus to move in this direction was already there before Julius Wellhausen and Bernhard Duhm laid the basis for the modern study of the Pentateuch and the prophets respectively.

What we find coming to the fore in the pre-Wellhausian era, then, is a developmental and genetic approach in this as in other areas of inquiry. Theologians of a rationalist stripe like Gabler read in the Old Testament a gradual unfolding of the truths of reason, in the process setting aside the miscellaneous moral and scientific crudities which were often deemed characteristic of the "semitic mentality." The many who, like Wilhelm Vatke, laid out the religious history of Israel on the procrustean bed of Hegelian dialectics read it as an interim stage preparatory to the absolute religion embodied in Christianity. The earlier exponents of *Heilsgeschichte* construed it as a *praeparatio evangelica,* a history structured by promise and fulfillment whose ultimate goal was Christ.[22] Whatever the model, the possibility of a positive evaluation of Judaism and of its ongoing existence after the rise of Christianity was never seriously entertained.

As suggested a moment ago, two developments in the second half of the nineteenth century profoundly affected the study of the Old Testament. The first was the discovery that the so-called Priestly Code (P), formerly known as the *Grundschrift* (G), belonged not to the beginning but the end of the process of formation of laws and narrative in the Pentateuch or Hexateuch. This discovery was in fact first made by Vatke as early as 1835, but it was several decades before it was taken up seriously and developed. In the *Prolegomena* of Wellhausen, who acknowledged having learned the best and most from Vatke, it provided the exegetical basis for a compelling reconstruction of the religious history of Israel. Briefly, the old nature religion based on family and clan was dealt a fatal blow by the Deuteronomic demand for centralization of worship in the seventh century. After that point "the warm pulse of life" (p. 78) could no longer be felt and the process of "denaturalization" was completed by the authors of the Priestly Code during and after the exile. By then the nation had been transformed into a church (p. 150), its traditions had been correspondingly reinterpreted and thereby judaized (p. 223), and the spirit of Moses had been "laid to sleep in institutions" (p. 398). Free prophecy lasted only as long as the monarchy. It could have no place in the post-exilic hierocracy, though its message was preserved in writing encased, as Wellhausen puts it, in the hard shell of an ecclesiastical institution.

This brings us to the other significant development, the rediscovery of prophecy as embodying a distinct type of religious individualism. Decisive for this new approach to prophecy, first clearly expressed in Bernhard Duhm's *Die Theologie der Propheten* published in 1875, was the thesis that the main legal corpora were later than classical prophecy and that therefore the prophets could not continue to be seen as primarily exponents of the laws.[23] In keeping with nineteenth-century moral idealism and certain dominant emphases in German Evangelical Christianity, the prophets were read as exponents of ethical individualism, an unmediated approach to God without benefit of priesthood and sacrificial ritual and, in brief, a religion in which personal experience counts for more than institutions and the traditions which they mediate.

As the title of his book already suggests, the whole point of Wellhausen's formidable array of exegetical arguments was to make possible a better reconstruction of the history of Israel and the development of its religious traditions. As he himself puts it:

> Criticism has not done its work when it has completed the mechanical redistribution; it must aim further at bringing the different writings when thus arranged into relation with each other, must seek to render them intelligible as phrases of a living process, and thus to make it possible to trace a graduated development of the tradition.[24]

This reconstruction has nothing in common with *Heilsgeschichte,* which Wellhausen dismisses contemptuously as "the approved recipe" (p. 235), since the elements most characteristic of the latter were introduced by late redactors and resulted in distorting or even falsifying the history. There is indeed a continuous and organic development, which the correct dating of the law codes allows us to perceive, but it ended in *Erstarrung,* the dead hand of ritualism, heteronomy and institutional control. The new understanding of and appreciation for prophecy, to which Wellhausen also contributed, only served to corroborate this scheme; for once classical prophecy is identified as the apex of religious development recorded in the Old Testament, the history which follows has nowhere to go but down.[25]

According to the Wellhausian model, then, the process of declension can be traced from Deuteronomy, through Ezekiel—the first of the epigoni—the Holiness Code (H, in Lev 17–26), the Priestly Code (P), Chronicles and on down into the Mishnah and Talmud. The epoch of the Second Commonwealth saw the ethical and ritual laws codified and canonized and the Jewish community firmly established as a church or theocracy. Judaism emerges as it will persist through the centuries, but for Wellhausen the impression is neither admirable nor edifying:

> The Creator of heaven and earth becomes the manager of a petty scheme of salvation; the living God descends from His throne to make way for the law. The law thrusts itself in everywhere; it commands and

blocks up the access to heaven; it regulates and sets limits to the understanding of the divine working on earth. As far as it can, it takes the soul out of religion and spoils morality. It demands a service of God, which, though revealed, may yet with truth be called a self-chosen and unnatural one, the sense and use of which are apparent neither to the understanding nor to the heart. The labor is done for the sake of the exercise; it does no one any good, and rejoices neither God nor man. It has no inner aim after which it spontaneously strives and which it hopes to attain by itself, but only an outward one, namely, the reward attached to it, which might as well be attached to other and possibly even more curious conditions.[26]

It remains to ask how, according to this way of thinking, early Christianity is seen to fit in. Right at the beginning of the *Prolegomena* Wellhausen correctly perceives that in dogmatic theology "Judaism is a mere empty chasm over which one springs from the Old Testament to the New" (p. 1); indeed, we might be tempted to add that the situation is not much different today. The Wellhausian reconstruction fills the chasm by linking the Church (sometimes referred to as "early Catholicism") with Judaism. The gospels themselves are a protest against Judaism, the religious individualism to which they attest takes up the forgotten message of the prophets, and Jesus casts ridicule on the works of the law and appears as a contender for the common morality. Thus the historical development which Wellhausen traces in the *Prolegomena* is replicated. "The Church is not his (Christ's) work, but an inheritance from Judaism to Christianity" (p. 512). The institution once again takes over, stifles the voice of prophecy and proceeds on its inexorable path toward the secularization of religion.[27]

At this point we need to remind ourselves that Wellhausen was neither a theologian nor a churchman and that he was not writing a theology of the Old Testament. His work was, of course, enormously influential. Assuming that the way the history of Israel and the development of its religious traditions are construed bears on the task of writing an Old Testament theology, as we surely may, it could hardly be ignored by the biblical theologian. It was (and is) possible, of course, to accept the exegetical arguments and the historical development to which they were seen to lead and yet reject Wellhausen's interpretation of this development. We can in fact go further and say that it is necessary to reject certain aspects of his thesis, given the advances which have been made over the last century. His views on, for example, the nature of religious institutions and of ritual, the character of Israelite prophecy, and the age and function of the

laws are clearly in need of revision or outright rejection. And no one, fortunately, needs to share his often expressed distaste for Judaism which,
though it can hardly be described as antisemitism, fitted only too well the
academic *Zeitgeist* at the time the book appeared.[28]

III

Rather than attempt an overall survey of developments in Old Testament theology since Wellhausen it might be more to our purpose to take
a closer look at two of the most significant essays which have appeared,
those of Hermann Schultz in the nineteenth and Walther Eichrodt in the
twentieth century. The first edition of Schultz's *Old Testament Theology*
appeared in 1869 and the fifth and last in 1896.[29] Beginning with the second edition (1878) he accepted the Graf-Wellhausen hypothesis and rear-
ranged his subject matter accordingly. As the sub-title ("The Religion of
Revelation in Its Pre-Christian Stage of Development") makes clear, the
material must first be presented historically and organically before a synthesis—based on the well-established God-man-salvation model—can be
attempted. The historical and systematic sections of the work are loosely
tied together by the theme of God working throughout the history of a
particular community to establish his kingdom (I, pp. 53, 56, 58)— which
history, needless to say, reaches its destination in the events recorded in
the New Testament (I, p. 59). Schultz does not naively assume that everything in the Old Testament is of equal religious value or contributes equally (or at all) to the forward movement of the history. The task of the Old
Testament theologian is to discern between "healthy" and "unhealthy" developments (I, p. 11) and this implies, though he does not say it explicitly,
that he must evaluate each phase of the history within the Old Testament
period as it progresses toward or deviates from the goal.

The first section of the work, then, consists in effect in a history of
the religion of Israel. Beginning with the pre-Mosaic period, it deals suc-
cessively with Moses, the time-span from Moses to Samuel, from Samuel
to the eighth century, the Assyrian age which is that of classical prophecy,
the period of Judah's trial and execution at the hands of the Babylonians,
resurrection under the Persians, and the closing era from Alexander to the
Hasmonean principate. Given the problematic interpretation of history in
Old Testament theology, it will be of interest to note why Schultz ends his
survey at this point. The main reason, it seems, is the dominance of scribalism which transformed Old Testament religion into "a sacred literature

absolutely complete and inviolable" (I, p. 60). In other words, the Old Testament canon in final form is the great divide between Israel and Judaism. The old religion shows no more signs of life, there is no longer any unity, and openness to foreign influences ("Palestinian, Grecian and Oriental") conspires to produce something quite different. At this point, then, the Old Testament theologian hands over to the historian of Judaism and of early Christianity.

We may note, in passing, that Schultz is oddly ambiguous in his attitude to Judaism. He takes issue with Kant for identifying Judaism with the "levitical corruption" of prophecy (I, pp. 35–6), yet goes on to speak of leviticism standing between prophecy and Christianity, condemns what he calls "the petty Pharisaic view of life" and identifies "the Jewish element" as externalism and heteronomy.[30] He attacks Rénan and Strauss for glorifying Indo-Germanic myth and philosophy at the expense of Semitic (and therefore also Israelite) religion (I, pp. 37–38), and yet goes on to affirm that the Aryan races have exhibited the highest and most attractive forms of nature religion (I, pp. 45–46). In his interpretation of the history something of the same ambiguity is generally close to the surface. The earlier "natural" phase, with its "simple and joyous existence" (I, p. 150), is contrasted favorably with the latest period characterized by the legalism of the scribes. In between is the high point, that of classical prophecy which culminates in the career of the Isaian Servant. Beginning with the Persian period we are invited to note how life and worship become increasingly artificial and how the letter of the law increasingly takes the place of that inward religious assurance which was the gift of prophecy (I, pp. 321, 331 etc.). In the closing era, beginning with the Ptolemies, "the consciousness of inward emptiness, and the feeling that the Spirit of Jehovah had departed, kept on increasing" (I, p. 406). Externalism, formalism, and legalism take over, the emergence of sects is seen as symptomatic of the decay of spiritual power and, in general, the "unhealthy" elements predominate over the "healthy." The conclusion is clearly drawn: "The two tendencies at work in Israel since the eighth century . . . are now accentuated and point clearly to their respective goals, to Christianity and to the Talmud."[31]

In the second, systematic part of his essay Schultz skillfully draws together the results of his historical survey arranged according to the traditional dogmatic scheme which leads up to soteriology: God and the world, man and sin, the hope of Israel. Perhaps in order to avoid the impression that it is simply a matter of religious ideas, he leads off with a section entitled "The Consciousness of Salvation." We note a certain shift of emphasis from the kingdom of God to communion between God and man in the covenant. Not unexpectedly, Schultz's own conservative Lutheran faith betrays its presence more clearly here than in the first volume. We are already alerted to it in the title of the first section just noted, circumcision and passover are described as the two sacraments of the covenants (II, p. 10—one suspects it would have been just as easy to have come up with seven!), the categories of *sola gratia* and justification by works are used to evaluate the religion of the post-exilic period (II, pp. 30, 42 etc.), the classical prophets preach morality and "the piety of the heart" as opposed to ritual holiness (II, p. 69), and so on. Whatever the intention, Schultz's second volume bears out the thesis of those who argue that a theology of the Old Testament must be not only Christian in a general sense but denominational.[32]

With the exception of Eduard König's very conservative *Theologie des Alten Testaments* which appeared in 1922, no further effort along these lines was forthcoming from continental Protestantism until Eichrodt published the first volume of his *Theologie* in 1933.[33] In some respects Eichrodt's work, which has come to be regarded as the most comprehensive and important produced to date, reads like an updated version of Schultz. There is the same emphasis on the historical and descriptive, though without the by now familiar division into historical and systematic sections. Also, the equally familiar God-man-salvation model is abandoned in favor of one which Eichrodt believes is dictated by the Old Testament itself: God and the people, God and the world, God and man.[34] Like Schultz, Eichrodt gives prominence to the continuity of divine action in establishing relationship with the community and the individual, and there is even the same oscillation between covenant and kingdom (e.g. I, pp. 13, 26). A certain sameness also appears in the treatment of religious developments throughout the period. While, as just noted, Eichrodt does not have a separate historical section, each major part of his structural and phenomenological presentation is worked through developmentally, usually ending with a treatment of the post-exilic period and "later Judaism" (*Spätjudentum*), and this in spite of his avowal that the theology of *Spätjudentum* is not really part of the Old Testament theologian's task (I, p. 35).

Of the many points at which Eichrodt's work has been criticized (e.g. the centrality and antiquity of the covenant)[35] the only one which concerns us for the moment is his treatment of this later phase of the history. While there are some significant differences compared to what we have noted in the work of Schultz and, *a fortiori*, in Wellhausen (e.g. a much more sympathetic assessment of P and, correspondingly, of the priesthood), the

overall impression is depressingly similar. The covenant has been reduced
to a legalistic formula (I, pp. 63–64), the law has led to a religion of mere
observances and casuistry which leaves the heart empty,[36] the rule of God
has come to be seen as a gloomy and irrational tyranny (I, p. 169), the love
of God has been overshadowed by fear and guilt (I, p. 258) and is practically no longer proclaimed after the exile (II, p. 299), and the practice
of religion is dictated more by fear than anything else (II, p. 313). These
are not isolated examples which have been brought together so to speak
against the grain of the argument. On the contrary, to anyone who reads
the work from beginning to end—and there are perhaps few who do so—
it will be apparent that they form part of a very consistent and explicit thesis. As Eichrodt himself puts it in the section on "The Removal of Sin":

> Thus at the very heart of the desire for salvation we find *once again* that
> inner disintegration of the structure of the Jewish faith (jene innere Ge-
> brochenheit der jüdischen Glaubenswelt) which *continually* confronts us
> in this specific context of the individual God-Man relationship (my ital
> ics).[37]

It may be useful at this point to remind ourselves that our purpose
is not to show that this or that Old Testament scholar is motivated to a
greater or lesser degree by anti-Judaism but rather to understand how the
post-exilic period (a rather unsatisfactory term[38]), which witnessed the rise
and earliest development of Judaism, has been interpreted or misinterpreted in Old Testament theology, and to assess the consequences which flow
from such interpretation or misinterpretation. The overall scheme which
we have observed in some of the major essays examined runs something
like this. The earliest period of the history, from the beginnings to the
emergence of classical prophecy in the eighth century, is assessed in different ways. In the nineteenth century, both before and after Wellhausen,
the assessment was generally positive. Early Israelite religion was close to
nature and the soil, its freshness and spontaneity had not yet been blighted
by rituals and institutions, and it worshiped a God who was involved in
every aspect of its daily life. It seems reasonably clear that the dominant
influence, especially in Germany, came from Romanticism which also led
to the somewhat parallel emergence of mystical *Volk* theories in the early
decades of the century. Discoveries and advances in exegetical method, archaeology and anthropology have necessitated a rather thorough revision
of this idealized picture, especially by emphasizing early Israel's place in

the life and culture of the Near East in the second and early first millennium BCE. From the eighth to the sixth century, the period of classical prophecy, Israel reached the apex of its religious development. With its emphasis on morality and spirituality, the religion of the prophets not only surpassed anything which had appeared previously but provided a measure by which all other expressions of religious life could be judged. The post-exilic period, which shades off into the history of Judaism in late antiquity, witnessed, finally, a progressive declension from the high religious ideals of prophecy.

It would require much more space than is available to us here to analyze and evaluate in detail the various reasons proposed by Old Testament theologians for this state of affairs in the last period of the history. Some of those which recur most often should, however, at least be mentioned. At the most obvious level (given the prevalent scheme) the kind of prophecy exemplified by Amos, Jeremiah and the Isaian Servant did not survive the exile. In its place—and in place of the monarchy—the priesthood and the scribes came to have increasing importance in regulating the life of the community. At the same time, the law came to be gradually separated from its native context in the covenant, becoming in the process an absolute entity in a way which tended to limit religion purely to the observance of specific precepts governing every aspect of daily life.[39] Symptomatic of profound change, finally, is the failure to record and interpret the history of events after the exile, a failure which reflects the conviction that the history of God's dealings with his people, or at least a decisive phase of that history, had now come to an end.

Before going on to outline a critique of this broad understanding of the Second Temple period we should state briefly how it functions in Old Testament theology. It seems to imply in the first place that post-biblical Judaism (which logically includes present-day Judaism) is a different entity from the Old Testament and represents, in effect, a disintegration of the theological unity which it is the purpose of an Old Testament theology to display and interpret.[40] Coming as it does between the Old Testament and early Christianity, it can providentially serve to illustrate the problem to which the New Testament provides the answer or, alternatively, the failure of a way of life (works, observances) which highlights by contrast the Christian dispensation (grace). Thus, a particular theological thesis can be transposed into chronological terms:

The spiritual loftiness of human obligation and
vocation . . . . Old Testament

reveals sin and failure .... Early Judaism
to which Christ provides the answer .... New Testament

It will, I hope, be appreciated that this model serves to structure only one way of doing Old Testament theology, albeit one which has dominated the field over the last two centuries,[41] and that it is applied in different ways and with various nuances by individual practitioners. On the other hand, its influence has reached beyond the bounds of Old Testament theology as, for example, in the contention of Bultmann that the miscarriage and inner contradiction of religious history in the post-biblical period actually contains a promise for those who read it from the standpoint of Christian faith.[42] A further clarification needs to be made, namely, that it is not yet intended to adjudicate on the theological propriety of this position, but rather to examine the interpretation of the Second Temple period on which, in one way or another, it is based. To put it briefly: if it were possible to offer a quite different interpretation of the religious history of this period, and of the relation of early Christianity to it, would this suggest a different and perhaps a more satisfactory way of posing the theological issue?

IV

The interpretation of the religious history of the period in question is a large matter and one that calls for much more careful consideration than it has received so far in works of biblical theology. All we can do here is raise some questions in a rather summary way with regard to the assumptions referred to earlier. Thus:

1. As noted earlier in this article, the biblical canon was in process of formation throughout the Second Temple period and in some important respects was still incomplete at the time of early Christianity. What we now know of the remarkable variety of viewpoints in Judaism in the latter part of this period, a variety which can be explained by intellectual and religious vitality rather than as symptomatic of confusion and disorientation, is entirely in keeping with this view. And since we must also recognize a similar theological pluralism in early Christianity, the common assumption that early Christianity simply "took over" the Hebrew Bible needs to be revised and the temptation to contrast the legalism of Second Temple Judaism with the Christian gospel needs to be resisted. In a broader sense, we would say that no Old Testament theology is likely to be suc-

cessful which does not take account of the formation of the Jewish scriptural canon as a decisive aspect of Second Temple history.

2. The history of prophecy does not come to an end with the exile, though it does, of course, undergo profound modifications due to the change in the social and political situation of the community. The study of the progressive transformations of prophecy during the Second Temple period, traceable in the so-called wisdom writings, the Chronicler's history and the anonymous additions to prophetic books, is an essential aspect of the religious history of the period inclusive of early Christianity.[43] Biblical theology has been ill served by studies which emphasize the "original message" to the detriment of "secondary" or "inauthentic" additions (as if these somehow had a lower theological status) and which suggest that the period subsequent to that of classical prophecy is one of decline and spiritual failure.[44]

3. Old Testament theology has experienced remarkable difficulty in integrating the so-called wisdom writings which form the bulk of the third part of the canon. The most recent essay, that of R. E. Clements, even omits them entirely.[45] Here again the problem is traceable to the model with which the author is working. If with Eichrodt, for example, one sets out with the assumption that covenant is the organizing category in the Hebrew Bible, compositions like Proverbs, Canticle, Qoheleth and perhaps also Job will inevitably be relegated to the periphery. The difficulty will be even greater for those who, with von Rad, center on the idea of a sacred history, since most of these writings do not suggest that revelation is uniquely or even primarily through historical events.[46] The failure of Old Testament theology by and large to do justice to the wisdom writings is particularly unfortunate in view of the connections between scribalism and the rabbinic schools and the issue of continuity with early Judaism. Here too we must ask what a positive evaluation of these writings as an integral part of the religious history would mean for Old Testament theology.

4. We come, finally, to the curious suggestion that the *Heilsgeschichte* somehow came to an end or stalled during or after the exile. This idea has been expressed in different ways but the intent behind it is not always clear. Von Rad states, for example, that the exilic period was devoid of *Heilsgeschichte* at least until the emergence of Cyrus; once the law came to be seen as a timeless reality, however, the forward movement of the history stopped for good.[47] This could mean simply that about that time people stopped thinking primarily in historical categories, and in fact the broad historical narrative which begins in the Pentateuch and is continued in the Deuteronomic history is not carried beyond the return from Bab-

ylon. While the loss of national independence may well have had this effect, we should also bear in mind specific theological motives such as, for example, led the Priestly writer (P) to omit an account of the military conquest of the land or the Damascus Document to pass directly from the destruction of Jerusalem to the founding of the sect to which its writer belonged.[48] It seems however—though von Rad is never very clear on this point—that he is thinking of a real hiatus of some kind in the divine activity with respect to the community. A further problem arises when we ask how this is related to his other major assertion that the prophetic proclamation brought about a radical discontinuity between the former dispensation and the subsequent history. What at any rate is significant about von Rad's *Theology* for our present purpose is the fact of discontinuity which led him, quite logically, to a typological linking of Old and New Testament and a virtual bracketing of post-biblical Judaism.[49] Let us add, finally, that others who have given pride of place to history avoid these problems by simply ignoring the Second Temple period.[50]

If the general impression conveyed in this essay is overwhelmingly negative, and if we have said little positively about the relation between Old and New Testament, we can only plead that we are as yet nowhere close to knowing how to write an Old Testament theology. It seems that first we must take Tanakh seriously on its own terms[51] which, given the way it came into existence, involves coming to terms with the Second Temple period inclusive of early Christianity as a phenomenon of Second Temple Palestinian Judaism. It involves further, as a necessary consequence, coming to terms historically and theologically with Judaism which, far from declining or disappearing at the time of early Christianity, only reached its most characteristic expressions several centuries later. In evaluating Judaism of the Second Commonwealth we will have to stop dealing in generalizations (often, as is only too obvious, occasioned by neglect if not ignorance) and get down to the task of incorporating serious and detailed studies into our theological perspective. As for the latter, we will have to admit that there are elements of infidelity and deformation at all points of the tradition—Ezekiel 20 even traces these back to the time in Egypt—as there certainly are also in the Christian tradition, here too perhaps in its earliest stages. Given its origins and nature, Christianity must of necessity address a critique to Judaism as Judaism must to Christianity, and such a critique will necessarily inform any attempt, Christian or Jewish, to give a theological account of the classical texts to which both bodies appeal. Is it inconceivable that such mutual testing be carried out in dialogue and cooperation? And what would an Old Testament theology look like which at least envisioned such a situation by taking Judaism with absolute theological seriousness?[52]

Unless I am mistaken, there are indications that, in view of the situation described in this article, many are now simply giving up on the possibility of an Old Testament theology. And of course there are plenty of theologians whose interest in the issues discussed in this article is no more than polite. I would argue, on the contrary, that the relation of Christian faith to the Old Testament and, by extension, to Judaism is central to the agenda of Christian theology today. To understand why, in spite of all the energy and skill which have gone into them, our efforts to date have been largely unsuccessful could be the beginning of a new and more promising chapter.

NOTES

1. The lists in question occur in Melito of Sardis and Origen, to which add that of Epiphanius (ca. 392) and the one appended to the *Didache* MS discovered by Bryennios in 1883. On this last see J.-P. Audet, "A Hebrew-Aramaic List of Books of the Old Testament in Greek Transcription," *JTS* 1 new series (1950), 135–54, which the author believes may go back to the second half of the first century. The "classical" talmudic text is T. B. Baba Bathra 14b-15a.

2. See my *Prophecy and Canon* (Notre Dame & London: University of Notre Dame Press, 1977) 3, 126–127, and several of the papers in Sid Z. Leiman, ed. *The Canon and Masorah of the Hebrew Bible* (New York: Ktav Publishing House, 1974).

3. Dan 9:2; 2 Macc 15:9; Prologue to Sir.

4. Discussion on the status of the Temple Scroll vis-à-vis canonicity has of course hardly begun, but see the remarks of Yigael Yadin, *Megillat-ha-Miqdash* (Jerusalem: Israel Exploration Society, 1978) I, 298–300. In this regard the Psalms Scroll from the eleventh cave at Qumran is also of first-rate importance, on which see M. H. Goshen-Gottstein, "The Psalms Scroll (11QPs^a)—A Problem of Canon and Text," *Textus* V (1966), 22ff and J. A. Sanders, "Cave 11 Surprises and the Question of Canon," in D. N. Freedman and J. C. Greenfield, eds., *New Directions in Biblical Archaeology* (Garden City, New York: Doubleday, 1969) 101ff. We are very poorly informed on groups in Judaism at that time like the Nasaraioi mentioned in early Christian sources who rejected the sacrificial system, as did the Ebionites and, to judge by Acts 7, the Hellenists whose spokesman was Stephen; on whom see M. Simon, *Jewish Sects at the Time of Jesus* (Philadelphia: Fortress Press, 1967) 103–106. The Samaritans and apparently also the Sadducees and Boethusians mentioned in talmudic texts regarded the Pentateuch alone as authoritative.

5. This is not the place to argue the point further. Suffice it to say that almost all the assumptions about the process of canonization in the Second Commonwealth period dutifully reproduced in the standard works of reference are in need of revision.

6. The point that the Qumran people thought of themselves as *within* the framework of the biblical period is made forcibly by Shemaryahu Talmon, "The Textual Study of the Bible—A New Outlook," in F. M. Cross and S. Talmon, eds., *Qumran and the History of the Biblical Text* (Cambridge, Mass: Harvard University Press, 1975) 378–381.

7. I refer the reader only to W. Bauer, *Orthodoxy and Heresy in Earliest Christianity* (Philadelphia: Fortress Press, 1971) and E. Käsemann, "The Canon of the New Testament and the Unity of the Church," in *Essays on New Testament Themes* (London: SCM Press, 1964) 95–107.

8. It is instructive to note how Käsemann, after expressing extreme skepticism about the possibility of getting back to the authentic tradition about Jesus (*op. cit.*, 98), simply assumes that Mk 7:15 is authentic. "This word of Jesus," he informs us, "strikes not merely at rabbinic exegesis and practice but at the very heart of the legislation governing ceremonial and ritual purity" (p. 101). The desire to make a theological point about the Christian's freedom from a way of life based on self-righteousness by works may help to explain why an exception was made in this case.

9. Mt 5:17–20. Note too that reconciliation with the "brother" is required before one can offer a gift at the altar (5:23). Further, a number of injunctions in this section seem to depend on the Holiness Code (Lev 17–26): 5:22 cf. Lev 19:18; 5:23–24 cf. Lev 19:5; 5:48 cf. Lev 19:2.

10. Beginning with the return from exile of the *benē-haggôlāh* and the consequent need to legitimate themselves as the true successors of the old Israel over against the "Palestinians" including the Samaritans. The history of separatism and sectarianism in Palestinian Judaism of the Second Temple period hinges on this issue of the identity of the true Israel.

11. On the Pietists—who seem to have been the first to use the term "biblical theology"—see R. C. Dentan, *Preface to Old Testament Theology* (New York: Seabury Press, 1963²), especially chapters I and IV, and on developments in Roman Catholicism my *A Sketchbook of Biblical Theology* (London: Burns & Oates, 1968), 1–15.

12. R. C. Dentan, *op. cit.*, 22–23.

13. J. C. K. Hofmann published *Weissagung und Erfüllung* in 1841, *Der Schriftbeweis* in 1852 and *Biblische Hermeneutik* in 1880. The last named has been translated into English by Christian Preuss under the title *Interpreting the Bible* (Minneapolis: Augsburg Publishing House, 1959).

14. Hermann Schultz, *Old Testament Theology* (Edinburgh: T. & T. Clark, 1892⁴), I, 59.

15. E.g. Gerhard von Rad: "The Old Testament is a history book; it tells of

God's history with Israel, with the nations, and with the world, from the creation of the world down to the last things, that is to say, down to the time when dominion over the world is given to the Son of Man"—*Old Testament Theology* (New York: Harper & Row, 1965), II, 357. What has been said will generally be true of studies dominated by a Christological-typological approach, e.g. W. Vischer's *Das Christuszeugnis des Alten Testaments* (Zurich: Zollikon, 1946[7]); *idem,* "Everywhere the Scripture Is About Christ Alone," in B. W. Anderson (ed.), *The Old Testament and Christian Faith* (London: SCM Press, 1963) 90–101; G. A. F. Knight, *A Christian Theology of the Old Testament* (London: SCM Press, 1959). The most recent critique of the salvation history-typological approach is that of A. H. J. Gunneweg, *Understanding the Old Testament* (Philadelphia: Westminster Press, 1978) 196–212.

16. See James Barr, "Story and History in Biblical Theology," *Journal of Religion* 56 (1976), 1–17.

17. See especially Pss 78, 105, 106, 136.

18. The most complete treatment is that of H.-J. Kraus, *Die Biblische Theologie. Ihre Geschichte und Problematik* (Neukirchen-Vluyn: Neukirchener Verlag, 1970). R. C. Dentan, *Preface to Old Testament Theology* (New York: Seabury Press, 1963[2]) has the merit of packing a lot of information into small compass.

19. The first-rate English translation, a good part of it by Robertson Smith, is available in Meridian Books, New York, 1957. It includes an expanded version of Wellhausen's article on Israel written for the *Encyclopaedia Britannica.*

20. G. F. Oehler, *Theology of the Old Testament* (New York: Funk & Wagnalls, 1883). This had the distinction of being the first of the Old Testament theologies to be translated into English.

21. *Ibid.,* p. 569. There is, however, a final footnote in which the author finds support in Franz Delitzsch's commentary on Ecclesiastes. The latter ends in fine style with the words, "And Ecclesiastes, upon its heap of rubbish, shows how needful it is that heaven should now open above the earth."

22. The most distinguished exponent of *Heilsgeschichte* in the nineteenth century, J. C. K. von Hofmann, offers the following definition and description: "The history recorded in the Old Testament is the history of salvation as proceeding toward its full realization. Hence the things recorded therein are to be interpreted teleologically, i.e., as aiming at their final goal, and thus as being of the same nature as the goal yet modified by their respective place in history. Since the course and the events of that history are determined by their goal, this goal will manifest itself in all important stages of its progress in a way which, though preliminary, prefigures it"—*Interpreting the Bible* (see n. 13) 135.

23. On this view, frequently attested in rabbinic writings, see my *Prophecy and Canon,* 116–120.

24. Julius Wellhausen *op. cit.,* p. 295.

25. Wellhausen argues that the gradual preponderance of written law, beginning with Deuteronomy, brought prophecy to an end (*ibid.,* pp. 398–404). The de-

generation of classical prophecy is already apparent in Ezekiel, first of the epigoni (*ibid.,* pp. 59, 403).

26. *Ibid.,* p. 509 (the passage is actually from the *Encyclopaedia Britannica* article (see n. 19).

27. He writes: "The distinction of religious and secular is a variable one; every formation of a religious community is a step toward the secularization of religion; the religion of the heart alone remains an inward thing" (*ibid.,* p. 512).

28. See my *Prophecy and Canon,* 17–23.

29. The references which follow will be to the English translation of the fourth German edition: Hermann Schultz, *Old Testament Theology* (Edinburgh: T. & T. Clark, 1892).

30. *Ibid.,* I, 408–409, 451, where he goes on to refer to "the spiritual caricature of Talmudic scholasticism."

31. *Ibid.,* I, p. 411.

32. Otto Eissfeldt, "Israelitisch-jüdische Religionsgeschichte und alttestamentliche Theologie," *ZAW* 44 (1926), 1–12. In reply Walther Eichrodt defended the more traditional understanding of the undertaking in "Hat die alttestamentliche Theologie noch selbständige Bedeutung innerhalb der alttestamentlichen Wissenschaft?" *ZAW* 47 (1929), 83–91.

33. Walther Eichrodt, *Theologie des Alten Testaments* (Stuttgart: Ehrenfried Klotz Verlag, 1933 [I], 1935 [II], 1939 [III]). References will be to the English translation in two volumes: *Theology of the Old Testament,* trans. J. A. Baker (Philadelphia: Westminster, I 1961, II 1967). Vol. I was translated from the sixth edition (1959) and Vol. II from the fifth (1954).

34. *Ibid.,* I, p. 33, taken from his teacher Otto Procksch, *Theologie des Alten Testaments* (Gütersloh: C. Bertelsmann Verlag, 1950), though with the order of the first two sections inverted. It is not entirely clear that this model is an improvement on that of Schultz *et al.* and, as has often been pointed out, it results in a great deal of wearisome repetition.

35. D. G. Spriggs, *Two Old Testament Theologies* (London: SCM Press, 1974), has gathered together most of the critiques of Eichrodt and von Rad and added several of his own.

36. Since it illustrates Eichrodt's way of relating *Spätjudentum* to the New Testament the passage deserves to be quoted in full: "The essence of the Jewish religion of the Law may therefore be seen as a regulation of the God-Man relationship which exhausts itself in endless casuistry, and leaves the heart empty. . . . It is impossible to find clearer evidence of the lack of a united religious attitude. The fact that Jesus and his apostles had recourse to the Old Testament in their description of the right attitude toward God witnesses plainly to the fact that in them the inner schizophrenia of Jewish piety (die innere Gespaltenheit der jüdischen Frömmigkeit) had been overcome, and that the liberation of Man for willing surrender to God had once more emerged into the light of day" (*op. cit.,* II, p. 315).

37. *Ibid.,* II, p. 464.

38. Too vague, and covering too long a period; indeed, logically, still going on. Persian, Ptolemaic, Seleucid, Hasmonean, and Roman are more precise terms.

39. In his well-known essay "The Laws in the Pentateuch," Martin Noth develops in a quite typical way this idea of the law becoming an "absolute entity" (*absolute Grösse*) in the later period; that Jews came to worship "dead ordinances and statutes" is seen to be typical of an ever-recurring tendency to inauthentic faith; see M. Noth, *The Laws in the Pentateuch and Other Essays* (Edinburgh and London: Oliver & Boyd, 1966), 85–107 especially 106–107.

40. No one has made this point more forcibly than James Barr; see especially his paper "Le Judaïsme Postbiblique et la Théologie de l'Ancien Testament," *RThPh* 18 (1968), 209–217. Also, *idem, Judaism—Its Continuity with the Bible* (printed by the Camelot Press, Southampton, for the University of Southampton, 1968).

41. It will be obvious by now that by far the greater number of influential essays in Old Testament theology emanate from German-language Protestantism.

42. See especially Rudolf Bultmann's essay "Prophecy and Fulfillment," in C. Westermann (ed.), *Essays on Old Testament Interpretation* (London: SCM Press, 1963) 50–75; also *idem*, "The Significance of the Old Testament for the Christian Faith" in B. W. Anderson (ed.), *The Old Testament and Christian Faith* (London: SCM Press, 1964) 8–35.

43. See my *Prophecy and Canon*, 124–138.

44. It may be added that most studies of prophecy tend to peter out at the exilic period. Gerhard von Rad, *The Message of the Prophets* (New York: Harper & Row, 1967), based on the second volume of his *Old Testament Theology*, assigns only two of twenty-four chapters to prophecy after the exile. Curiously, Haggai and Zechariah are assigned to the Later Persian period (p. 245).

45. R. E. Clements, *Old Testament Theology, A Fresh Approach* (London: Marshall, Morgan & Scott, 1978) on which see *Expository Times* 90.7 (1979) 193–195.

46. This criticism of von Rad has been stated several times by James Barr; see his review of von Rad's *Theology* in *Expository Times* 73 (1962) 142–146; also "Revelation through History in the Old Testament and in Modern Theology," in *Interpretation* 17 (1963) 193–205; *idem, Old and New in Interpretation* (London: SCM Press, 1966) 65–102.

47. Gerhard von Rad, *Old Testament Theology* (New York: Harper & Row, 1962) I, 126, 91.

48. CD I 1–8; note that the absence of God from Israel's history is expressed by saying that he hid his face from Israel and its sanctuary.

49. Typology seems inevitably to rule out, or at least render very difficult, a positive evaluation of post-biblical Judaism, as noted by James Barr, "Le Judaïsme Postbiblique et la Théologie de l'Ancien Testament" (see n. 40), 212.

50. As, for example, G. Ernest Wright, *God Who Acts* (London: SCM Press, 1952).

51. The only Old Testament theology I know of which has attempted this is that of the Roman Catholic scholar John L. McKenzie, *A Theology of the Old Testament* (Garden City, N.Y.: Doubleday, 1974). While he readily admits that he has reached conclusions and made judgments as a Christian, he set out to write a theology of the Old Testament as if the New Testament did not exist.

52. For an excellent beginning, see the book by the Swiss Roman Catholic theologian Clemens Thoma, *A Christian Theology of Judaism,* trans. Helga Croner, Stimulus Book (New York: Paulist Press, 1980). It was published too late to be evaluated here.

The "Old Testament"
in the Protestant Tradition

André Lacocque

Looking back at 2,000 years of "Old Testament" reading in the Christian Church, one comes unmistakably to the conclusion that few phenomena in human history reveal a greater ambivalence, or rather ambiguity. The Christian Church has historically both revered the Jewish Scriptures and felt deeply embarrassed with them. It has both paid tribute to the people of the Bible and stolen from them their sacred testimony, their soul.

True, the Reformation has done much to rescue us from the mire of that equivocation by restoring Scripture as the ultimate authority in and for the Church, but other ambiguities have remained or have resulted from the Reformation. The fact is that Christian hermeneutics had almost from the start taken a wrong path, and that the Reformers were still too much the heirs of the Middle Ages and of their exegetical habits (inherited from the Church Fathers), to feel free enough to blaze an entirely new trail. Moreover, as we shall see below, the Reformers' attitude toward the Jews, which could have made all the difference, was far from creative, despite a transitory intuition of Luther's at one point.

More importantly, there was for the Reformers, as for the former generations (and, one may add, for the subsequent ones until this day), an authoritative use of the "Old Testament" by the New which they had no boldness, and indeed no desire, to call into question. Such an approach by the New Testament can be summarized by what Paul writes to the

Corinthians in his first letter (15:3–4): "Christ died for our sins in accordance with the Scriptures; he was buried and was raised on the third day in accordance with the Scriptures."

Thus, the Hebrew Scriptures—I shall hereafter use the term "Prime Testament" since "Hebrew Scriptures" and, worse, "Old Testament" are unsatisfactory—had been annexed by the Church and made a Christian book speaking in types and figures of Jesus Christ. Now, Luther, e.g., was adamantly opposing the allegorizing explanation of Scripture, but he certainly was not ready to dispute the typological reading of it. One may not, he says, have recourse to allegories "unless either the text exhibits them, or (allegorical) interpretations can be cited from the New Testament" (WA 42[173]). But these do not for him include Christological explanations, for they are expressly warranted by the New Testament, that is, they are seen as the literal meaning of the texts by the Christian Bible itself.[1]

We shall return below to that crucial hermeneutical issue of multiple vs. single meaning of the Prime Testament texts. Let us for now emphasize again the ambiguity we started with. The Bible as a Christian book clearly robs the Jews of their own Scriptures and thwarts from the outset any attempt at reading the Prime Testament in its own right and integrity. But, on the other hand, the very consistent apologetical effort on the part of the New Testament writers to base on Jewish Scriptures their demonstration of Jesus' Messiahship, and on the part of Christian commentators to find "the testimony to Christ in the Old Testament,"[2] make clear at least three points.

1. The Prime Testament is the incomparable warrant of Jesus' Messiahship and of the faith of the Church (cf. Acts 24:14).

2. At the level of the New Testament the *kerygma* was primarily addressed by Jews to Jews.

3a. Implicitly and explicitly, the Prime Testament's nature is understood as fundamentally pointing toward something transcending the text itself. (So Jesus is presented as explicating that transcendent aim of the Prime Testament as referring to his own person; cf. Mt 4:1ff; Lk 4:1ff.[3])

3b. Between the Scriptures and Christ, there is no discontinuity, but continuity (cf. Heb 1:1–2), the continuum being the common inspiration by "the Holy Spirit." 1 Pet 1:10–12 reads: "The prophets who prophesied of the grace *that was to be yours* searched and inquired about this salvation; they inquired what person or time was indicated by *the Spirit of Christ within them* that they were serving not themselves but you, in the things which have now been announced to you by those who preached the good news to you through the Holy Spirit sent from heaven, things into which angels long to look" (*RSV;* emphasis mine).

Let us take serially these three points under the following rubrics: (I) The Problem of Canon(s); (II) The Problem of the People and Tradition of Israel; (III) The Problem of Bible Hermeneutics. In conclusion (IV), I shall try to indicate some possible direction for the hermeneutical research.

I THE PROBLEM OF CANON(S)

It is out of the question to retrace the history of Bible canonization, or even to discuss theologically the opportunity or inopportunity of canonizing the books of the Prime Testament. The matter at issue here is the duality of Canons in the Christian Church. This question is, I contend, the point of departure for our study, as indeed all other issues revolve around this one. Clearly, as a matter of fact, were it not for the boosting of the New Testament to the same level with the Prime Testament and even to a status superseding the latter, the whole of our problem would be utterly different. And, indeed, it was unavoidable that, *de facto* if not *de jure,* one of the two canons in the Christian Church would take precedence over the other (the "unity" of the two being a wishful thinking, like the "double nature of Christ, perfectly God and perfectly man," which remains purely theoretical). John Bright rightly states: "To say that the Old Testament can retain its place in the Church only if specifically Christian meanings can be found in its texts[4] comes perilously close to saying that it can be regarded as canonical Scripture only when given a meaning other than the one it plainly intended."[5]

I have discussed elsewhere—also much too briefly, a flaw which cannot be corrected here due to the drastic limitations of this article—the problem of Canonization of the New Testament as one of the most urgent issues for modern theological reflection.[6] I have tried there to make a clear-cut distinction between the canonicity of the Prime Testament and the alleged canonicity of the New Testament. The two sets of documents are, as a matter of fact, mutually incomparable. Primitive Christianity is founded on the Prime Testament as Scripture; as such the early Church has no Scripture of its own which would not be shared by the other members of their Jewish community. Moreover, and this point is crucial,[7] the Prime Testament as document was preceded and followed, surrounded,

by the community of Israel. *Per contra,* the New Testament precedes the
Church and presides to its constitution. The prophets of old were within
their people's fold and are unthinkable without it. But the Church is "built
upon the foundation of the apostles and the prophets, Christ Jesus himself
being the cornerstone" (Eph 2:20). Calvin, by the way, takes advantage
of this text to pointedly show that Scriptures are not founded on the
Church's authority, but the other way round.

The very notion of Canon is transformed by the Christian Church.
Whereas for the Synagogue the Canon of the Prime Testament means that
a specific compendium of documents, effectively although minimally, represents all aspects of Israel's soul, so that the Jewish living tradition is
not thereby exhausted, the Church had a very different rationale in accepting the same Canon. Here, as Christ was seen as the eschatological
event, the concept of Canon was accompanied by the idea of its being
closed. Nothing conceivably could be added to the fulfilled Scriptures.
Consequently, the Church's "oral tradition" is of a different nature from
Jewish oral tradition. What should have remained on the level of an ac-
companying oral tradition for the Christians, viz., the New Testament,
has been promoted to the rank of Scripture, so that to the extent that
the ecclesial tradition is dealing with the Gospel, it is a tradition in mono-
logue with itself.

The early Christian writings were all "parerga," occasional, circumstantial, writings, not meant for generalized use, and still less for being
promoted to the rank of canonical texts.[8] Writes Pierre Grelot (whose
orthodoxy is beyond doubt): "The writings of the New Testament . . .
are all circumstantial documents with immediate aims. . . . (They are) par-
tial exposés, sketches, allusions, turned short development. . . ."[9]

Furthermore, the topic of this study invites to go deeper into the
problem. The canonization of the New Testament writings coincided with
the Christian onslaught against Judaism and the concomitant hardening
of the Church's dogmatism. The whole process is to a large extent an
anti-Jewish move which entailed a systematic devaluation (short of evacuation, a step made by Marcion and countless others) of the Hebrew Scriptures. Paralleling this, the more the holy character of Christian texts was
emphasized, the more de-Judaized (i.e., according to the conveniently ad
hoc jargon, "spiritualized") they appeared to their readers. As, however,
it was felt impossible to purely and simply reject the "Old Testament,"
the latter was annexed by the Church, indeed stolen from the Jews. The
Jews were disowned of their Scriptures which, it was taught, had never

been understood by their mechanical writers. As Rosemary Ruether says: "Salvation was now found solely through faith in the messianic exegesis of the Church."[10]

This was unavoidable as the co-existence of two Canons is an inner contradiction. As we shall see in the following part, once the step of canonizing the New Testament was made, the last dike against a flood of antisemitic feelings broke. Even the very nature of the Gospel was altered.

II THE PROBLEM OF THE PEOPLE AND TRADITION OF ISRAEL

The Prime Testament as Scripture was able to protect the Church against a philosophical environment characterized by idealism and dualism. It is therefore not surprising to discover that, with the devaluation of the "Old Testament," all the trends in Christian antiquity converge toward a dichotomistic view of reality. One can even wonder to what extent the devalorization in question is not after the Stoic idea of the passage from a sham world of the senses (the "Old Testament") to the real world of the immutable (the New Testament). In the universe of ideas, it is of course unthinkable that Scripture and Israel be one. The Jewish dimension appears to be too relative, material, "sensorial." Scripture indeed must belong not to people, but to the supra-human. So, e.g., Clement of Alexandria has no room for anything Jewish in the Bible. There is, he says,[11] one Testament from the origins of the world, coming from one God through one Lord Jesus, constituting one chosen people. And St. Augustine completes the picture in characterizing that chosen people as the community of the just who, since the beginning of the world, have had in fact Christ at their head.[12]

Thus—I shall again insist on that point later—"Christ" has swallowed all of Scripture and all of history. He so much fills the horizon that there is place left for no one and nothing else. Indeed, "Christ" is the label on the Christian myth, and the New Testament is its "hieros logos." Hermeneutically, as we shall see in the following part, this means that Christ is the *spirit* of Scripture, while the "Old Testament" is merely its flesh. The literal meaning is not only insufficient, but it is misleading as it puts a veil upon the eyes of the readers (cf. 2 Cor 3:14).

That negative judgment on the Synagogue is found throughout Christian history from the time of the "Fathers" to the sixteenth century and beyond. Erasmus—not to speak of the infamous declarations and pamphlets of Luther against the Jews—sees Israel as a people that God has rejected.[13] The Counter-Reformation does not, to be sure, dispute that point. Partisans and adversaries of the Reformation are of the opinion that the former people of God must leave behind their material and institutional apparatus and join the veritable *qua* spiritual community of the saints, i.e., the Church (*sic*). For the promise of God, to the shame of narrow-minded Jews, is not for this world, but for the next, after the resurrection of the dead. P. Grelot in our day frowns upon the limitations of the Sinai covenant in which "the divine punishments are exclusively of a temporal order; the retribution after the grave is thus totally ignored."[14]

But Israel of old was not all short-sighted. That is why Christian apologetics may also have recourse to another arsenal. The people of the old covenant, says the influential St. Augustine, was already a "Christian people" (Sermon 300).[15] Besides, Christian tradition in general distinguishes, inside Israel, between the *majores* and the *minores*. Even the former have seen the mystery of Christ only through a veil. There is much truth in the following quote of H. Windisch: "The apostle Paul is the man who took upon himself to unveil the veritable character of the Old Testament announcement of redemption, and to snap from the hands of synagogal rabbis their holy book."[16] One may, however, find it somewhat unfair to blame the Jewish blindness for not reading "Adam" instead of "Edom" and "look for" rather than "inherit" in Amos 9:12 (cf. Acts 15:17 after the Septuagint) or for not understanding Isaiah 52:5 as a judgment against the Jews, rather than the Assyrians (cf. Rom 2:24), and Amos 5:25–27 as chastizing Israel for their idolatry, rather than praising them for living on the sole fidelity of God in the desert (cf. Acts 7:41–43).

There is, from the point of view of such negative attitude toward the Jews, a real continuity down to the Reformation and beyond. True, there is from the Middle Ages to the Reformers a considerable change of tone and substance. The monk Vincent at Lerinum (sixth century) could say: "Care is to be taken that we hold that which has been believed everywhere, always, by everybody."[17] And the Council of Trent (sixteenth century) concurs: "It is for Mother Church to judge of the true sense and interpretation of the holy Scriptures."[18] What a difference of conception when we hear Wycliff! "Though there were a hundred Popes and every monk were made a cardinal, their opinion in matters of faith is to be valued only insofar as it is founded upon Scripture."[19] It is not necessary in such a limited article as this to insist on the attitude of Martin

Luther and John Calvin—with their mottos of "justification through faith" and *"sola scriptura"*—since the statement of Wycliff summarizes so well.

The Post-Reformation era is represented by diverse movements I shall briefly review at this point for the sake of synopsis.

(a) *Fundamentalism* affirms a hermeneutical principle according to which the "Old Testament's" inspiration is recognized only when Jesus is found permeating its pages. Those are not the Jews' Scriptures but God's. The Jews have been used as unconscious instruments by God. Some individuals among them, it is true, to the extent that they were types of Christ and participants in his Spirit, saw the light (Abraham, Moses, David, Isaiah), but this was not enough to lead their stiff-necked people to salvation.

Christ came for a new people, replacing the old one. In fact, *mirabile dictu,* the "second" people is in fact the "first," since it was from the beginning the only people God had in mind. Israel *kata sarka* ("according to the flesh") has only been the type of spiritual Israel now revealed in (the right wing sects of) the Christian Church. The Jews have *stricto sensu* never been the Elect People. They could have become the reality they metaphorically represented, but they forsook their chances. They have rejected their own Messiah who solely was able to usher them into the Kingdom of God. Thus "Israel" as a name should not mislead us; it designates from the outset a *spiritual* reality, badly twisted into material and worldly substitutes by the Jews. Their sin is in choosing a land and a king of their own instead of the Kingdom of God and the Son of Man. Unworthy vessels for the pure gold of God's treasure, they will nonetheless, because of the service rendered to humanity—however reluctantly like Jonah—be joined at some time to the community of the saints through their conversion to Christianity.

The "Old Testament's" true reading is Christological. The prophets have prophesied about Jesus of Nazareth. Were it not because the crossing of the Red Sea prefigures the baptism of the Christian in Christ's blood, the event would be secondary, by far surpassed by Daniel's salvation from the den of lions, a flagrant sign of Christ's resurrection from the grave.

Fundamentalism paradoxically insists that biblical personages are historical, even when the case is most improbable, e.g., Jonah or Job, but their historicity is without integrity. They are hybrid "historical allegories." The same applies to the texts. They are in fact pretexts. They never mean what they say. Hence the understandable Jewish "lack of intelligence": they have been deprived of or have refused the key of interpretation. For there is a radical hiatus between the literal meaning (misleading) and the spiritual meaning (edifying). Rabbis had traditionally distinguished a four-level understanding of the Text, going from the literal *(pešat)* to the sacred *(sod)*, but each sense was contained in the preceding one, so that the *pešat* boxed in the three others, and the *sod* was the innermost shrine with three external layers for its protection. Christian Fundamentalism has dislocated the ensemble. The *sod* is the real and indeed only meaning of the text; it has swallowed up all the others. This is so true that modern Bible scholarship and its historico-critical approach is at best a vain exercise, and at worst a contribution to the blindness before the Bible, of which the Jews have been historically the prime example.

Of all classic Christian systems of interpretation, Fundamentalism is the most "expensive." All reality which is not "Christ" is dissolved, at the cost of making "Christ" a myth then deprived of the objectivity of the Scriptures, history, and people of Israel. But it is also the most coherent system. One key opens all doors. Hence the fascination exercised by Fundamentalism on generations of "tired heroes."

Fundamentalism remains untouched by Auschwitz, but not by the State of Israel. Auschwitz is one more demonstration that "Israel according to the flesh" has been forsaken by God. The event belongs together with the destruction of the Temple in 70 CE. The State of Israel is more complex. It demonstrates again that the Jews choose the material over the spiritual. But this time, the move may prove providential. The ingathering of the Jews in their land brings us on the way to the fulfillment of famous prophecies of the "Old Testament" and of St. Paul's promise in Romans 9–11 (cf. 11:25f.).

(b) At the antipode of Fundamentalism is the nineteenth-century Protestant *Liberalism*. It had become somewhat embarrassing, in an era of rationalism and scientism, to appear as religiously gullible. Man's *Weltanschauung* had been subject to three successive phenomenological "reductions" at the hands of Galileo, Darwin, and Freud. The earth was not any longer the center of the universe; man on earth was only the result of animal evolution; man's ego was deceptive, his "center" was bewildering. In such a dismantled universe, there was left nothing reliable, not even the historicity of events presented as such by the Bible.

Liberalism often is a synonym for skepticism. Theology becomes a by-product of philosophy and/or psychology. It imposes "external canons of evaluation on the Old Testament," and "since a value judgment is by definition an individual matter ... a subjective norm is substituted for an objective one. . . . No longer did men look to the Bible as the Church's supreme rule of faith and practice. Rather, the Christian individual in a real sense assumed authority over the Bible. . . ."[20]

With respect to the role of the Prime Testament for modern man, the response is far from uniform. The following words of Adolf von Harnack are well known: "To have cast aside the Old Testament in the second century was an error which the Church rightly rejected; to have retained it in the sixteenth century was a fate which the Reformation was not yet able to avoid; but still to keep it after the nineteenth century as a canonical document within Protestantism results from a religious and ecclesiastical paralysis."[21] Other liberal theologians shy away from such radicalism. They "keep" the Hebrew Scripture but cast doubt upon the possibility of reading the Prime Testament in the light of the Christ event. For the latter itself is problematic. Nothing of what the New Testament says about "Christ" is reliable. "Jesus" is not a known quantity susceptible of shedding light on an "Old Testament" considered as the unknown. Thus, by the same token, the Prime Testament retrieves a certain integrity of its own. Prime Testament and New Testament equally raise a great number of problems of "authenticity." The cleansing of the Temple by Jesus is a priori not more historical than Jonah in the fish's belly. And the central tenet of Christian faith, viz. Jesus' resurrection, is not any more an established fact than Daniel's companions saved from the crematorium.

On the other hand, once the Prime Testament and the New Testament are being put on the same level of uncertainty by the Christian liberal, their respective interpretations are compartmented. "Old Testament scholarship" and "New Testament scholarship" are different sciences. For Graf, Ewald, Wellhausen, and their many disciples, there is no necessary relation not only between the two Testaments, but also between the different parts of each Testament, or for that matter between pericopes of the same biblical book. Moreover, and on a philosophical level, neither is there a necessary relation between the Bible scholar and the believer. A Wellhausenian student of the Bible reads "his" Prime Testament one way in his study and a totally different way in his local church. As a scholar, at least, he feels unbound to the community of faith, to the denomination, to allegiance, and even to the texts he is studying.

(c) Reviewing above the Fundamentalist approach to Scripture, we noticed that the history of Israel had been in the process emptied of all substance; the personages were reduced to allegories, and the texts themselves to pretexts. Expectedly, Liberalism brings us to the other extreme: *Historicism,* where only what is objectively historical is reliable. Like Fundamentalism, Historicism is an expensive proposition. Very little indeed can be salvaged from radical historical skepticism, and what remains belongs anyway with an exotic set of beliefs of an exotic people who mixed indiscriminately the historical and the mythical. This makes "Israel" more a fiction than a reality. And the documents which inform us about it are so biased that the image they provide is the reflection of a sect, not of a nation. Their sole credential is that they "succeeded" while other sects and parties—at times more "interesting" or more spiritually "refined" than the victorious trend—were defeated. Thus Judaism is a more or less artificial offspring of a more or less artificial intellectual construction. Today's Jews are not "Israel." Auschwitz has no theological meaning, nor does the State of Israel, although both events are "prodigiously interesting."

(d) Between the two world wars was born a movement in opposition to Liberalism, viz. *Neo-Orthodoxy*. In the convulsions preceding the birth of the new "Order," the need was felt of something more substantial than Liberalism. Philosophical skepticism is hardly comforting in the midst of State terrorism and genocide. Then Liberalism appears as an intellectual exercise, a luxury reserved for a scholarly elite in an economy of abundance. On the contrary, in a world permeated with tragedy, critical conclusions to the effect that a certain text is non-historical, that a certain moral imperative is relative, that a narrative is of a foreign origin, or that a prophetic oracle is of a prejudicial nature do not help much. In a changing world, the problematic itself is altered. The issue of historicity, e.g., so crucial for Liberalism as to be confused with "authenticity," has now shifted to the issue of credibility. Now, credible is not just rational, for tyrants act in the name of "functional rationality,"[22] thus discrediting a certain aspect of reason. From the vantage point of materialist analysis, Judaism and Christianity are sheer aberrations, opiates for gullible people.[23]

But, even in Neo-Orthodoxy, the methodological conquests of Liberalism could not be ignored, whatever the pressure of new circumstances. There was no way to play the "game" of exegesis by other rules anymore. How then was one to accept the methodology of Liberalism, and to reject its conclusions? The response of Neo-Orthodoxy was: dialectics, or the *coincidentia oppositorum.* From this perspective, historical is no synonym for trustworthy. The non-historical in the *kerygma* takes us merely upon another level of communication. A biblical narrative, for example, may be a-historical scientifically speaking, but become historical through the faith and commitment of an historical community from which and for which the narrative gets its *raison d'être*. For "historical" covers not only what is *historisch* (i.e., assessable as objective by scientific methods) but also what is *geschichtlich* from an existential point of view, using non-logically measurable *existential* norms. From *historisch* to *geschichtlich*, we have passed from the particular to the universal. Thus, the Prime Testament is at the same time the book of a particular Jewish community *and* a foundational document of the universal Christian Church.

The text is to be treated as literature in its fabrics, and as sacred Scripture in the *kerygma* it transmits. The diversity of forms has little effect on what is conveyed thereby. In short, the distinction is made by Neo-Orthodoxy between what pertains to reason in the document (which indeed can be a-historical in many cases) and what belongs to the *kerygma* (which is beyond historicity). So, it becomes possible to maintain the fundamental skepticism of the liberals as regards the literary complexes and the modalities of their transmission. It becomes concurrently possible to affirm the Reformation central tenet that Christ is the soul of all Scripture, the *kerygma* of both "Old Testament" and New Testament. Consequently, there can be a reconciliation between the theologian and the believer. Whether, however, this reconciliation was based on a caricature of the Prime Testament is to be considered in the following section. Be that as it may, we conclude this part of our study with the words of Brevard Childs: "It became increasingly clear that the rise of the historical critical study of the Old Testament had, once for all, broken the dependence of Christian scholars upon traditional Jewish learning. . . . (It also introduced) an enormous hiatus between the description of the critically reconstructed literature and the actual canonical text which has been received and used as authoritative Scripture by the community."[24]

III   THE PROBLEM OF BIBLE HERMENEUTICS

(a) This new section has been largely introduced by the preceding one. I intend here to deal not with the schools of interpretation as above, but with the methods themselves and especially with Typology. Our review must, however, start with *Allegory,* as it is the method by and large used by the New Testament in quoting the Prime Testament. Our study above of Fundamentalism will allow brevity on this topic. As Robert M. Grant says: "The Alexandrines . . . deprive the whole biblical history of its reality. Adam was not really Adam, paradise was not really paradise, the serpent was not a real serpent."[25] According to the ninth-century Isho'dad: "The psalms and the prophets who spoke of the captivity and the return of the people, Origen explained as teaching the captivity of the soul far from truth and its return to the faith."[26]

As said above, allegory is largely used by the New Testament (cf. Gal 4:25; Heb 7:2; Gal 3:16; 1 Cor 5:7f.; Phil 2:17, etc.). The method is based on a conception of the text as *autonomous*. That is why allegory has a totally different import whether used by Jews or by Gentiles. In the former case, the evacuation of Israel from the text is, to a certain extent at least, compensated by Israel's presence in the person of the allegorist (e.g., Philo of Alexandria).

Not so when the allegorist is a Gentile. As O. Cullmann pointedly wrote: "From an historical perspective, the need for an allegorical interpretation of the Bible is born when theologians, while retaining the Bible's authority, realize that there is a hiatus between their own convictions and biblical doctrines. So Origen who interpreted Scripture after Greek philosophy, or later the Catholic Church whose interpretation was after dogmas. So especially is it for eighteenth-century rationalism which interpreted the Bible after 'natural' truth."[27]

It is indeed "Greek philosophy" to look for "ultimate meaning in elements which only contribute to, but do not independently state, ultimate meaning."[28] Paul Ricoeur's formulation is, in my opinion, definitive: "Allegory implies that the true meaning, the philosophical meaning, preceded the fable, which was only a second disguise, a veil deliberately thrown over the truth to mislead the simple." And he adds: "I am convinced that we must think, not *behind* the symbols, but starting from the symbols, *according* to symbols, that their substance is indestructible, that they constitute the *revealing* substrate of speech which lives among men."[29]

(b) *Typology* as an hermeneutical method sees in the Prime Testament's "promise" the *type* of things to come as witnessed in the New Testament, "fulfillment" of the promise. "The fundamental idea is one of a very concrete formal dependence; the object which is coined depends upon the form-giving object through modeling, coining or sealing . . . (cf. 2 Cor 3:7; Acts 7:43; 23:25). But as the coin in its turn is the reproduction of the original, it is invested vis-à-vis the subsequent copies with a *normative value*. It is then the prototype, the normative sample, the *example* to imitate (1 Thess 1:7; 2 Thess 3:9; Phil 3:17; 1 Tim 4:12; Tit 2:7; 1 Pet 5:3), or the model for copy (Acts 7:44 translating the Hebrew *tabenît),* the form (Rom 6:10; cf. 1 Tim 1:16; 2 Tim 1:13) . . . (St. Paul) calls *tupoi* the events

of the old covenant (Rom 5:14; 1 Cor 10:6, 11); the antitype designates
(then) the *model,* even if historically it came in existence after the foreshadowing copy. . . ."[30]

Typology must be understood within the broader complex of the multiplicity of meanings of the text, according to a long tradition present both
in the Synagogue (we mentioned above the rabbinic four-story exegesis)
and in the Church. Origen saw three levels of meaning, the "flesh," the
"soul," and the "spirit." Not surprisingly, the "flesh" was for the Jews.
John Cassianus (ca. 425) distinguished in the text historical, tropological-
moral, allegorical-Christological, and anagogical-eschatological senses. St.
Augustine also saw four levels of meaning: history, aetiology, analogy, and
allegory. It is in reaction against the allegorizing Alexandrines that the
school of Antioch (with Diodorus, Theodore of Mopsuestia, *et alii*) proposed the method of typology. The Antiochenes strongly affirmed the literal meaning of the text and rejected allegory as "utter inanity " or
"insanity," but, as K. Grobel writes, what "Theodore so valiantly exclud-
ed with one hand, as allegory, he and the whole school of Antioch admitted with the other hand—as typology. Admittedly there is a difference
in degree, but the underlying assumption of dual (if not plural) meaning
is the same."[31]

A difference in degree only? Yes, for although even today among the
greatest "Old Testament" scholars such as M. Noth, G. von Rad, W. Zimmerli, etc. typology is advocated as hermeneutical method; it does not read
the Prime Testament in its own right and integrity. St. John in the New
Testament is on that issue categorical, and modern scholars should med-
itate on what the evangelist says before adopting a similar hermeneutics
(cf. Jn 3:37f.; 5:39, 45; 15:21). For typology implies the following misunderstandings:

(1) It negates the Prime Testament's specificity. G. Fohrer says: "We
should then (if using the typological method) conclude that the Christological meaning specific to the Old Testament words was hidden to the
men of the Old Testament and could be grasped only retrospectively, from
the point of the New Testament. It would imply a total dismissal of meaning from the Old Testament; for what type of prophet would it be that does
not understand what he preaches?"[32]

(2) It must discriminate within the Prime Testament which texts can
be Christologically typified. W. Eichrodt says: "(Typology) will hardly
avoid the blame of being arbitrary, all the more so as it must leave aside
a good deal of the Old Testament."[33]

As a matter of fact, typology introduces a fundamental confusion of categories. It promotes *metaphor* to the level of *type*. Pierre Grelot, for example, in his book already mentioned above, sees the exodus from Egypt as susceptible to be interpreted on three different levels: historical, for it started by being an event of history; prophetic, for it was the type of Jesus' "passage" from this world to the Father (Jn 13:1), and of the Christians from a sinful condition to the life in Christ through baptism (1 Cor 10:1–2); eschatological, for it is ultimately fulfilled in the passage with Christ to celestial glory (cf. Rev 15:3: the saints sing Moses' song).[34]

In this concatenation of senses, one link at least is patently missing—all the more unfortunately as it would have corrected Grelot's misunderstanding. I am referring to Second Isaiah's use of the exodus theme to metaphorically describe the return of Israel from Babylon to Zion. There is thus, if one wills, a "typology" inherent to the Prime Testament itself. But there is with the New Testament's or G. von Rad's typology a decisive difference. The prophet's use of the exodus motif is *prospective* and *metaphorical*. It means that, for Second Isaiah, the restoration provides no superior sense to the event of the coming out of Egypt—a sense that the Book of Exodus had tried in vain to convey until the sixth century. The exodus is an event with its total integrity; the restoration in the sixth century is also an event with total integrity. But the prophetic message conveyed by the latter, its theological import, is in reference to the primal exodus, the foundational event of leaving Egypt for the Promised Land.

The authors of the New Testament reverse the movement. From prospective, their typology becomes retrospective. Their justification is in their conviction (of an apocalyptic nature) that no other event ever will in the future better deserve to become the antitype of all types, the reality of all metaphors. Christ is more Abraham than Abraham, more David than David, and the Christ-event is more the exodus than the exodus, more Sinai than Sinai. But the dynamism in such a formulation gets lost as soon as the hermeneutical back and forth movement between scriptural types and Christic antitype is "frozen" in a *doctrine* of the "Old Testament." For with the "passage" from type to antitype, there is no ontological leap from "shadow" to "reality,"[35] but from an event, by nature limited, fragmented, transient, to its eschatological illimitation, or to what I shall call below its "eventuation."

In a certain sense, all events participate in the central event, whatever this latter may be. Clearly, for the primitive Church, the cross-resurrection was the end-event, and the whole Pauline system of realized eschatology is based on that conviction. But when such apocalyptic fervor was frustrated by an indefinite postponement of the *parousia,* typology, from a practical, paraenetic, ad hoc, opportunistic expedient, became an herme-neutical system, backed by an established Church, whose settlement could afford the lingering of the end. A taxonomy prevailed according to which the Church's warrant was the New Testament in contradistinction to the "Old Testament" warrant for the peregrination on earth (before reaching the paradisiacal Church) of a people geared to the material instead of the spiritual, to the transient instead of the eternal, to a humiliated status in-stead of the glorious.[36] St. Augustine therefore feels entitled to say: "The early promises which seem to be there proposed, mean in a hidden way a spiritual recompense"[37]—a proposition considerably radicalized by Pas-cal: "(The prophets) had to deal with carnal people and to make them the depositaries of the spiritual testament. . . . Therefore prophecies convey a hidden, spiritual, meaning—of which the (Jewish) people was enemy—under a carnal form—of which the people was friend."[38]

Such statements paved the way to Auschwitz. But we rather return to the problem of metaphor vs. type. As Grelot puts it, "Figures are at the outset of language; they belong to its fundamental structure" (p. 430). That is why there was no way for Christians to do away with figures; the Christian language continues to use the very images molded in Israel's his-torical experience (God is "father, king, lord, husband, shepherd"). It is therefore problematic whether, from Prime Testament to New Testament, the shift is from image to reality. Certainly the exodus was no mere figure of style for historic Israel, and the Kingdom of God is no reality without figurative representation for the Church ("Behold, the Kingdom of God is like . . .").

Thomas Aquinas is therefore well inspired when, sensing that over-simplification of typology, he distinguishes between *texts* and *things*.[39] It is at the level of "things" that the cross may be said to be the antitype of a number of Prime Testament types; but at the level of "texts," no Prime Testament formulation is relativized by the New Testament. *On the con-trary,* I would say, as the New Testament is but an appendix (of crucial importance) to Scripture, the Christ-event to which the New Testament brings its testimony as ultimate fulfillment absolutizes, i.e., teleologizes, es-chatologizes, the Prime Testament formulation (law, creed, oracle, psalm, narrative, proverb, etc.).

Typology does not render justice to this point. As J. Barr says, "Even if typology could be defined . . . as a relation between historical entities and (be) supposed that it is thereby adequately discriminated from an allegory which relates a historical text to a non-historical meaning . . . it would only raise another question, viz., whether the 'historical' meaning of the text as used in the typology could be fitted with the contextual meaning of the text in its own environment and historical setting."[40] For even though G. von Rad cautions that typology "must hold itself to the *kerygma* that is intended" and "confine itself to the *credenda*" instead of "running wild" in interpreting "historical and biographical details,"[41] it remains that it is a reductionistic method which is acceptable on the level of homiletics (in parallel with the Jewish midrash), but not on the level of exegesis. In brief, exegesis is foundational for typology, but typology is no exegetical method.

Moreover, it is necessary at this point to make a clear distinction between the Jewish and the Gentile readers of Scripture. True, there is in the Church a figurative use of the Prime Testament (or typological, sometimes even allegorical) which externally resembles the rabbinic midrash. Does it legitimize it? The text, it must be emphasized, is Jewish. There is no text without the Jew; there is no Jew without the text. Such are the parameters of biblical commentary. The Prime Testament can be "handled" with the greatest liberty as long as such use does respect Israel's identity with the text and does not alter it. Rabbis or Gospel writers feel that free because the relation of their Jewish community with the text is *direct*. Israel dialogues with Israel; present Israel consults historic Israel.

Such a direct rapport is impossible for the Gentile; he comes "second" (cf. Rom 1:16; 2:9-10). His relation with the text is always indirect; he can dialogue with the text only through his dialogue with the People of the text[42] (in the Church this indirectness is acknowledged, but the individual "Jesus Christ" has pushed aside and replaced Israel). In the Christian handling of the text, any "free" use—implying a direct relation which does not exist in this case—unmistakably alters the text into a philosophical treatise or a religious sacrosanct formulary.

The Gentile must by necessity discover the *world* of the text, which is not his world.[43] There is only one way: the historico-critical approach. This is the sole guarantee that the reader does not alter the text or shape it according to his foreign philosophies. That way, he encounters a Jewish text in its Jewish context, in its genuine Jewish *Sitz im Leben,* the product of the history of Jewish traditions, imbedded in a Jewish formulation, transmitted by Jewish traditionalists and masoretes, for the use of a Jewish audience, with the aim of forwarding to future Jewish generations the covenantal relationship between God and Israel.

This, to be sure, does not imply that Israel, rather than the Pope in Rome, is infallible in its interpretation of the text. I said that Israel's relation with Scripture is *direct,* which is a far cry from saying that it is automatic. A relevant example is provided, among others, by the protest of

Jewish disciples of Jesus against a tradition obscuring, in their opinion, the real import and spirit of Scripture ("You have heard that it was said . . . but I say to you . . .").[44] Thus, the directness of the relation with the text does not imply inerrancy in the rapport. It is appropriate that the Jews as well, like their Christian counterpart, use the critical tools of exegesis, but not in order to discover a text which would be foreign to them, for indeed it is "the mental, traditional, religious and verbal matrix" of their identity. That it happens to be also "the mental, traditional, religious and verbal matrix in which the Christ comes to born"[45] is a powerful demonstration of the identity of Christ and his people. Their common being lies in their unique *parole*, to speak in the style of F. de Saussure and P. Ricoeur.

It is of course at this very point that the text escapes the historico-critical methods' totalitarian claim to exhaust its meaning. Thus, G. Ebeling sees in hermeneutics less of an effort to understand a language than the quest for the meaning of reality *through* language. P. Ricoeur would call it the quest for the referent of language. There is here a healthy reaction against a *formal* approach to an *object* (which can be comprehended), and an attempt to share in the movement itself of *parole* within the text.

(c) *Rudolf Bultmann*, in the words of Ricoeur, "has perfectly understood that (the) primacy of the object, (the) primacy of meaning over understanding, is performed only through the understanding, through the exegetical work itself. It is necessary therefore to enter the hermeneutic circle. . . . To understand the text, it is necessary to believe in what the text announces to me, but what the text announces to me is given nowhere but in the text. This is why it is necessary to understand the text in order to believe." Or, in summary, "To understand, it is necessary to believe; to believe, it is necessary to understand."[46]

But Bultmann's hermeneutics goes much beyond this affirmation of an "hermeneutic circle." He takes a definite Heideggerian stand which must be studied here—all too briefly—for two reasons. First, no other hermeneute has been more influential in modern Bible scholarship. Second, Bultmann's negativity in regard to the "Old Testament" is a challenge we must meet.

The Lutheran exegete draws radically different conclusions from ours from the indirectness of the relation with the text (cf. above). The "world" of the "Old Testament," he says, is not our world.[47] True, it has been claimed also by the New Testament as its own, but it is because of the Jewishness of its authors and of its original milieu. What this proves is that the New Testament must be submitted to an *Entmythologisierungs* process in order that such a world may become our world. Hence, the actual rejection of the "Old Testament" by Bultmann as the source of the New Testament myth. (His Lutheranism is irredentist: he persists in using the worn-out category of *Gesetz* vs. the New Testament *Gnade*.)

Whether this view is Marcionist-Gnostic is much disputed.[48] If Gnosticism is characterized as evacuating history, then Bultmann is certainly under fire. G. Ernest Wright, e.g., asks, "Does not the existentialist background of (Bultmann's) viewpoint actually dissolve the historical, so that one lives, alone, in the presence of the new existence, the eschatological deed of forgiveness wrought in Christ? Is not the fulfillment and the 'eschatological event' the end of significant history in this perspective?"[49]

In the presence of one another is a text and a reader. Israel is absent, and, with Israel, the "primary tradition"—in contradistinction to any Lutheran baggage, or any philosophical *Vorverständnis* which cannot but be secondary. Karl Barth saw how gravely threatened by Docetism was the Bultmannian approach.[50] There is indeed Docetism as soon as the text is abstracted from its Jewishness, and the reader is an island. Ultimately both are a-historical. That is why G. Ebeling, himself a disciple of Bultmann, stresses that hermeneutics corresponds with the very movement of history and of reality, i.e., is in intrinsic relation with its object.[51] Here then history is recuperated, although Ebeling is more interested in the Church's theology and predication than in Scripture's people and history.

The Roman Catholic reads Scripture indirectly, but the indirectness is not the one I have stressed above. Israel has been replaced by an ecclesial tradition. The Protestant claims to read Scripture directly, thus shortcircuiting a relation which should not take "a short cut, without having made the long detour of the question of being[52] without which these existentials ... are nothing more than abstractions of lived experience, of a formalized *existenziell*."[53]

Clearly, the crux of the problem lies in the understanding of history. I shall in my conclusion venture some vectorial suggestions.

IV PROSPECTIVE CONCLUSIONS

"Revelation is, at the moment when it takes place, the total revelation of the living God, his eternal Word *for and in that moment which looks toward* a new moment and, above all (by the impulse it gives the immediately following one), *looks toward* the crucial moment which is the summit and the key of revelation. ... In the moment which follows the present one, the revelation which follows is a *new* Word and every bit as *abso-*

lute.... For the newness of revelation is linked to the newness of the moment...."[54]

Samuel Amsler concurs with this affirmation—in my opinion at the summit of his book: "At the very hour when God will make the event yield all of its fruits, then at last, *in the light shed by its ulterior context,* the event shall manifest its full meaning."[55]

What Lys and Amsler are saying is that God's revelation in each instance is always complete, so that the schema "promise-fulfillment"—so dear, e.g., to W. Zimmerli—must be revised, and that anything relativizing our "C.E." time (cf. O. Cullmann) is wrong. Even when Jesus Christ is seen as the paradigm *par excellence* of history, he cannot fill so much of the horizon as to swallow history, so that we "of the generations after" come "too late" (Cullmann). There is no cumulative science of God finding its fullness in Jesus Christ (Wellhausen and Protestant Liberalism). Jesus Christ is not the chronological result of the "Old Testament," but its "axiological meaning."[56] In other words, one cannot say that, before Christ, all was unfulfilled prophecy, for prophecy and fulfillment go together. Any fulfillment is a new promise striving toward another fulfillment. The issue is considerably clarified by Th. C. Vriezen, when he writes: "Fulfillment (does not) mean that the time of hoping-without-beholding and of hoping for the future has now come to an end because the reality has become visible and tangible. For the appearance of Jesus also demands faith: the faith that God's salvation has become manifest in him whose outward appearance does not give any proof of his mission. *Fulfillment does not mean that the promise comes to an end and is replaced by the very thing that was promised, but it means that now the promise itself becomes completely unambiguous and consequently effective.'*[57] This point has been particularly well understood by J. Moltmann when he places Christ's resurrection outside of the customary framework of Hellenistic epiphanies of eternity and shows that it *confirms* the promise in broadening its validity to include all men.[58]

Therefore, if, according to St. Paul, Scripture can be summarized with the one word "promise" (Rom 1:2; 4:14ff.; Gal 3:17ff.; etc.), we still need to get a grip on what this means. As the quotation of S. Amsler above shows ("in the light shed by its ulterior context, the event shall manifest its full meaning"), there is here a conception of history as in continuity and even as having an organic unity. Thus W. Pannenberg's contention is that the whole of universal history reveals God. I shall not emphasize Pannenberg's position, however, because, with respect to our present topic, I find it unstable. On the one hand he stresses the continuity of tradition (hence, of history) from the "Old Testament" to Jesus and also that "we do not stand in the continuity of Israel's tradition, except through Jesus," but then he comes forth with this surprising statement: "Only then (with Jesus Christ) for the first time was the God of the Jews revealing himself as the God he really is."[59] Be that as it may, it would appear difficult in a Pannenbergian perspective to maintain the centrality of Israel's *particular* history and peoplehood while affirming at the same time that God's revelation in *universal* history is visible to "uninhibited perception." Now, "uninhibited" is to be understood philosophically. It does not mean—as it should—a perception made possible only within the framework of the particular covenantal relationship between God and Israel. For particularism is the *conditio sine qua non* of universalism. It is because the light is concentrated in Zion that Israel is the beacon for humanity (cf. Is 49:6).

Like so many other scholars of our time, Pannenberg has not drawn the lessons of Jewish genocide. For the continuity of history can only be seen in retrospect, but when even in retrospect that continuity is broken by an unassimilable event such as *Auschwitz,* then the question is the following: Is history itself *(Geschichte)* at that point non-revelatory, or is our power of interpretation of history *(Wort)* at fault? In the former case, Pannenberg's "universal history" (à la Hegel) becomes senseless; in the latter, Zimmerli's "word of demonstration" becomes impotent.[60]

We are seemingly at an impasse. It is so, however, because one has lost the view that history is inseparable from its interpretation, i.e., an oriented series of events seen by Israel as providential in the light of their anticipated *eschaton.* There is thus in Israel a sense of *project* of history, springing from its "archaeology" and pulled by its *telos.* Now, as Hermann Gunkel, for instance, has amply demonstrated, there is between *Urzeit* and *Endzeit* a commonality which brings Israel to apply to the one and to the other a similar interpretation. That unique interpretation also informs the understanding of the present as the in-between of *Urzeit* and *Endzeit.*[61] That is why E. Troeltsch speaks of a "principle of similarity of all historical occurrence, which to be sure is not identity, but rather leaves all necessary room for differences, but for the rest presupposes in each case a kernel of common similarity, on the basis of which the differences are to be understood and tested."[62]

In short, there is in the absolute only one Event, already revealed and "named" from the origins ("the ulterior context" of S. Amsler; the "teleological"). Archaelogy and teleology: two that are one. I call the presence of the central Event in every historical event the principle of *eventuation,*[63] meaning that every event from alpha to omega reflects

Event, names the Event, gives shape to the Event.[64] The eventuation of history is its orientation and meaningfulness. In the words of P. Lestringant, "God's work can be summarized in a single act: he chose to himself a people so as to save them and dedicate them to his service."[65] This single act is permeating the whole of history, so that there are no two elections or two peoples in succession, but one elected People to whom are joined ("grafted") all those who "have heard that God is with" Israel (Rom 11:17, 19, 23–24; Zech 8:23).

Such is the content of the "eventuation." The primitive Church saw in Jesus of Nazareth the Christ, i.e., the principle of eventuation reflected in all past events experienced by Israel in dialogue with her God, and in all future events as all of them—and now we put in its true context the Cullmannian expression—are "coming too late," i.e., *too late for providing a different content* to the eventuation of history from alpha to omega.

Hence the New Testament does not pay lip service to the Scriptures in quoting texts of the Prime Testament, nor does it perpetuate an obsolete "world" of myth. It was on the contrary crucial to show that Christ is the kernel of history, of any event of history, i.e., of the encounter God-man. He is *cor temporum*. Only from this perspective is it meaningful to speak of Scripture inspiration, revelation, and authority.[66] What is inspired, revealed and revealing, what is authoritative, is the Event, which every event experienced and recited by Israel reflects.

The Prime Testament is the crossroad where from the meeting of people as interpreter and history as interpreted is born a *parole* whose referent is God. The New Testament is an appendix saying what is the living soul of that *parole,* the name of that Event, but certainly not its termination.

NOTES

1. Cf. Kendrick Grobel, "Interpretation," in *Interpreter's Dictionary of the Bible* (Nashville: Abingdon, 1962) II, 718–724.

2. Cf. Wilhelm Vischer, *The Witness of the Old Testament to Christ* (London: Lutterworth, 1949).

3. Cf. John Bright, *The Authority of the Old Testament* (Nashville: Abingdon, 1967), p. 138: "The Old Testament does indeed relate a *Heilsgeschichte,* a history of redemption, but it is a strange *Heilsgeschichte,* a *Heilsgeschichte* that does not arrive at *Heil,* a broken *Heilsgeschichte,* a truncated *Heilsgeschichte.* The Old Testament is a book that is theologically incomplete; it points beyond itself."

4. Cf. below on hermeneutics.

5. John Bright, *op. cit.,* p. 91.

6. Cf. André Lacocque, *But As For Me* (Atlanta: John Knox Press, 1979), pp. 111ff.

7. It has been made also lately by James Barr, in a lecture given at the University of Chicago in October 1979.

8. Cf. Edgar J. Goodspeed, *The Meaning of Ephesians* (Chicago: Chicago University Press, 1933).

9. Pierre Grelot, *Sens chrétien de l'Ancien Testament, Esquisse d'un Traité dogmatique* (Tournai: Desclée, 1962), p. 15 (my transl.).

10. Rosemary Ruether, *Faith and Fratricide* (New York: Seabury, 1974), p. 78.

11. Clement of Alexandria, *Stromata* 6, 13.

12. Augustinus, *Enarrationes in Psalmos* 35, 3–4.

13. Erasmus, *Opera* (Froeben ed.) V, 73f.

14. Pierre Grelot, *op. cit.,* p. 203 (my transl.).

15. Quoted by Pierre Grelot, *op. cit.,* p. 140. Cf. also Thomas Aquinas, Ia IIae, q. 106, art. I ad 3 (P. Grelot, p. 158): "All those to whom the law of grace was applied did thereby (already) belong to the New Testament" (my transl.).

16. Hans Windisch, *Paulus und das Judentum* (Stuttgart, 1935), p. 65 (my transl.).

17. *Commonitorium* II, PL L, 640, quoted by Kendrick Grobel, *op. cit.*

18. Quoted in Kendrick Grobel, *op. cit.*

19. John Wycliffe, *Trialogion* IV c. 7; cf. Kendrick Grobel, *op. cit.*

20. John Bright, *op. cit.,* pp. 96, 108.

21. Adolf von Harnack, *Marcion, das Evangelium vom fremden Gott* (Leipzig: Hinrichs, 1924²), quoted by John Bright, *op. cit.,* p. 65.

22. The expression is used by Max Weber and Karl Mannheim. Cf. my forthcoming *Where Was God at Auschwitz?*

23. So is also by the way poetry, a vain exercise of reactionary societies, or myth, sheer legend for retarded people.

24. Brevard Childs, *Introduction to the Old Testament as Scripture* (Philadelphia: Fortress Press, 1979), pp. 38, 40.

25. Robert M. Grant, *The Bible in the Church: A Short History of Interpretation* (New York: Macmillan, 1948), p. 74.

26. Quoted in *ibid.,* p. 75.

27. Oscar Cullmann, "Les problèmes posés par la méthode exégétique de l'école de Karl Barth", in *Revue d'histoire et de philosophie religieuses,* 1928, p. 81 (my transl.).

28. James Barr, *Old and New in Interpretation* (New York: Harper & Row, 1966), p. 107.

29. Paul Ricoeur, *The Conflict of Interpretations: Essays in Hermeneutics* (Evanston: Northwestern University Press, 1974), p. 299.

30. Samuel Amsler, *L'Ancien Testament dans l'Eglise: Essai d'herméneutique chrétienne* (Neuchâtel: Del. & Niestlé, 1960), p. 30, n. 2 (my transl.).

31. Kendrick Grobel, *loc. cit.*

32. Georg Fohrer, *Messiasfrage und Bibelverstaendnis* (Tuebingen, 1957), p. 7 (my transl.).

33. Walther Eichrodt, "Les rapports du Nouveau et de l'Ancien Testament," in J. Boisset, ed., *Le problème biblique dans le protestantisme* (Paris, 1955), p. 109 (my transl.).

34. Pierre Grelot, *op. cit.*, p. 295.

35. Despite the philosophically dangerous and misleading expressions of the Epistle to the Hebrews, which considers the relationship of Christ to a *static* "Old Testament."

36. Cf. at the cathedral of Strasbourg, France, the statues of triumphant Church and humiliated Synagogue facing each other.

37. Augustinus, *Quaest. in Hept.*, 4, 33.

38. Blaise Pascal, *Pensées* 570 (Paris: J. Chevalier, 1937) (my transl.).

39. James Barr as well distinguishes between a "good" and a "no longer admissible" typology. The former is "applied to historical events" and "is based on historical correspondences," while the latter is "applied to persons, human characteristics, religious institutions, and so on." Gerhard von Rad and Martin Noth, he says, have emphasized that necessary distinction—both, in Claus Westermann, ed. *Essays in Old Testament Hermeneutics* (Richmond: John Knox Press, 1963). Cf. James Barr, *op. cit.*, pp. 103f.

40. *Ibid.*, p. 111.

41. Gerhard von Rad, in Claus Westermann, *op. cit.*, pp. 36f.

42. "There is an interlacing of the destiny of Jew and Gentile such as the latter does not find God except through involvement with the former. . . . (There is) dependence of Gentile on Jew within the total history, tragic and expensive, of salvation with the people of God": James Barr, *op. cit.*, pp. 164f.

43. Cf. below on Rudolf Bultmann.

44. Cf. Wolfhart Pannenberg, "The Revelation of God in Jesus of Nazareth," in J. M. Robinson and J. B. Cobb, eds., *New Frontiers in Theology* (New York: Harper & Row, 1963) III, p. 111: ". . . in Jesus' person, the Jewish tradition entered into conflict with itself." One must, however, be careful not to oppose Jesus to the Law. "When (Jesus) says to his disciples: 'But I say to you,' or 'The Son of Man is lord even of the sabbath' (Mk 2:28), they must as well understand: 'But the Law says to you.' In him, the Law manifests itself as a person; it reveals itself as the perfectly one will of God, to which at last responds the perfect human obedience"—Pierre Lostringant, *Essai sur l'unité de la révélation biblique* (Paris: Je Sers, 1942), p. 54 (my transl.). The author adds (p. 94): "There is no fear to be mistaken in affirming that the so painful conflict between Paul and the Christians who remained faithful to Judaism happened above all on the exegetical terrain" (my transl.).

45. James Barr, *op. cit.*, p. 141.

46. Paul Ricoeur, *op. cit.*, pp. 390, 389. Clearly, this "hermeneutic circle" fits

perfectly the Gentile approach to the text, but much less so the Jewish commerce with a document Israel authored for the exclusive recipience of Israel.

47. Its cosmological conception, e.g., is totally inadequate for modern readers. So is its theology; cf. the thundering God on Mount Sinai in Exodus 19, or on Mount Carmel in 1 Kings 18, etc.

48. Cf. e.g., C. Michalson and E. Voegelin, in Bernhard W. Anderson, ed., *The Old Testament and Christian Faith: A Theological Discussion* (New York: Herder & Herder, 1969).

49. G. Ernest Wright, in *ibid.,* p. 180.

50. Karl Barth, *Dogmatik* III/2; ditto, *Rudolf Bultmann, ein Versuch ihn zu verstehen* (Zurich, 1953), p. 19.

51. Gerhard Ebeling, *Wort und Glaube* (Tuebingen, 1960), p. 337. English edition, *Word and Faith* (Philadelphia: Fortress Press, 1963).

52. I add here that "the question of being" is exclusively mediated by Israel.

53. Paul Ricoeur, *op. cit.,* p. 399.

54. Daniel Lys, *The Meaning of the Old Testament: An Essay on Hermeneutics* (Nashville: Abingdon, 1967), pp. 97f. Lys pointedly stresses that "God reveals himself . . . not something—even if it be something *of himself*" (p. 101).

55. Samuel Amsler, *op. cit.,* p. 114 (my transl.); cf. pp. 119, 121, 127f, 146, 148, etc.

56. Daniel Lys, *op. cit.,* pp. 163f.

57. Theodore C. Vriezen, *An Outline of Old Testament Theology* (Newton, Mass.: Ch. T. Branford, 1958), p. 100 (emphasis mine).

58. Jürgen Moltmann, *Theology of Hope* (New York: Harper, 1967).

59. Wolfhart Pannenberg, *loc. cit.,* pp. 102, 104, 109.

60. Cf. Walther Zimmerli, in Claus Westermann, *op. cit.,* pp. 89ff.

61. Cf. Oscar Cullmann, "The Connection of Primal Events and End Events with the New Testament Redemptive History", in Bernhard W. Anderson, *op. cit.,* pp. 115ff.

62. Ernst Troeltsch, *Ges. Schriften* II, 732; quoted by J. M. Robinson and J. B. Cobb, *op. cit.* III, 31.

63. Cf. *The Oxford Universal Dictionary:* "to eventuate" means to have a (specific) event or issue, to turn out, to result in; to bring to the issue.

64. Martin Heidegger also attempts to grasp that reality and speaks of "das Ereignis," as Paul Ricoeur reminds me (oral communication).

65. Pierre Lostringant, *op. cit.,* p. 35.

66. Cf. the embarrassment of James Barr, in *The Bible in the Modern World* (New York: Harper & Row, 1973).

PART III
THE BIBLE AS RECORD
AND REVELATION

Record and Revelation:
A Jewish Perspective

Martin A. Cohen

I

That the Bible is a record is an inarguable truism, but profound disagreement attends the consideration of what exactly it is a record of. The fundamental divergence revolves around two questions: Is the Bible somehow divinely revealed? Or is it a human construct, similar to every other human document we possess?

Though deceptively simple, much rides on the answer to these questions. Two religious constellations, Judaism and Christianity, ultimately derive from a claim of biblical revelation. At stake is nothing less than the credibility and authority of their institutions. Derivatively affected are other religions, notably Islam, which are rooted in similar textual revelations.

These questions could not be openly posed prior to the modern world, when there were Christian kingdoms, Moslem kingdoms and Jewish communities living within them quasi-autonomously under talmudic law. In these polities ecclesiastical authorities stood at the ganglia of ultimate political power. For any deviation from the authorized views on revelation in their respective faiths they could impose the severest of social as well as spiritual sanctions.

Today the questions may be posed with relative impunity. If socio-political control is still exercised by ecclesiastical authorities, it is usually without national support and limited to voluntary associations. And these questions not only *may* be asked; they *must* be asked because of the potent challenges to Judaism and Christianity from other religious and areligious perspectives.

To the obvious query as to which of the two fundamental perspectives on the Bible is correct there is no obvious answer. The answer depends upon the inner world of our pre-rational assumptions. All remonstrations to the contrary, we cannot argue the truth of our affirmations in any area unless we first consciously or unconsciously make assumptions about the nature of the universe that will accommodate our postulates and accompany them to our conclusions. Whether so-called scientific or otherwise, all our ratiocinations ultimately develop from quantum leaps of faith. Our assumptions define all our experiences, however refined they themselves may be in the process. A circularity of reasoning thus ineluctably envelops every system of thought.

We must therefore candidly admit the impossibility of demonstrating biblical revelation unless we first in some sense assume its possibility. At the same time, we cannot deny biblical revelation unless we adopt assumptions that preclude its possibility.

Biblical revelation belongs to the genus of general supernatural revelation. Two realities regularly acknowledged by the most scientific minds argue in favor of such revelation. One is the underlying mystery of the universe, the baffling residuum in every field of human probing when all else is rationally accounted for. The other is the mystery of inspiration and insight which leaps over conventional routes of thought to catalyze disparate information into new configurations of useful creativity. Furthermore, the luxuriant variety of revelations recorded in almost every age and place argues more cogently for revelation as a universal reality than as a universal delusion.

The assumption of revelation in principle does not compel belief in the specifics of any of its alleged concretizations. Such commitment depends upon additional assumptions and in turn upon their corollaries and derivatives. Because of endless assumptive possibilities, revelational systems are regularly at variance with one another, and frequently even self-contradictory.

Even denying the claims of revelation, we must acknowledge their common human dimensions. All presumed revelations are transmitted through channels of human perception, be they dreams, trances, signs, inspirations or literary documents. All are communicable to other humans through the bridge of language. All reflect their ambient society. All respond to specific needs within that society. All possess ideological, social, economic, political and psychological coordinates. If originally confined to individuals, the promulgation of revelations attests to consequences involving groups.

Revelational records championed by groups become institutional statements witnessing the struggles for position and power characteristic of every society. Their aim in these struggles is threefold: to neutralize the hostile, attract the receptive, and retain the *fides,* the loyalty, or, as it is called in religion, the faith, of the already committed. All revelational records are thus apologies, born of the need for self-definition and refined through the dialectic of challenge and defense.

Institutions built on revelational systems have branded conflicting revelations as false and, if similarly premised, as heretical. Whenever they have had the power to do so, they have suppressed all alternatives to their own. Ultimately, the differences between authentic or "true" revelations and inauthentic or "false" revelations are assumptively grounded, institutionally based, and politically determined. To attempt to divorce the spiritual dimension of the concept of revelation—or, for that matter, any other theological concept—from its human and societal dimensions can therefore only be delusive.

II

The various components of Judaism and Christianity provide diverse interpretations of biblical revelation. However, the internal differences among the various sub-groups of Judaism and Christianity are not as striking as the ones that separate these major constellations of faith. For Christians the Bible traditionally consists of what they call the Old Testament and the New Testament, though from ancient times on some groups have rejected the Old Testament. The Roman Catholic and Greek Orthodox Churches include the books called Apocrypha by Protestants and Jews. The Christian Bible is weighted theologically toward the New Testament and the incarnation. The revelation implicit in the incarnation logically supersedes the revelation of the biblical text. The text thus serves the ancillary function of harbinger and support of the New Testament's Christ figure.

For Jews the only Scriptures regarded as sacred are those called "Old Testament" by Christians. But these books are not regarded by Jews as susceptible to supersedure. Nor are they called "Bible" or viewed as a single book. Rather they are seen as a collection of twenty-four books, each belonging to one of three sections: the *Torah,* or Pentateuch, or, as it is often called, the Five Books of Moses; the *Neviim*, or Prophets; and the *Ketuvim*, or Sacred Writings. The three sections are known by no collective name except the acronym *TNK* (vocalized *Tanakh*). Although the entire TNK is regarded as holy, its first section, the Torah, is held as the holiest and most fundamental text of Judaism's sacred tradition.

Thus, the primary scriptural "book" for the Jews is of smaller scope than the "Bible." Simultaneously, it is of far greater compass. This is due to the fact that in the sacred tradition of Judaism the word "Torah" is construed to mean all Sacred Scripture in Judaism, including the Neviim, and Ketuvim of the TNK, and, beyond it, all subsequent works in our sacred tradition. These include the Mishnah, the Gemaras, the Midrash, the Responsa, the commentaries, the novellae, the codes, and, beyond that, all worthy human knowledge, ethical, philosophical, scientific, humanistic and artistic. The term "The Torah" is always used to designate the Pentateuch and often the Tradition. Without the definite article, the word Torah may refer to a specific Pentateuchal law, to the Tradition, or to learning in general.

There is a further sense in which *the* Torah, that is, the Five Books of Moses, is distinguished from all other works. The Pentateuch is called the Written Torah (*Torah she bi-Ketav*), while the non-Pentateuchal elements of Torah, at least insofar as concerns the sacred tradition, are called *Torah she be'al-Pe* or the Oral Torah or Oral Tradition. The NK belong to an intermediate category. They are often regarded as *Torah she bi-Ketav*, although in a sense they too belong to *Torah she be'al-Pe*.

All of these considerations are essential for an understanding of the Jewish view of scriptural revelation. Clearly, given these perimeters, the Jewish view must necessarily differ from Christian approaches to revelation in ways beyond the mere inclusion of the New Testament, with or without the Apocrypha, into the Christian Canon.

The sacred tradition of Judaism recognizes a wide variety of possible revelations, but it affirms only one fully authentic revelation, original, unrepeated and supreme. That is the revelation of Torah. In fact, Judaism's sacred tradition unmistakably declares this position by expressing the concept of revelation through the Hebrew term *Torah min ha-Shamayim*, that is, "Torah (given) from Heaven." Also utilized is the term *Torah mi-Sinai*, "Torah (given) from Sinai," which is an identical reference from terrestrial perspective. The term *Torah min ha-Shamayim* was coined by the early rabbis and has been utilized traditionally in Jewish theological writings ever since. The word *hitgalut*, now used for revelation in the generic sense, was not known until post-talmudic times; it was one of the many lexical inventions of Jewish philosophers in the Middle Ages.

Like other fundamental Jewish theological concepts, *Torah min ha-Shamayim* is complex, and its details are occasionally in conflict. In no small measure this results from the fact that Judaism has never possessed an official creed and is not primarily creedally oriented. Its theological ideas, founded on the TNK, received their classical formulations during the early rabbinic or Tannaitic period (ca. 75–215 CE). There was always room for variations in their details, and, except where prohibited by Jewish authority structures, their principles were always open to challenge. Yet, for all of this, the general contours of *Torah min ha-Shamayim,* like those of other basic theological concepts in Judaism, remain unmistakably clear.

Judaism's sacred tradition affirms that the Torah was given by God to Moses in heaven. Moses had ascended to the peak of Mount Sinai, where God had bent the heavens to touch the earth. There God's glory, which means God himself, descended with the sacred doctrine, prepared in advance of creation, and the blueprint for all its details.

Most fundamentally, the Torah is the Pentateuch. Underpinning it is the Decalogue. Extending its scope are the Neviim and Ketuvim (the NK) and the Oral Tradition in its broadest sense, "all the commandments, their principles and particulars," as well as the principles of interpretation by which the Oral Tradition is derived. It comprises as well all scholarly disputes and divergences of opinion, all future insights and innovations, and "even that which a conscientious student would expound before his teacher."[1] On such subjects additional to the Torah, it holds that "all these were already spoken to Moses on Sinai."[2]

The basic stratum, the Torah itself, is unlike any other document. It is a perfect text, entirely original, without superfluity, omission or defect of other kind. It is intended for all times and circumstances. It is entirely atemporal. Its sequential events really possess no essential sequence, *en mukdam u'meuhar ba-Torah* (there is no "earlier" or "later" in the Torah).[3] The Torah in its totality is eternally present. Its ostensible imperfections, contradictions and duplications, diverse orthographies and grammatical gratuities form intentional cables of meaning to be plumbed. Its every letter, jot and tittle soar beyond the confines of patency to the realm of mystery and arcane universal truth. *Torah min ha-Shamayim* possesses six fundamental characteristics: eternity, transcendence, miracle, mystery, perfection and holiness.

God delivered this entire Torah to Moses in a single instant through the conduit of the holy Hebrew tongue. Moses recorded it, as if from dictation, and transmitted it to his people. According to a Hasidic formulation, rooted in the Talmud and Maimonides, the recipients of the revelation at Sinai heard only an *aleph*.[4] A laryngeal stop, the most effortless of consonants, the *aleph* may be regarded as the primal ground of all articulated speech.

Judaism's sacred tradition records revelations other than the Supreme Donation at Sinai. The Torah and Oral Torah contain within them nearly the full gamut of revelational possibilities. Nor are the recipients of these revelations always Jews, as can be seen, for example, in the appearance of God's angel to the Aramean prophet Balaam (Nm 22:8ff) and even to his donkey (22ff), and the critical dreams sent to Abimelech, king of Gerar (Gn 20:3), and the Egyptian butler and baker (Gn 40:16ff) in the Joseph cycle. All these revelations are part of the unfolding of *Torah min ha-Shamayim*. Judaism's sacred tradition does not deal explicitly with revelations in the literature of other faiths.

Torah min ha-Shamayim is as central and indispensable to Judaism as the Incarnation is to Christianity. It is not a mere fortuity that the Christian Pentecost celebrates the descent of the Holy Spirit upon the apostles, while the Jewish Pentecost in tradition commemorates the *Mattan Torah*, the giving of the Torah from heaven.

The above understanding of *Torah min ha-Shamayim* is unknown to the TNK. Though its roots may be considerably older, it first appeared in the early second century CE. It presents a general rabbinic position in contrast to the Sadduceean, which rejected *Torah she be'al Pe*, and the Christian, which, under Philonic influence, focused on the Incarnation as the primary revelation.

Within their common theological matrix the early rabbis and their predecessors developed diverse corollaries for their factional disputes. The details of the concept *Torah min ha-Shamayim* now central to Judaism's sacred tradition represent one such position. They were conceived by the incomparable Rabbi Akiba ben Joseph (ca. 50–135 CE), whose multifaceted brilliance dominated his age and who more than any other luminary merits the title Father of Rabbinic Judaism.

Judaism's sacred tradition lionizes this sage. A talmudic discussion reveals unprecedented support for the view that the *halakha*, or legal procedure, "is according to Akiba even if he differs from his Master."[5] Elsewhere the Talmud even goes so far as to record a legal discussion in which Rabbi Tarfon, regarded as Akiba's teacher, says to him, "Akiba, whoever separates from you is like one who separates himself from life."[6] Again, it says that "matters not disclosed to Moses were revealed to Rabbi Akiba."[7] More boldly, it states that Akiba could "see by means of the Holy Spirit,"[8] and that God had said of him that "he was worthy to behold my Glory."[9] Akiba's ideas, including those on *Torah min ha-Shamayim,* were developed by his followers or "school."

We lack adequate evidence for most factional ideologies among the early rabbis, but we possess considerable information on the most enduring alternative to Akiba's position within the Jewish tradition. This was the position of Akiba's contemporary, Rabbi Ishmael ben Elisha (first half of the second century CE), and his "school." While accepting the principle of *Torah min ha-Shamayim,* Ishmael diverged sharply from Akiba's transcendental interpretation. Ishmael did not see the Torah text as an endless mine of symbols. He believed instead that "the Torah speaks in human language,"[10] that it sought to convey literal meaning, and even that it possessed a composite character. The Torah, the Ishmaelans believed, was not given all at once. Only the Ten Commandments were given at Sinai, the rest section by section in subsequent revelations in the Tent of Meeting and the plains of Moab. In its composition Moses relied on other sources, among them older documents. He even included some material of his own creation. Nor did Moses write the entire Torah; at least several sections derived from other hands, including the last eight verses of Deuteronomy, which discuss events beginning with Moses' death. Furthermore, the Ishmaelan group pointed out, the Bible's inconsistencies, contradictions and obvious changes of God's word point to human intervention in its transmission.

The Ishmaelan position on *Torah min ha-Shamayim* was never completely abandoned. It surfaced in various forms and with embellished details. But the Akiban view prevailed and became the source of authority for Jewish institutions and leadership. This Jewish understanding of revelation came into conflict with the competitive revelational claims of Christianity and Islam. Fierce in some periods and in others banked, this conflict inheres in all contacts between these faith constellations.

During the Middle Ages, *Torah min ha-Shamayim,* along with its Christian and Moslem counterparts, confronted the arrival of Greek philosophy in Western Europe. The resultant "conflict between reason and revelation" left the intellectual leadership of Islam, Judaism and Christianity with three broad options of response. Should they categorically reject Greek thought? If so, they would alienate many who viewed it as a font of truth. Should they instead categorically reject their respective traditions? If so they would lose their positions, which directly or indirectly derived from the ecclesiastical hierarchies in their respective societies. Or should they synthesize the newly found "reason" and the inherited revelation? To do so would entail a compromise of both.

As usually happens, the synthesizers proved the most creative. In Judaism a small number came close to rejecting *Torah min ha-Shamayim.* The first and most renowned was Issac Albalag (late thirteenth century) who expounded a doctrine of double-truth apparently borrowed from contemporary Averroists but utilized independently as well in contemporary Christian circles by thinkers like Duns Scotus (ca. 1270–1308). This doctrine prevents a collision between reason/philosophy and revelation/faith by permitting them to coexist on different planes.

Most synthesizers insisted on a single-track approach. They staunchly defended revelation and utilized Greek philosophy for the rationalization of such concepts as God, creation, the soul and prophecy—but not revelation itself. In Judaism, Saadia, Ibn Daud, Maimonides, Gersonides, Crescas and others pay little attention to the concept. If Bahya ibn Pakuda emphasizes Judaism's revealed literature as the source of ethics and Albo holds its revealed law to be superior to conventional law, neither enters into a defense of the concept itself.

Only Judah Halevi (1070?–1141) explicitly argues for God's revelation to Moses on Mount Sinai. His case rests on history rather than philosophy, and his appeal derives from the two basal dimensions of history: experienced event and reflective tradition. For Halevi revelation was an event witnessed and corroborated by the entire people of Israel assembled at Mount Sinai, that is, 600,000 men of military age according to the Torah and therefore a multitude in excess of two million people. Halevi says: "The people prepared and fitted themselves to receive prophetic inspiration and actually to hear the words of God. This came to pass three days later." And he concludes that "these grand and lofty spectacles, seen by thousands, cannot be denied."[11]

For Halevi, the experience of revelation has been faithfully transmitted through the Oral Tradition. Of its records, he specifically mentions the Mishnah as "so striking that everyone who scrutinizes it genuinely must become aware that no mortal is capable of composing such a work without divine assistance."[12] Yet even Halevi does not defend the full Akiban position. He is Ishmaelan in his critique of talmudic content and his assertion that Moses included inherited laws in the Pentateuch.

III

An even more formidable challenge to the traditional Jewish and Christian views of revelation came with the rise of modern secularism. The concept of secularism, though utilized in contemporary Jewish thought, is not native to Judaism. The distinction between the sacred and the secular arose in the Christian world. Judaism's division between the sacred and the profane distinguishes not between divisions but between conceptions of life.

The secular world has altered the normative medieval outlook on life. It has limited ecclesiastical authority to a realm arbitrarily dubbed "religious" and has placed assumptive reliance on the ordering potential of human reason channeled through empirical research. On this foundation it has constructed disciplines of knowledge and applied them to the direction of all human concerns from nature to nations. The disciplines applicable to the Bible, though often at variance in methodology and results, have confronted all belief in biblical revelation with irrefragable arguments in favor of the gradual and totally human composition of the entire TNK. Archaeology, anthropology, religious history, comparative literature and philology have emphasized the natural outgrowth of the Bible from analyzable settings in the ancient Near East. The natural sciences have undermined the accuracy of the Bible's cosmological, geological and physical presuppositions, while sociology, economics and political analysis have been providing coherent natural explanations for its structural interactions. Psychology has cast doubt on revelational claims in general by suggesting that even if honestly reported, they may have resulted from delusion or hallucination. Incidentally, the Koran takes pains to defend Mohammed's revelation against the charge of madness.

The traditional Christian and Jewish concepts of revelation have been further challenged by the modern world's greater awareness of the conflicting thought-systems of non-Western religions. The result has been an imperious battering at religion, and, within it, the quest, with thinkers like Julian Huxley, for "religion without revelation." In both the Christian and the Jewish worlds, the reaction to the new challenge has spanned the entire spectrum of possibility. It has led to denials of revelation on the one extreme and its unqualified reaffirmation on the other in the fundamentalist Christian "perfect wording theory." Significantly, the strongest Christian fundamentalist defenses came with the Oxford Declaration and the Catholic Syllabus of Errors, both in 1864. These were promulgated a mere five years after the publication of Darwin's *Origin of Species,* four years after Bishop Wilberforce's disastrous attempt to defend biblical faith against T. H. Huxley, and one year after Ernest Rénan's scandalizingly rationalistic *Life of Jesus.*

The general thrust of syncretizing Christian approaches has been to salvage some aspect of revelation from the vise of modern scholarship. All are characterized by reliance on subjectivity, and, particularly with the existentialists, on affective encounter with the Divine through Scripture. The most important are classifiable around the concepts of "perfectly revealed meaning," "essential truth" and dialectical and existential theology.

For a variety of reasons, the secular world affected European Jewish communities later and more slowly than their Christian counterparts, but the results were equivalent. Many Jews embraced naturalism and rationalism. Some became votaries of *Le Grand Etre* or its more conventional deistic counterparts, while others diminished in concern for traditional belief. Fundamentalist Jews, both pre-modern and modern Orthodox, even if elsewhere committed to reason and science, have rejected the possibility of a humanly developed Torah and declared Torah and Tradition to be beyond the bounds of modern criticism. This constitutes the core of the most cogent modern Orthodox defense of *Torah min ha-Shamayim,* by Samson Raphael Hirsch (1808–1871).

Simultaneous with the persistence of these polar alternatives, a variety of accommodations to the modern world have appeared in the last three centuries. All reveal their respective environments and usually the influence of leading contemporary non-Jewish philosophical thought.

The first significant such effort was that of Moses Mendelssohn (1729–1786), the father of all modern Judaism and in particular Orthodoxy (not Reform, as is sometimes claimed). Influenced by the universalist philosophies of the Enlightenment to deny the particularism of the Jewish thought-system, he described Judaism as a "revealed legislation." By this he meant that of Judaism's multifaceted tradition, only its legal component was divinely disclosed, though he does not specify whether his concept extends beyond the Written Torah to embrace the Oral Tradition.

Other thinkers have devised alternatives to Mendelssohn's eclecticism. Some Orthodox Jews have sought to apply *Torah min ha-Shamayim* to the TNK alone and release the Tradition to analysis. More opposed to Mendelssohn's view is the position of Solomon Steinheim (1789–1866) that God revealed doctrine rather than law and that reason must subordinate itself to its content. Another philosopher, Nahman Krochmal (1785–1840), expressed belief in the super-natural Sinaitic revelation of "righteous and all-encompassing laws, statutes and judgments,"[13] but did not explicitly espouse the full Akiban position.

At the same time, Krochmal's evolutionary theory of Jewish history, influenced particularly by Giovanni Vico and Johann G. Herder, may be regarded as a transition to the concept of "progressive" revelation. Krochmal's view of history as the unfolding of the Divine Spirit carried the corollary of revelation as the process and progress of the consciousness of this Spirit.

Prismed through the philosophies of Immanuel Kant, Friedrich W. Schelling and Georg W. F. Hegel, the evolutionary tendency dominated nineteenth-century Jewish syncretistic theology. Abraham Geiger (1810–1874), the father of Reform Jewish theology, distinguishes between eternal spirit or kernel in Jewish ideals and the diverse but progressively developing forms or husks of their articulation. Solomon Formstecher (1808–1889) explains revelation as the communication of the moral and aesthetic ideal. He distinguishes between what he calls prehistorical revelation, by which he means the innate presence of these ideals in the spirit, and historical revelation, by which he intends their progressive disclosure to the consciousness of an individual.

Samuel Hirsch (1815–1889) relates divine revelation to the changing circumstances in people's lives, while for Max L. Margolis (1866–1932), it is the mysterious burgeoning of a religious idea that stimulates creative energy. The neo-Kantian Hermann Cohen (1842–1918), with a differently oriented liberal perspective, separates revelation from the historical moment, and conceives it as the will of God working through a spontaneously reciprocal human reason.

In the twentieth century existentialism has provided the dominant syncretistic force. For the existentialists, revelation involves not passive receipt but encounter and dialogue with God's Presence. The manifestation of this revelation is not objective or communal but highly personal and subjective, while its content is principally affective rather than cognitive. The views of both Martin Buber (1878–1965) and Franz Rosenzweig (1886–1929) fall into this category, with Rosenzweig stressing God's initiation of the process out of love. From a somewhat different perspective, Abraham Joshua Heschel (1907–1972) holds revelation to be a mysterious expression of God's concern for man communicated to a recipient who is a witness and therefore not passive.

Denying the possibility of distinctive Jewish values, Emil Fackenheim (1916–) affirms a revelation which "is its own sole content," and which carries an assertion of the existential relevance of the individual in the wake of its affirmation. The presupposition of a revelation at a specific time and for a distinctive Jewish destiny he regards as essential for a religious concern with Jewish life and law. On the other hand, profoundly spiritual thinkers like Ahad Ha-Am (1856–1927) and the founder of Reconstructionism, Mordecai Kaplan (1881–) find no room for revelation in their thinking and dismiss it as wholly subjective.

Some thinkers who uphold the Akiban position on revelation occasionally embellish it with other elements. Among these are the dimension of personal mystical insight in Abraham Isaac Kook (1865–1935) and the experienced Presence of God in the writings of Joseph Soloveitchik (1903–).

IV

Attractive as the modern Jewish syntheses may be, they all suffer from an abandonment of the traditional *Torah min ha-Shamayim,* even in an Ishmaelan sense. This is the result of their tacit capitulation to the challenges posed by modern scholarship. They have replaced *Torah min ha-Shamayim* with a variety of conceits, which they occasionally claim to be derived "from within" Judaism, but which on closer scrutiny turn out to have been influenced by alien sources. For example, the implication in Jewish "encounter" theories of revelation that a new mode of individual life results from such encounter is more reminiscent of the Christian position of revelation's extrication of humanity from its "predicament" or "forlorn condition" than of anything traditionally Jewish.

Many contemporary Christian theologians have compromised their concept of literal biblical revelation. Yet, except for occasional radical thinkers, they have made every effort to salvage the centrality of the Incarnation for modern humanity. The equivalently central concept in Judaism is not chosenness or covenant or an amorphous and infinitely interpretable general revelation, but the specific concept of *Torah min ha-Shamayim.* That concept not only serves as the indispensable link between the Jew and God, but it also informs the entire belief-system of Judaism and sustains all its derivative authority structures. The Mishnah explicitly denies "a share in the world to come" to anyone who denies the principle of *Torah min ha-Shamayim.*[14] All sacred Jewish literature therefore assumes *Torah min ha-Shamayim,* and *Torah min ha-Shamayim* accompanies, even where it does not inform, all Jewish prayer.

Samuel S. Cohon (1888–1959) was correct in his appraisal that "the traditional view of revelation [in Judaism] requires radical restatement."[15] But there is no way to circumvent the fundamental reality that in any such restatement the sacred tradition of Judaism stands without support unless a contemporarily cogent case can be made for *Torah min ha-Shamayim*.

Ultimately any such case is, of course, an apology for the uniqueness of Judaism, precisely as a case for traditional Christian revelation must stress the uniqueness of Christianity. Such apologies will not be palatable to individuals of whatever tradition who would deprive religions of their distinctiveness. In this regard one can only express the profoundest respect for the Second Vatican Council, which, despite its sincere efforts for friendship and understanding among people of all traditions, yet possessed the courage to declare:

> The Catholic Church rejects nothing of what is true and holy in these religions. She has a high regard for the manner of life and conduct, the precepts and doctrines which, although differing in many ways from her own teaching, nevertheless often reflect a ray of that truth which enlightens all men. Yet she proclaims and is in duty bound to proclaim without fail Christ who is the way, the truth and the life (Jn 14:6). In him, in whom God reconciled all things to himself (2 Cor 5:18–19), men find the fullness of their religious life.[16]

A cogent contemporary Jewish apology for *Torah min ha-Shamayim* must fulfill six conditions:

1. It must preserve the traditional concept of *Torah min ha-Shamayim*, preferably in its Akiban exposition.

2. It must treat human reason and the so-called scientific method as instruments of divine truth and accommodate the uncontested results of their application to the world at large and to TNK and Tradition in particular.

3. It must plausibly account for conflicting revelations from both outside and within the Tradition.

4. It must cohere integrally with the other theological principles and corollaries of the Tradition.

5. It must address contemporary needs in a manner unmistakably competitive with alternatives offered by other revelational as well as non-revelational systems.

6. Its claims must be "objectively," that is, publicly, verifiable within its own assumptive system.

The apology sketched below will be assumptively rational/scientific and methodologically heuristic. For pedagogical purposes, supposing *Torah min ha-Shamayim* to be unknown and "scientific" knowledge to be reliably known, it will seek the transcendent in the immanent and the divine in the human. Its philosophical orientation, without abandoning logic or psychology, will nevertheless focus on history, recognizing that, however interpreted, history operates with "givens" on whose contours and content there is the best hope for a working consensus.

The apology attempts impressionistically to induce the conclusion of *Torah min ha-Shamayim* by arguing for the continuing perceptibility in Torah and Tradition of the six cardinal dimensions of *Torah min ha-Shamayim*. If arbitrary, the structure of these coordinates is auxiliary to the fundamental goal.

The dimension of eternity derives from the values of Torah. The term "values" is here used restrictively. It denotes the fundamental motivations disclosed in the actions and attitudes of human organisms, individual or collective. In this sense, values are visceral, not cerebral, and distinguishable from the hierarchy of concepts, ideals or goals which constitute the articulated rationalizations of values. Values are influenced by experience, including cognition, but they simultaneously also shape experience. In no human organism are the standards of truth, right, goodness and beauty ever autonomous; they are all derivatives of its emotional axiological foundation. It is impossible to skirt the conclusion that both logically and temporally they are rooted in visceral commitment, or, to put it theologically, in gargantuan leaps of faith.

To speak of values ineluctably entails conceptualization. Yet such cerebration must always be tempered by a sensitivity to its otherwise unattainable object. Judaism's insight into the logical priority of values may be discernible in Ishmael ben Nahum's statement that *derekh erets* preceded the Torah by twenty-six generations.[17] Though usually blandly rendered as "good manners," *derekh erets* suggests less ethics and morality, which according to Tradition derive from Torah, than their inherent and logically prior value supports.

Rarely articulated, values thus furnish the conduits for the channeling of raw emotions. In this sense, they serve as an organism's superego, and, when embodied in specific propositions, as the marrow of its creed. Yet values are most effectively disclosed not in disembodied creed, that is, in untested superego, but in actions, that is, in the superego's deflection by the ego as it confronts the realities of life.

In every organism values may be altered by time and circumstance or neutralized by unresolved conflict. But in direct proportion to their basic stability, individuals and groups retain fundamental values across the years, decades, and, in institutions, often centuries.

Like other traditions, Judaism possesses values that have survived change and contradiction. Through mazes of evanescent accretions and mines of contradiction, its fundamental values continually and consistently resurface in ethics, law, theology and lore of the faith-people Israel from its biblical texts to its contemporary responsa. These values may be formulated as follows:

1. The Ultimate Unity of Being
2. The Intrinsic Purposefulness of Existence
3. The Pervasive Sanctity of Life
4. The Fundamental Centrality of Humanity
5. The Innate Goodness of Individuals
6. The Essential Equality of People
7. The Inherent Perfectibility of Society
8. The Ennobling Duty of Creativity
9. The Sublime Altruism of Compassion

In other words, Judaism's value system is universal, confident, spiritual, supportive, optimistic, meliorative, teleological, Promethean and irenic. It is important to note its emphasis on compassion, whose Hebrew may also be translated as love. For those who fail to recognize the centrality of this concept in Judaism, it should be pointed out that the commandment to "love your neighbor as yourself" is first found in the Torah (Lv 19:18), and that it was Rabbi Akiba who gave currency to the Aramaic term *Rahamana,* "the Loving [or Compassionate] One," as a designation of God.

Numerous groups share with Judaism some or many of the above characteristics, but the originality of the Jewish value system, particularly with its distinctive nuances, can be cogently defended. Like all others, this value system consists not of discrete philosophical propositions, but of an organic perspective or emotional set toward the world.

A further if daring case can be made for the identification of Torah values as the essence of God. It would derive from the meaning of the biblical concept *daat elohim.* Though usually literally translated "knowledge of God," investigation discloses that the term is regularly used in an affective rather than cognitive sense.

The dimension of transcendence derives from the Torah's role among the faith-people Israel. From the time the Torah became the constitution of the faith-people Israel it has existentially functioned as a divine text, above time, beyond error, and relevant to every conceivable condition. The conviction that it represents the visible embodiment of God's will on earth led to the exaltation of the Torah text in prayer and preaching, to its regular and sequential liturgical recital in triennial or, more customarily, annual cycles, and above all to its enshrinement in the synagogue's holy ark. As God's complete word for humanity, the Torah has furnished the consummate pattern for the texture of Jewish life. At least until the advent of the modern world, Jews individually and corporatively have turned to the Torah for guidance in all areas of life, including the ritual, the behavioral and the ideological.

The guidance they have received has derived even more from the symbolic potential of the Torah text than from its literal meaning. Across the centuries Jews have indeed regarded the Torah text as an organic whole, with its messages eternally present without *mukdam* or *meuhar* ("earlier" or "later"), and its concepts, sentences, phrases, words, letters and eccentricities all mysterious vessels capable of the profoundest meanings.

Of course, all the *Torah she be'al Pe* that they drew out—all the laws, commentaries, codes, ethics and scriptural translations—they deemed to be not novelty, but expositions of the Torah text.

That all future Torah was deemed contained in the Torah text is nothing other than Tradition's way of explaining the unfolding of the *Torah she be'al Pe*. But that this unfolding is equivalent to the modern concept, if not the details, of the development of Torah there can be no doubt.

This is perhaps nowhere more impressively dramatized than in the story of God's preview to Moses of Akiba's academy. The point of the story is that Moses understood nothing of the proceedings until, in citing the source of a decision, Akiba declared, "The practice is according to Moses from Mount Sinai."[18] Rabbi Joshua ben Karha went so far as to declare that "whoever studies the Torah and revises it not is like a sower who reaps not."[19]

Tradition's recognition that in effect Torah has developed brings it into concert rather than conflict with the modern critical disciplines applied to biblical and post-biblical sacred texts. In opposition to Tradition, these disciplines may suggest the conclusion that *Torah she be'al Pe* and *Torah she bi-Ketav* are in every sense human constructs. But there are two areas in which the commitment of Tradition and the demands of science symbiotically agree. One is that the unfolding or development of *Torah she be'al Pe* reveals changes which are in effect intended to furnish a cogent application of the Torah text to the altering conditions of life. The other

is that underlying and directing the changes, which often deflect and occasionally even contradict the Pentateuch's explicit meaning, is a constant
criterion which unites Torah, TNK and Tradition.

Within the above indicated perimeters, that constant has been the Torah's informing value system. Though aware of the infinite flexibility of the
Torah pattern in the Torah text, successive centuries of Jews have nevertheless interpreted it in such a way as to reinforce commitment to its axiological a prioris. If Judaism's sacred Tradition defines love of God as
humility, forbearance and fortitude, if it explains Temple sacrifices as lessons in peace, and if it understands the reference to Jacob's sword and bow
as manifestations of the sharp potency of his orisons, it is because in these,
as in countless other instances, it has looked through the frame of the Torah's words to the world-creating *aleph* of its unarticulated values. Devi-
ations from this channeling have characteristically been unenduring and
explicable contextually with the aid of contemporary scholarship. Ample
evidence is available to support these conclusions.

Tradition compares the Torah to fire. With equally traditional imag-
ery, it could be said that the fiery light of Torah values requires reflection
in the Torah text. Only through the cynosure of the Torah text has the
constellation of eternal Torah values continuously reflected upon the altering exigencies of existence.

Against the seeming chaos of the world, these Torah values have
made the Torah text a map, whose "ways are ways of pleasantness and
whose every path is peace" (Prov 3:17). Against the seeming aridity of the
world, they have made the Torah text "a tree of life, bearing happiness to
all who securely hold it" (Prov 3:18). Against the seeming darkness of the
world, they have made the Torah text a lamp eternal, "the precious vessel
by which the world has been created."[20] Modern scholarship can fully detail how the Torah came to exercise this function. But why it was the Torah text rather than any other record is a question unanswerable by cause
and effect, or, for that matter, any other mundane assumption.

The element of miracle derives from the dissemination of Torah. This
dissemination the Jewish community could never have accomplished
alone, for all its zeal for Torah, if for no other reason because of the extreme paucity of its numbers. The dissemination of Torah has therefore
primarily been the work of the Christian world, though the contribution
of the Moslem world has also been impressive. Through Christianity, the
Torah, especially with the NK, has spread to every corner of the world.
As foundation and precursor of the New Testament, Torah and TNK have
become the basis for Christian faith, learning, philosophy, literature, art,

music and other forms of worthy creativity. In other words, Torah became a foundation for Western civilization, and, when all its dimensions are considered, its most important one.

For demonstrable reasons, Western civilization became the most dynamic and ultimately the predominant of world civilizations. This facilitated the luxuriant dissemination of Torah and TNK, which have been copied, translated, commented upon, edited and reprinted more than any other texts in the world. Translations of the Bible for pre-literate peoples have made the Torah the logical basis for their introduction to literacy and Western culture, even if other biblical books have actually been the first used. If, as has been unreliably stated, the Koran has been the most widely read work, the TNK has unquestionably been the most influential. It has been a portable sanctuary bringing enlightenment, knowledge and hope to the remotest communities of mankind.

It has also brought them its underlying values. Although at times deflected by other attitudes in both New Testament and Christian tradition, including a vein of opposition to the Old Testament in general, the record of these values of Hebrew life has been enshrined in Christian society from its beginnings. As Morton Enslin writes:

> The point often overlooked is that the kind of life which Paul felt worthy of in Christ is precisely the type of life which as a Jew he had been from birth trained to revere, as he had found it revealed in Scripture.[21]

Through the ages, Torah values prismed through the Bible provided the rule by which faithful Christians have measured their societies, churches, communities, homes and personal lives.

Above all, the dissemination of Torah and TNK has contributed to the frustration of those who have sought to obliterate the name of the Jews. Especially in the Christian world, it has kept ever present the consciousness of the biblical Hebrews, the Jewish foundations of Christianity, and the special role that appears to have been assigned to the Jewish people by history or history's Source.

The dimension of mystery derives from the Torah's people. Modern disciplines can chart every phase of the experience of the faith-people Israel. Yet the more they do the more amazing the totality becomes.

Factors beyond Israel's control have always conditioned the contours of its history. They determined the path of the Exodus and the entry into the Holy Land. The strategic position of the Holy Land exposed the Hebrews to the most powerful nations and latest ideas. Its defenselessness compelled them to seek survival in knowledge and service, and its challenges enabled them to induce a universal God, a universal ethic and a universal goal.

Once so formed, the faith-people Israel were compelled to enter a new phase. When Rome destroyed their Temple and State (70 CE) they became wanderers. Individuals and families might remain rooted for centuries, but none were henceforth fully secure. Besides, the centers of Jewish life shifted along a route paralleling the march of Western civilization. In this long experience the patterns of Jewish life have always been similar. As a group we have been permitted to enter only new or renewing societies. Our skills and the political advantage of our defenselessness have been our tickets of admission. To encourage our productivity, societal leadership has granted us freedoms and the wherewithal for contentment. It has generally impelled us to material pursuits involving knowledge and risk.

We have, where permitted, regularly succeeded in acculturating, but never in fully assimilating, largely because we have been regarded as a caste. In good times societal leadership has protected us. In bad times, if their own position was endangered, they have always been able to scapegoat us by galvanizing anti-Jewish sentiments into antisemitic attacks.

As we observe Jewish history, a mysterious conclusion emerges. Wherever we have trodden, our greater or lesser security has always revealed the extent of the implementation of Torah values in the ethics, morality, and laws of the society as a whole. Willy-nilly we as a group have thus amazingly always been witnesses for Torah among the peoples of the earth. That Jews have never enjoyed complete serenity in any society can be traced to the fact that none has as yet fully applied the Torah's value system. Characteristically, the Tradition recognizes that the application of these values can be effective only if worldwide. It calls the time of such application the days of the Messiah, when all shall sit under their vines and fig trees, with none to make them afraid.

The dimension of perfection derives from the Torah's task. This task is nothing short of the universal insemination of the perceptible derivatives of Torah values in all individuals and societies. It involves the dissolution of all obstructions in the form of oppression, subjugation and exploitation, whether physical, emotional or spiritual, which to date have been present in all societies, including those of greatest freedom. Tradition calls the process leading to this goal "the completion of the world" or *tikkun olam*. It speaks of the duty "to complete the world in the kingdom of the Almighty" (*letakken olam be Malkhut Shaddai*).[22] The Lurianic kabbalists graphically describe the process as the patient collection of the divine sparks resident in the universe's imperfections in order to restore its pristine and atemporal wholeness.

For Tradition, the attainment of this goal will herald the messianic era. At that time, in a new covenant, as Jeremiah says, the Torah will be written on human hearts; that is, Torah as value will be internalized, Torah as application will be reflexive, and therefore Torah as pattern will be superfluous. The rabbinic statement which boldly declares that "the Torah studied in this world is evanescent (*hevel,* "[like] a breath,") compared to the Messianic Torah"[23] obliquely attests to the essentiality of Torah as values and to the goal of their ultimate universalization.

Though utopian, the messianic goal of Torah values is not, like Condorcet's (1743–1794) *Esquisse,* a doctrinaire belief in humanity's unfettered refinement. Long before the reinforcing insights of contemporary psychology and the social sciences exposed the scabrous ids and masked egos of individuals and institutions and the perversion of their ideal systems into cant, Judaism fully recognized the contempt for Torah values that derives from the recalcitrant and chronic corruptibility of all human organisms. Yet it has traditionally viewed this condition as willful rather than inherent and remediable through undular if not linear progress. In face of the utter fecklessness of all ultimates founded on corruption, it offers the universalization of Torah values as the only practical alternative for the world.

To struggle for this end becomes the duty of all humanity, and not so to strive its most grievous dereliction. What might be called a Nietzschean rejection of loving-kindness—symbolic of the total system of Torah values—is characterized by Judaism's sacred Tradition as one of Sodom's heinous sins. Little wonder it is that oppressors of humanity have seen noxious foes in all proponents of the Torah's goal.

But the duty weighs most heavily upon the faith-people Israel. Mysteriously ordained by history (if not its Source) as witnesses for the presence of Torah values in life, this faith-people has recognized that as long as oppression, subjugation and exploitation affect even the humblest of mankind, the world is marked by imbalance and the Jew's lot is precarious. The Jew therefore has no choice but to lead in the inculcation of Torah values in the world, knowing that the reward for this task will yield no superiority, but only equality with a total humanity actualized at last.

The leadership in this task is discharged not by professed velleity, but by performed activity. It involves taking specific stands on specific issues of import whenever and wherever indicated by the realities of life. It calls for teaching, preaching and actively pursuing the implementation of humanizing change "for the blessing of all," as the prayerbook says, "and the hurt of none; for the joy of all and the woe of none; for the life of all and the death of none."[24]

Given the paucity of its numbers, the faith-people Israel can fulfill this task neither by might nor by power. Only by the spirit, by the small, still voice of suasion and the unarticulated values implicit in example can it hope for an end to "the kingdom of arrogance" and the advent of the day when *daat elohim* shall cover the earth as the waters cover the sea.

The dimension of holiness derives from the Torah's integrity. Manifest in its comprehension of existence, this integrity is publicly validated through four concentrically related tests:

(a) *Theoretically, by consistency.* Torah values organically harmonize the various interpenetrating realms of life, which, with Judah Halevi, following Aristotle, we may conveniently divide into categories of increasing complexity: the mineral or lifeless, the vegetative or living, the animal or sentient, and the human or spiritual. Within ever-changing frames of contemporary reference the Torah accounts for the complexities within these realms. It reduces the contradictions between them and meaningfully resolves the divergencies between human/spiritual experience and the concretized expressions of its values. Above all, it brings harmony into the wild luxuriance of nature and suffuses with sanctity all that is profane.

(b) *Practically, by conduct.* It cannot be sufficiently emphasized that adherence to Torah values by individuals and groups is measured not by creedal expression but by example. Therefore confluence with Torah values even in the absence of the Torah text is universally possible through axiological commitments and derivative conduct by individuals and groups, without regard to birth, nation, creed or institutional commitment. Sensitive to the wide variety of alternative value-systems, Judaism would, in a way similar to contemporary Catholicism, regard as validly revealed all articulations consonant with Torah values. From the Torah's statement that "a prophet like Moses has not again arisen in Israel," an early rabbinic source declares, "but such has arisen among the nations of the world." Judaism recognizes the possibility of multiple paths to Sinai's summit and demands only worthy conduct for the privilege of ascent. Of all the exclusivist revelations, Judaism alone assures the "righteous of the nations" full salvation, or, as Tradition states, "a share in the world to come."

(c) *Intellectually, by conviction.* The study of the formulated superstructure in TNK and Tradition of the affectively accepted system of Torah values leads to the rationalization of life by the precepts and principles of Torah and therefore to the surer management of their implementation. The study of Torah without the logically and temporally prior affective acceptance of Torah values is deprecated by Tradition: "What is said of someone who studies Torah (i.e., *Torah she bi-Ketav*) and Mishnah (i.e., *Torah she b'al Pe*) and follows the Sages but deals not honorably and speaks not decently to people?" the Talmud asks. It answers: "Woe to so-and-so who studied Torah! Woe to his father who taught him Torah! Woe to his teacher who taught him Torah!"[25]

(d) *Spiritually, by conversion*—that is, by the enthusiasm for existence, courageous faith, thirst for justice, urge to creativity, and selfless devotion to individuals and humanity which unmistakably identify Torah-dedicated and Torah-learned individuals as living carriers of the Torah's light. Their celebration of life testifies eloquently to a qualitative transformation in their lives, when somehow the irruption of the transcendent into the immanent and the sacred into the profane has brought them individually or corporatively to the mountain of Sinai. Historically and personally, the mountain of Sinai represents the moment when time meets eternity, when capacity meets capaciousness, when inspiration meets realization, when preparation meets fulfillment. Judah Halevi added yet a fifth realm, the prophetic, to his categories of existence. In its place or in addition one must include the experience of *Torah min ha-Shamayim*.

As with the children of Israel described in the Torah text, this conversion can result only from the free exercise of will in reflective and attitudinal preparation. Such transformation does not compromise their humanity, but when it comes it makes new organisms of individuals and groups. In conscious harmony with Torah values and the Torah pattern it brings an alacritous acceptance of the Torah task, or, as Tradition calls it, the *ol ha-Torah* ("the yoke of Torah"). This liberating transformation yields the unmistakable reward of an integrity of life indissolubly bound to universal Purpose, or, as described by Tradition, to partnership with God.

Experienced by individuals, such conversion is witnessed corporatively by the faith-people Israel, whose survival, if in part determined by uncontrollable externalities, has no less dramatically depended upon its own will to live for the fulfillment of its mission through the *ol ha-Torah*. Explicitly included in Judaism's distinctive messianic hope is the equivalent conversion of all humanity, not theologically to Judaism or institutionally to the Synagogue, but axiologically to the universe's unifying Force. Thus united above their formal differences "like a single band to do God's will with perfect heart," as the Jewish High Holy Day liturgy declares, the peoples of the earth will existentially, without need of verbal utterance, bear witness to the advent of that time when "the Lord shall be One and the Lord's name shall be One" (Zech 14:9).

V

In their explanations of Jewish theology, some contemporary thinkers follow philosophers, processes, patterns and rubrics borrowed from sources outside the Tradition and often from other faiths. Yet traditionally Judaism has always ordered its principles in distinctive configurations. Techniques borrowed from the outside world, like those in the above study, have been harnessed to the substantive rationalization of the Tradition-as-is, with its inherent alignments, emphases, and, even where they exist, contradictions.

In the Tradition, reason is a servant, not an enemy of *Torah min ha-Shamayim*. Faith and knowledge are not contradictory, but the obverse and reverse of the identical coin of divine creation. However deep the divine message may be, the Jew cannot believe that God speaks in inpenetrable riddles or that the supernatural is delusive. Reason, study and reflection are, as it were, ministering angels leading humanity lovingly along the path to God.

In the Tradition, all theology as well as all value flows from *Torah min ha-Shamayim*. Therefore, to the extent to which any approach succeeds in describing *Torah min ha-Shamayim* in modern terms, it opens the way for equivalent explanations of the other cardinal concepts of Jewish thought.

In our new world of growing ecumenism and mutuality, it is the author's prayer that no individuals of lofty tradition and worthy faith feel constrained to blunt the distinctive contribution of their respective sacred heritages for the sake of dialogue, but that rather the dialogue become a means for understanding differences no less than similarities and for preventing any hurt resulting from our beliefs. Above all he would call to mind the words of the Jews' modern prayer, reflecting a millennial stance, that "with zeal tempered by wisdom and guided by regard for other people's faith"[26] God will grant us the grace to fulfill our task.[27]

NOTES

1. TJ *Peah* 1, 17a; TJ *Megillah* 4, 74d; TJ *Hagigah* 1, 76d.

2. *Ecclesiastes Rabbah* 5, 7.

3. TB *Pesahim* 6b.

4. This explanation, offered by Rabbi Mendel of Rymanov (d. 1814), is discussed by Gershom Scholem in his *On the Kabbalah and Its Symbolism*, Ralph Manheim, transl. (New York: Schocken, 1971), p. 30.

5. TB *Kethuboth* 84b.

6. TB *Kiddushin* 66b.

7. *Numbers Rabbah* 19, 6.

8. *Leviticus Rabbah* 21, 8.

9. TB *Hagigah* 15b, *according to Rabbenu Hananel.*

10. TB *Kerithoth* 11a. For a fuller discussion of the Akiba and Ishmaelan positions, see Abraham J. Heschel, *Torah mi ha-Shamayim b'Ispaklaryah shel ha-Dorot* (London, New York, 1962–1965), 2 vols., *passim.*

11. Judah Halevi, *Cuzari,* part I, section 87. For an English translation, see H. Hirschfeld, *Jehuda Halevi's KITAB AL KHAZARI* (London: Cailingold, 1931), pp. 53f.

12. *Ibid.,* part III, section 67; Hirschfeld, p. 169.

13. Nahman Krochmal, *More Nevukhei ha-Zeman*, S. Ravidowitz, ed. (Berlin, 1924), p. 43.

14. TB *Sanhedrin 10, 1.*

15. Samuel S. Cohon, *Jewish Theology* (Assen, 1971), p. 131.

16. Austin P. Flannery, ed., *Documents of Vatican II* (Grand Rapids: Eerdmans, 1975), p. 739.

17. *Leviticus Rabbah* 9, 3.

18. TB *Menahoth* 29b.

19. TB *Sanhedrin* 99a.

20. TB *Aboth* 3, 14.

21. Morton Enslin, "The Bible in Christianity", in *Encyclopaedia Judaica.* Vol. 4, col. 924.

22. This phrase is to be found in the *Aleynu* prayer, in the concluding section of every daily service. Cf., e.g., Joseph H. Hertz, *Daily Prayer Book* (New York, 1948), p. 298.

23. *Ecclesiastes Rabbah* 11, 8. Cf. also *ibid.,* chap. 2, beginning.

24. *Union Prayer Book* (New York, 1961), I, 265.

25. TB *Yoma* 86a.

26. *Union Prayer Book* I, 34.

27. This article is a pilot presentation containing the essence of a book-length study in preparation on the subject. Limited by constraints of space, it is unable to cite more than the directly quoted sources or fully develop all of the arguments it mentions or adumbrates. Some important sections, like the demonstration of the

relationship of *Torah min ha-Shamayim* to the other cardinal points of Jewish theology, have had to be entirely omitted, while other areas like the relationship of *Torah min ha-Shamayim* to other revelations have had to be limited to passing mentions. For others, fuller treatment may be found in such of the author's articles as "Are the Jews the Chosen People?" (*Dimensions,* Spring 1968, pp. 1–5); "The Mission of Israel after Auschwitz," in Helga Croner, Leon Klenicki, eds., *Issues in the Jewish-Christian Dialogue*, Stimulus Book (New York: Paulist Press, 1979), pp. 157–180; "Midrash and Maaseh: The Structure and Function of Jewish Preaching" (in preparation); "The Mission of Israel in Historical and Contemporary Perspective" (in preparation).

Bible Interpretation: Has Anything Changed?

Monika K. Hellwig

I

Anyone who has been active in Jewish-Christian dialogue for several decades will want to ask once in a while: In the light of the many advances in biblical scholarship, has the Jewish-Christian dialogue become any easier, any more substantial, any more honest? The answer may at first sight be rather disappointing. Just as, on the Jewish side, *Tanakh* is not the sole or isolated point of reference but stands within *Talmud* and *Midrash* and a process of transmission, so on the Christian side the Bible is not the sole or isolated point of reference but stands within Church confessions and traditions that are not immediately susceptible to scholarly reinterpretation of biblical texts and themes. Moreover, perhaps more on the Christian than on the Jewish side, the variation in susceptibility to biblical scholarship is extremely wide. To the fundamentalist and the ultra-liberal, for instance, hard-won gains of painstaking biblical scholarship tend to be equally irrelevant—for the one because there can be no reinterpretation, the meaning being assumed to be self-evident to the reader who comes in faith, and for the other because reinterpretation need not rest on such a laborious process.

To put this another way, the churches have been formulating their doctrine for centuries. At each stage the doctrine was being developed with reference to the biblical text as it was understood at that time. But the doctrine has a history of its own and an authority of its own in the Church.

172

When later biblical scholarship suggests that an earlier doctrinal formulation was based on a mistaken understanding of the biblical text, the Church concerned is presented with a problem. The official teaching is not simply rewritten to match the new biblical understanding. A conflict, sometimes a bitter conflict, is set up. This conflict will involve tensions between biblical scholars and systematic theologians, but it will also involve tension between scholars and those who exercise an official scrutiny of orthodoxy in the churches. Because Jewish tradition does not have anything like an official *magisterium* it may be difficult for Jews to understand what is at stake. In most Christian churches, most notably in the Roman Catholic Church, scrutiny of orthodoxy is carried on by people whose authority is based not on their scholarship but simply on the office to which they have been appointed. The appointments are not usually made with an eye to the learning of the person concerned but with an eye to his being able to function in an administrative capacity.

Moreover, within the Christian churches and among them, there are very wide differences in the ways that Scripture is used and interpreted. These range from a fundamentalist to an existentialist interpretation. The fundamentalist takes the Bible at face value, interpreting it word for word quite literally according to the meaning that seems to be the obvious one. More usually, this meaning is taken directly from whatever translation is being used, without regard for the fact that a good deal of interpretation has already been done in the process of translation and that many passages would lend themselves to alternate readings. More usually it is also done without regard to the literary history of the texts, their cultural context or the style, idioms and rules of composition that governed them in their own time. Obviously, biblical scholarship is a cause of bitter contention to the extreme fundamentalist churches or groups within churches. It cannot really make a difference to their understanding of the message of the Bible. At the other end of the spectrum are various interpretations, of which the extreme existentialist interpretation may be taken as typical. They tend to reject everything that is particular, everything that belongs in the cultural context of the text, everything expressing the religious understanding and expectation of the time the text was written, as irrelevant to the religious message. They try to sift the message out from its cultural form to arrive at the "pure" meaning in universal, basically human, existential terms. This leaves the reading very vulnerable to unrecognized projections of the particular bias and prejudices of the reader's own culture. With so wide a range of possibilities and many carefully specified positions lying between the two extremes, it is obviously not possible to answer the question of this essay in relation to all Christian churches or all positions within the churches.

The following, therefore, can only be an assessment of where we stand from the point of view of a particular Christian position. As will be evident from the foregoing essays by Blenkinsopp and Lacocque, there is a significant Catholic-Protestant differential in the role which the Bible plays in Christian faith and doctrine, and there is a further range of positions among Protestant churches. This essay will present the positions which are acceptable within the Catholic context, while commenting also on the contributions of Protestant scholars.

II

The role of the Bible in the Christian community has always been a complex one. As the section-heading of this part of the volume implies, there is in the first place the distinction to be made between the Bible seen as a record of events that have happened in history, and the Bible seen as an account of the revelation of God and God's purpose in creation and history. This essay will take these one at a time. It is in the Bible seen as record of past events that greater progress has been made and greater promise is contained for the Jewish-Christian dialogue.

Reflection on the Christian creeds and the structure of liturgies since early days suggests that the Bible as a record of events really begins for Christians with the gospels of the New Testament and looks back from there into the Hebrew Scriptures for interpretive categories. It is true that in the extant literature of the first Christian centuries[1] the term "the Scriptures" means exclusively the Hebrew Bible, while Christian writings of the beginnings are more generally referred to as "the apostles." Nevertheless, there can be no doubt that for the Christian community history is founded upon and interpreted by Jesus of Nazareth and the Christian story begins there. It is, of course, on this unrecognized fact that some of the crassest false judgments by Christians against Jews have been based. For many centuries Christians have spoken and written as though any Jew in good faith would necessarily conclude from the Hebrew Scriptures to the messiahship of Jesus. The corollary of this is that those who remain Jews are in bad faith, and that the Jewish community has no right to exist as a contemporary with the Christian.

The more general recognition of the inner logic of the Christian use of the Hebrew Scriptures has now penetrated sufficiently into the circles of systematic theologians that it would not be respectable or acceptable to establish the Christhood or messiahship of Jesus on such grounds today. There is, in other words, a general acknowledgment by those who have studied theology that the Hebrew Scriptures have as their primary meaning that which is discerned therein by Jewish piety and tradition—a meaning that is complete without the New Testament. The meaning that Christians discern there, in the light of their experience of Jesus the Jew and his impact on their world, is a reinterpretation, not the primary and evident meaning of the Hebrew texts themselves. Obvious as that may be to modern Scripture scholars and to Jews, it has been accepted slowly and reluctantly by theologians and is by no means shared even now by all the Christian people or their pastors. Yet it is a basic and crucial area of advance for the Christian-Jewish dialogue because Christians cannot take Jews seriously until this is established.

The question of the Bible as the record of God's dealings with his people in history functions somewhat differently in the Christian-Jewish relations with respect to the Hebrew Scriptures and with respect to the New Testament. With respect to the Hebrew Scriptures, a strictly fundamentalist interpretation of what is written there gives the Christian substantial foundation for taking the Jewish tradition and stance seriously. It is otherwise with a fundamentalist interpretation of the New Testament—for instance, the references to the Jews in John's gospel, the infancy narratives of the gospels of Matthew and Luke, all the accounts of the passion and death of Jesus, the resurrection narratives, and a number of the miracle stories, as well as many Pauline passages. In all of these cases a fundamentalist reading necessarily condemns contemporary Judaism as inauthentic, possibly even insincere, simply because the fundamentalist reading sees the messiahship of Jesus (and perhaps even the divinity claim) as authenticated by overwhelming and publicly verifiable evidence. It is only a more nuanced and critical reading of the New Testament, with its claims of what happened in the heart of Israel in the life, preaching, death and resurrection of Jesus, that there lies any possibility of granting good faith on the part of Jews then and now in their rejection of the Christian claims for Jesus.

In case this is not clear enough, perhaps some examples should be given. A fundamentalist reading of passages in the Pentateuch will indeed lead a Christian to say that God's election rested upon Abraham and his offspring forever, that the land of Israel is given by God to Israel in perpetuity, and that God has made with the children of Israel a covenant in perpetuity that can never be abrogated. The Christian reading, however, cannot and will not stay with the Hebrew Scriptures but will continue into the "New Testament" to learn God's word concerning the outcome or fulfillment. A fundamentalist New Testament reading will yield the understanding that "God can make children of Abraham out of these stones here" (Mt 3:9), and that "You (the followers of Jesus, whether Jews or Gentiles by birth) are now the people of God, who once were not his people" (1 Pet 2:10). This thesis will be amplified and reinforced by further search of the New Testament, and suggests on a literal reading that God indeed is faithful to his promises but that the "true Israel" which falls heir to those promises is identified with Jesus, the faithful remnant, and those who have gathered around him. So the fundamentalist reading, which seemed so promising in relation to the Pentateuch, ends by excluding all legitimate claims for Jews who remain Jews after the Jesus movement separates itself from the national identity of Israel and from the Temple, the Law and the Land.

In this author's experience, Jews who engage in the dialogue are not always aware of this. It frequently happens in conventions and workshops that some of the Jewish participants will be at pains to elicit from the Christian partners an endorsement of a very fundamentalist interpretation of focal passages of the Hebrew Scriptures, particularly those relating the land of Israel to the covenant of God with the Hebrews. Yet, if they succeed they drive the Christian partners to an equally fundamentalist interpretation of the problematic passages of the New Testament by the inexorable logic of the Christian perception of Scripture. This perception views the New Testament, and the gospels in particular, as the core of the record of God's dealings with the human community, and therefore as the last bastion to resist critical analysis. If other parts of the Scriptures are to be taken in pre-critical literal understanding, then all the more so must the New Testament, which seems to discern the followers of Jesus as the "true Israel" inheriting the promises, leave other Jews in sinful schism. Clearly, there is no real "take-off point" for a profitable Jewish-Christian dialogue that does not rest upon a critical study of Scripture. A meaningful dialogue can begin when the Bible is recognized not as a literal account of what happened, but as a collection of interpretations of what happened. This allows for a legitimate variety in the approaches to and interpretations of the same reality.

When we turn from the Bible as record to the quest for revelation in the Bible, there are again some preliminary distinctions to be made. To the Christian, the Bible is not the revelation of God simply, but rather the testimony of the revelation of God. To the Christian, Jesus is the central revelation of God—Jesus with his Hebrew piety, his Jewish sense of covenant and election, his Jewish sense of God as caring Father and simultaneously as all-powerful Master of the universe, his Jewish longing for the reign of God to be fully realized, his Jewish understanding of community within the covenant with God. What Christians have claimed from the beginning is not so much that Jesus has brought revelation to the Gentile world, but that in his person he is the revelation of the Father and the outreach to all nations.

Beyond this initial affirmation there are distinct differences between Protestants and Catholics, and among Protestants there is a variety of positions. Best known of these latter is the extreme version of the Lutheran stance, *sola scriptura;* it is by the Bible alone that we have access to revelation, because it is the only ultimately trustworthy witness. The Catholic understanding is more inclusive: the Bible is one expression of the witness of the Church to revelation. In this understanding, Jesus centrally mediates the encounter with God; the Church as the collectivity of those who have been touched by him mediates the encounter with Jesus (who is the revelation or encounter with God) in its community life, its values, its rituals, its prayer; and among the ways that these are passed on or communicated is that collection of writings, canonized in the early centuries of the Church and left intact since then, which includes the collection of the Hebrew Scriptures (in its more inclusive form) and the collection of the writings "of the apostles" (actually a collection of very early Church documents incorporating the traditional preaching of the "good news of Jesus as the Christ" handed down by the apostles). Thus, for Catholics, the Bible is not the only trustworthy witness; it is the apostolic community as such that is the only ultimately trustworthy witness, and it is the Church as a whole that holds the responsibility for transmission and interpretation. Yet the Bible holds a privileged place, precisely because the corporate discernment of the Church has selected these documents and no others as the most solemn literary testimony to the revelation of God. While the Bible itself requires Church interpretation, the texts taken as a whole also function as the criterion of orthodoxy of subsequent developments in the tradition.

Thus, for all Christians the Bible holds a central position as testimony of the self-revelation of God. It is held to be inspired. For most Christians this does not mean that every word is thought to have been, so to speak, dictated, but rather that the whole message conveyed is that which God wills to have conveyed. It is also held to be inerrant, which follows logically from the claim of divine inspiration, but this does not mean that all factual information in the Bible is correct. Inerrancy rather means that the Bible unfailingly testifies to the self-revelation and the call of God. It is accepted by almost all Christians that the various writers of the biblical texts took for granted the science, geography, history, astronomy and so forth of their time. If their perceptions were incorrect in these matters, this is thought to be unimportant inasmuch as it does not interfere with the religious or spiritual message of the text.

One of the reasons that Christians from New Testament times onward felt free to do the kinds of things they did with the texts of the Hebrew Scriptures, adapting them to their own use to convey a message about redemption through faith in and fellowship with Jesus as the Christ, is that they discerned in the text both a literal and a further, spiritual sense. The literal sense is that which the original author intended and the original listeners or readers would have understood. This would include any figurative or allusive language that was apparently intended by the original author. The spiritual sense is understood as going beyond the human author's intention and being due to the inspiration of God which brings that author to write something that can be understood in a further way, and which brings the worshipping, believing community to understand further, deeper meanings in it.

Implicit in this understanding is, of course, a certain conception of what is meant by revelation. It assumes that the self-revelation of God is pre-verbal and given multidimensionally in human experience. Except in a derived and secondary sense, revelation would not be identified with a set of propositional formulations. It would be identified with the truth that such formulations attempt to express, necessarily always in an inadequate way. That truth itself is read in the human experience of the believing community, also necessarily always in an inadequate way. Therefore there is always room for a deepening and refinement of faith (the obverse side of the coin of revelation) and thus also for a deepening and refinement of the appropriation or understanding of the revelation. There is room to question one's own understanding and interpretation in the light of critical biblical and historical studies and in the light of complementary and contrasting interpretations. There is room for this because, if revelation is given multi-dimensionally in the totality of experience, though brought to central focus in the person of Jesus, then Christians of all generations stand at the source of the revelation in their experience within the Church and are not only recipients of the end-product of a process of revelation that happened long ago to other people.

In case the very condensed language of the previous paragraph is not

clear to all readers, the same thing can be said in simpler language, though
at the price of losing all the necessary nuances that keep the statement
within actual orthodoxy in Catholic and related traditions. An over-simplification might run as follows: How does God "speak"? Not in so many
words, but in experiences at all levels, experiences of nature in the world,
experiences of conscience within the human person, experiences of hope
and promise in history. How do people receive revelation or "hear" what
God says? In the first place by reflection on experiences in a humble and
receptive attitude, and in the second place by learning, from the traditions
that are taught to them, how to interpret their experiences and "hear"
God speaking in them. How does that happen for Christians specifically?
They come to understand Jesus as the central experience in which God
speaks, is present to them and unveils himself to them. Therefore they begin to interpret everything else in the light of the person and event of Jesus
in the world—in the light of the impact he had by what he was, what he
did and preached, the death he died and the explosion of his intensified
presence among his followers after his death.

For Christians, revelation has a universal aspect and a particular aspect. The universal aspect which is shared with all peoples, is that, cumu-
latively in all that happens in the world, God shows himself as powerful
compassion, drawing human beings and all things into existence by the
creative force of love, and masterful enough to bring the creation of his
love to fulfillment beyond all tragedy and human infidelity and failure, so
that no one and nothing is simply tossed into the margins of history as evolutionary waste product. The particular aspect of God's self-revelation as
Christians apprehend it is the person of Jesus of Nazareth. This is so
strong a focus that the Christian conversion consists not of the moment
in which one says "Jesus is so like God," but in the moment in which one
says, "Now I realize that all previous knowledge of God was nothing but
a prelude to this, that God is so like Jesus—like Jesus in his trust, his being
for others, his unreserved self-gift even to the point of death by criminal
execution, his unqualified fidelity in face of the infidelity of others, his un-
measured compassion which at the same time is exigent of a total self-gift
on the part of the believer, his insistence on meeting people according to
their needs and not according to their deserts."

This is the core of revelation to the Christian. But this cannot be formulated in so many words, once and forever, either in the Bible or in other
formulations in the tradition of the churches. This revelation is received
in the relationship set up with Jesus of Nazareth by the believer and by
the community of believers in every generation and in every culture and

situation. In other words, revelation is on-going. Revelation is happening now and always, inasmuch as the meaning of Jesus as the disclosure of the compassionate God continues to unfold as history unfolds and Christians try to live as followers of Jesus in the course of that history. Jesus is certainly seen as illuminating the history before him, and this is why Christians read the Hebrew Scriptures in the light of the Christian experience of Jesus and of the impact he has made on their lives and understanding and historical experience and expectations. But Jesus is also seen as illuminating history after his time, as the living dialogue between him and his followers goes on through his presence in the community. This means that there is always more to learn, more to discover, about the grace and power of the compassionate God in history and about his call and promise to human beings.

In this context of the understanding of the Bible and the ways in which the Bible is related to revelation, Christians need not come with closed minds to the encounter with Jews. In this context they ought rightly to be in a continuing process of true dialogue,[2] open to insights from the dialogue partners that might transform their understanding of revelation and the content of revelation in a far-reaching way.

III

The crucial theme around which Jewish-Christian dialogue must revolve, when it becomes seriously theological and meets on the common ground of Scripture interpretation, is that of election and covenant. This theme and the discussion of it between Jews and Christians have a long history. As noted in the foregoing essays, the earliest Christian discussion of it is in the New Testament itself, especially in Romans 9—11 and in Hebrews 8—9. These are difficult and very elaborately allusive passages. In the course of the centuries, a too superficial reading of them has offered an all too easy foundation for Christian antisemitism. Modern scholarship, attempting to come to terms with Christian antisemitism, has looked into these passages again in a more exigent way.[3]

Election in the Bible is the choice that God is seen to have made—the choice of the Hebrews as his chosen witness people in the world and its history. It is a choice that is expressed in the stories about Abraham, Isaac and Jacob, and again in the stories about Moses, the exodus of the Hebrews from the slavery of Egypt, the Sinai encounter and the promised entry and possession of the land of Canaan. It is a choice that is understood to be based not on any special merit of the Hebrews or their ancestors or their leaders, but in the last analysis simply on the compassionate and transcendently free will of God who chooses to have things so. In Christian thought the notion of God's free election is applied most especially to Jesus, and through association with him to all who believe in him and surrender themselves to become his followers and to serve God by their association with him. In one way or another, Christian thought claims that Jesus inherits the election of Israel and that therefore those who are incorporated into him in the churches become heirs with him of the election of Israel. This is rather basic in defining the self-image or self-identity of Christian churches and communities.

Covenant in the Bible is the unqualified, unlimited alliance that God makes with his people to be their God and identify with them so that their enemies will be his enemies, their concerns his concerns, their pain his pain. Christians freely acknowledge that the special covenant of God from ancient times was made with Israel, the people of the Hebrews. However, they claim that the new covenant is made in Jesus and sealed with the blood he shed in death. They see themselves as participants in that new covenant, making them forever the "people of God."

The problem in hand is that Christian faith and teaching claims to be founded on a "new covenant," which is so called obviously in distinction to the "old covenant" of Israel. The question of the legitimacy of the two traditions then becomes a question of the relationship of the "old" and "new" covenant. The question arises whether there is one covenant renewed and enlarged to include the Gentiles, or whether there are two separate covenants. Beyond this, if it is more consonant with the Christian texts to think in terms of one covenant, does the one renewed covenant become the inheritance of Christians alone (including Jewish and Gentile Christians) to the exclusion of non-Christian Jews because they are seen as having cut themselves off from the covenant people, and thereby have lost their claim to the covenant? Unfortunately, the text from Hebrews could be interpreted in this way, and as long as Christians think their Sacred Scripture should be interpreted in this sense, there can be no dialogue between equal partners, but only conversion efforts.

Continuing, however, the model of one covenant, one could also think of it in terms of the renewed and widened covenant which is still in process of renewal and to which Jews who were left behind (perhaps through no fault of their own or their ancestors) continue to be invited in the course of history. The text from the Letter to the Romans could certainly be interpreted in this way, especially in view of the language about the grafting of the branches. This interpretation does at least have the advantage over the one given above that it speaks more kindly and truthfully about the Jews of the past. However, it still does not grant any legitimacy to Jews of the present or the future; it really looks forward to a world without Jews. This does not offer a sufficient basis for a dialogue among equal partners.

The one covenant could, however, be seen as having, so to speak, two aspects:[4] it is the "new covenant" inasmuch as, reduced to radical simplicity, it is thrown wide open to the Gentiles, returning to the rudimentary covenant of Abraham, that is, before the complexity of the Sinai covenant, yet seen as one and the same; it is at the same time the "old covenant" that continues in its own right and as the root and foundation in a continuing way of the new. Such an understanding would indeed open the way for dialogue at a serious level, because it suggests a model that allows each partner to grant legitimacy to the other in the present and future. The main problem with this model from the Christian side is that it is so difficult to reconcile with the literal text of the two Scripture passages cited above from the Letter to the Romans and the Letter to the Hebrews. Therefore it raises in an acute fashion the question of how far Christians can go with the New Testament texts to interpret a meaning beyond what the author intended, or to restrict the relevance of what was said to the immediate context and circumstances in which it was said.[5]

Turning to the two-covenant model of interpretation, one is also confronted with a number of possibilities, some much more helpful for dialogue than others. There can, for instance, be two covenants of which one is the old and now outdated and the other is the new that takes its place. The text from the Letter to the Hebrews strongly suggests this model. In that case, those who cling to the old after the inception of the new are either perverse or badly mistaken; in either case the only truthful relation with them is to attempt to convert them. Clearly, it offers no basis for a real dialogue because it offers the Christian no basis for genuine respect for the position of the Jew.

The two-covenant theory can also offer a model in which the new covenant is replacing the old gradually, because it is the divine purpose to keep some people in the old covenant for the time being, although it is clear that in the end all must come within the Christian ambit. Certainly both passages alluded to can be interpreted in that way. The obvious problem with this in the Christian dialogue with Jews is that the latter enjoy only a temporary and conditional legitimacy, which is ordered ultimately to the conversion of the Jew to Christianity. It should be pointed out, however, that the model is not altogether useless for dialogue. Although it does not lead the Christian to see the Jew as a truly equal partner, it does at least demand an attitude of docility toward the Jewish testimony, as it implies that the continuing divine purpose has to do with the continuing witness role of the people Israel in the world. It might even be taken to mean that Christians have not yet fully understood their own covenant and are in need of further tutoring by Israel to initiate them into their own covenant with the God of Israel.

The two-covenant theory offers, of course, a much bolder ecumenical option. There could be two covenants, contemporaneously valid, neither destined to subsume the other in the end-time, but both destined to be consummated in an unforeseeable and ineffable pattern of reconciliation with God and each other in the end-time. The obvious advantage of this option is that it establishes equal partners in the dialogue. A further advantage is that it is based on an attitude of humility in the human effort to understand the plans and purposes of God. There seems to be some warrant for it in the Letter to the Romans in that, after Paul's various speculative efforts to make sense of the situation of schism in the people of God which he sees about him, there is indeed the acknowledgment of the inscrutable nature of the plans of God. It would be difficult to find warrant for it in the Letter to the Hebrews. It would also be somewhat difficult to reconcile it with the claim made so frequently one way or another in the various documents of the New Testament, namely that Jesus is the one mediator between God and the human race, the cornerstone, the universal redeemer, and that salvation is by faith in him as the revelation and redemption of God.

It may be asked how these options have actually functioned to date in the attempts at Jewish-Christian dialogue and where these options leave us regarding prospects for the future. These options, or some of them, have been considered since the writings of Karl Barth and the aftermath of the Nazi era stimulated thought on Christian antisemitism. Karl Barth himself offered a very detailed and nuanced analysis of the biblical understanding of covenant in both Hebrew Scriptures and New Testament,[6] but the doctrinal assumptions underlying his analysis seem to prevent it from being immediately helpful in dialogue today.

About a decade after Barth's analysis was written, Bernard Lambert offered the solution that "the story of salvation is a story of waiting"[7] and that the great law of the *oikoumene* is suffering and mercy, in a context that respected both the text of Scripture and the ambiguities of our experience and our expectation.[8] Later in the 1960's, A. Roy Eckardt made a comprehensive study of the positions taken to date, grouping them under the "rhetoric of continuity" and the "rhetoric of discontinuity," showing doctrinal and biblical difficulties and complexities involved in the positions and finally proposing a single, unfolding covenant with two complementary sides.[9] Contemporaneously, Kurt Schubert[10] and others began the task of re-evaluating the Christian-Jewish covenant dilemma in terms of a more critical contemporary Scripture scholarship and the newer possibilities it opened up. By 1977 so much more discussion and reflection had taken place that Michael McGarry, in discussing the Christological implications of the dialogue, was able to compare many positions by two different criteria: continuity/discontinuity and two covenant/single covenant.[11]

The outcome of this last, carefully done, analytical survey suggests that the one covenant/two covenant distinction is not as important as is sometimes claimed, because discontinuity or continuity can in fact be expressed in both. The logical analysis of the options as given above suggests the same conclusion. The McGarry analysis further suggests that Christians have not yet offered a model for full ecumenical partnership of Jews which is not in some way very vulnerable to doctrinal or biblical objections.

IV

The above may be too abstract and schematic for the general reader. At the risk of greatly distorting the whole picture, it may be set out simplistically as follows. Scholars within the Christian context have for a number of decades been asking themselves how they can acknowledge the continued existence of Israel as legitimate. Some have answered that within the boundaries of orthodox Christian belief it cannot be done. Israel, that is, the Jews as a covenant people, should have ceased to exist because their covenant was fulfilled in Jesus and his followers. If they still exist, that has no religious significance. This means in effect that Christians see present-day Judaism as a false religion and Jews mainly as candidates for proselytizing activities.

Obviously, this is unsatisfactory to most scholars who see an historical and a logical connection between these suppositions and the persecution of Jews. The question then arises as to how Judaism may be "legitimated" as a contemporary faith commitment in terms of a Christian theology. Scholars for some time engaged in a discussion based on the claim of a special covenant with God. One aspect of this was the debate whether one should think of two covenants, the "old covenant" of God with Israel and the "new covenant" with Jesus and his followers, or whether it was better to think in terms of one covenant of God with the human race in which different groups at different times participate in different ways. The logical options have been set out above. If we think in terms of one covenant it allows us to think of different simultaneous ways of participating in it. Israel may be thought of as a continuing witness people with a task precisely in terms of its separation, its ritual code, and its closed community organized around the observance of Torah, while the special task of the Church, the followers of Jesus, is the continual universal offering of salvation to all the nations, which is in some sense the very opposite of the exclusivity of Israel. Yet precisely this difference might be seen as a necessary complementarity within God's redemptive purpose in the world. The major difficulty with this apparently happy solution is that it is difficult if not impossible to justify by the New Testament texts that deal with the issue.

The alternate option, thinking in terms of two covenants, actually allows for the same possibility. The two covenants need not be seen as successive in time, with the new abrogating the old. They could be seen as complementary, the new growing out of the old and continuing in counterpoint with it through history, in an amicable relationship or in a sort of friendly wager. At least there would be the possibility of constant mutual enrichment through each other's experiences and insights. The result, in a sense, is the same, and the objection from the New Testament texts, notably the Letter to the Romans and the Letter to the Hebrews, is also the same.

This is why scholars have abandoned the one covenant/two covenant debate as a blind alley. What is evidently at stake is rather the continuity that is established between the "old covenant" and the "new covenant." A sharp discontinuity is evidently hostile to the continued existence of Israel as a witness people. In other words, to write of Jesus and of the Church as abrogating the covenant of Israel leaves no place in history for the legitimate continuance of Judaism. The task of legitimation is that of establishing a theological account of Israel which allows of continuity. Moreover, it is not enough to say that Jesus and his teaching and mission and Church flow directly from ancient Israel as its fulfillment rather than its contradiction. It is necessary to see the impact of Jesus on the world in its continuing unfolding as continuing to proceed somehow from Israel. So far, models have been proposed but none have really been accepted by the Christian theological community.

It would seem that the reason for this lack of a truly workable model is in part the fact that not just a few ecumenically minded scholars and churchmen but the whole body of scholars, churchmen and believers are involved in the determination of the legitimacy of a model in relation to the accepted faith. The whole body of Christians, even in one denomination, however, are usually reluctant to rethink any position and are not motivated by a sense of ecumenical urgency. But the more important reason for the lack of a truly workable model is that it clearly requires a very bold style of biblical interpretation, which not only churchmen but also scholars are reluctant to undertake. This is the type of Scripture interpretation that was known and practiced in the patristic age, that is, in the very early centuries of the Church's existence. Reflection was being done quite frankly out of the on-going experience of living the Christian life, and Scripture was used as a resource of language, story and symbol to express the present reality experienced. If modern Christians were free to do this on the understanding of the on-going revelation in the community of the faithful, they could approach the biblical text quite differently as a living resource that grows and expands with maturity in the Church's experience. The contemporary attitude of churchmen and scholars to the Scriptures sees them as a static "deposit" rather than as a dynamic force.

As suggested by the logical analysis of the options above, a fully satisfactory basis for dialogue between equal partners would need to be in the third category of either the one covenant or the two covenant options. To achieve either of these positions by analysis of what the biblical authors of Romans and Hebrews themselves intended to say would be specious. There remains, therefore, only the possibility of showing some grounds on which Christians today might be justified, in full loyalty to their own Church tradition, in setting aside the literal, that is, originally intended, meaning of the texts.

It would seem that one might tentatively venture such a move along the following lines. The text of the Bible, as explained above, is not to be equated with revelation simply; it is one testimony within the on-going life of the Church, though a privileged testimony. Revelation is the encounter with God in experience, and the content of revelation is what is learned in multi-dimensional experience. We cannot appropriate it until we participate in the experience, and we cannot express it until we have appropriated it pre-verbally. Thus the meaning of Scripture itself emerges in dialogue with the on-going experience of the community. It is by centuries of living the Christian way that we discern what to extend into universal application and what to set aside as the culturally conditioned thinking of the particular biblical author. Thus, we have long ago set aside the exhortations found in the New Testament to slaves to bear their condition cheerfully and to masters concerning proper treatment of slaves. We have set them aside because centuries of Christian living have convinced us it is unnecessary, immoral and un-Christian to give any countenance to the institution of slavery. On questions about the role of women in society, we are still engaged in the struggle over what may be set aside as culturally conditioned. In both cases, however, there is no doubt that it is a matter of contradicting the literal sense of the passages concerned, that is, the intended meaning of the biblical author.

It is in such a context that one might be able to say that these documents are indeed inspired by God, part of the Canon of Scripture, sharing in the inerrancy of Scripture and yet not to be followed in our times on these particular points. Furthermore, the content of revelation is never adequately understood or adequately captured in any language; therefore there is always room for progress in understanding and in formulation in words. Finally, because God's dealings with us must always be expressed in analogies drawn from human relationships, we must regard these analogies with a certain suspicion and reserve, and we cannot let the logic of the analogy dominate the logic of our historical experience of participation in the process of redemption. The on-going revelation becomes a principle of hermeneutics; we do not deny the truth of experience in order to keep the logic of our inadequate language intact; rather we must then reshape the language used to describe the experience.

Between the one covenant and two covenant models the present author continues[12] to prefer the one covenant model. The choice would seem to be arbitrary in the sense that no demonstration could verify which is closer to the reality. However, in terms of appropriateness, it seems better to suggest that divisions and discontinuities may be perceived at our end, but with God all is unified and coherent; all are called, perhaps in different ways; both are chosen, evidently by different routes; it is one God who calls, and therefore ultimately there is one call, one creation, one covenant. Moreover, this appears to be closer to the sense of the unity of all the covenants in the Hebrew Scriptures.

Finally, it may be said that the prospect of adoption of the more radical approach to ecumenism which depends on the more radical approach to Scripture interpretation is a remote one, and that it is to be hoped the dialogue will be pursued earnestly in the meantime. What is the prospect? It seems to this author that the best that can be hoped for is that, whatever the positions that are taken and that are bound to be in some sense a contradiction of the position taken by the other party, there might be on both sides a humble acknowledgment that we live by hope and that none of us sees clearly the outcome of our hope, that God is greater than all our knowing and striving, and that the appropriate attitude on both sides is that of a friendly wager that one's own is the more direct route to the ultimate salvation.

NOTES

1. E.g., in the Apostolic Fathers.

2. Cf. Pope Paul VI, *Ecclesiam Suam* (Washington, D.C.: U.S.C.C., 1964).

3. Besides standard Scripture commentaries, see the bibliography in A. Roy Eckardt, *Elder and Younger Brothers* (New York: Scribner's, 1967).

4. Cf. Bernard Lambert, *Ecumenism* (New York: Herder, 1967), chap. XI, pp. 445–490. Also, Helga Croner, Leon Klenicki, eds., *Issues in the Jewish-Christian Dialogue: Jewish Perspectives on Covenant, Mission and Witness*, Stimulus Book (New York: Paulist Press, 1979), esp. pp. 66–70.

5. Opinions among scholars differ widely on the licitness and advisability of interpretation beyond the author's intent. Thus Eckardt, *op. cit.,* has: "It would be less grievous to state candidly that the apostle was in error than to interpret him as saying something more than he says" (p. 56).

6. Cf. Karl Barth, *Church Dogmatics* (New York: Scribner's, 1956), Part IV, Vol. I, pp. 22–78. Barth's interest is mentioned here because he stimulated much of the later discussion. His position is not discussed for three reasons. First of all, it is simply and totally irrelevant to the present discussion except inasmuch as it should be acknowledged as the key initiative that started the ball rolling. Second, it was written before the fruits of the last several decades of Scripture studies were available to systematic theologians. Third, a presentation of Barth's theses concerning the election and covenant of Israel, taken outside the whole context of *Church Dogmatics,* would read more like an advanced step in prejudice than a step in ecumenical dialogue. This last is due to the characteristic strain of historical pessimism in Barth's thought. In fact, although he appears to contradict himself in the course of his several works and even between different volumes of *Church Dogmatics,* his basic position appears to be that he sees a continuing role for Israel but one that is purely negative where the role of the Christian Church is positive. To understand his position sympathetically one would have to study *Church Dogmatics* in its entirety. To perceive why we cannot take the position seriously in the contemporary discussion, it is sufficient to read attentively A. Roy Eckardt, *op cit.,* pp. 58–63. That book is readily available and it would be useless to repeat the demonstration here.

7. Bernard Lambert, *op. cit.,* p. 488.

8. *Ibid.*, chap. XI.

9. A. Roy Eckardt, *op. cit.*, chaps. IV, V, VIII.

10. Kurt Schubert, "The People of the Covenant," in John M. Oesterreicher, ed., *Brothers in Hope* (New York: Herder, 1970), pp. 132–158.

11. Michael B. McGarry, *Christology after Auschwitz* (New York: Paulist Press, 1977).

12. Cf. Monika Hellwig, "Proposal Towards a Theology of Israel as a Religious Community Contemporary with the Christian", microfilm, Ph.D. dissertation, Catholic University of America, 1968; "Christian Theology and the Covenant of Israel," in *Journal of Ecumenical Studies* 7 (1970), pp. 37–51; "Why We Still Can't Talk," in Robert Heyer, ed., *Jewish/Christian Relations* (New York: Paulist Press, 1975), pp. 26–31.

Afterword:
From Argument to Dialogue—
Nostra Aetate Fifteen Years Later

Leon Klenicki

> No person outside Israel knows the
> mystery of Israel. And no person
> outside of Christianity knows the
> mystery of Christianity. But in their
> ignorance they can acknowledge each
> other in the mystery.[1]

The Declaration on the Relation of the Church to Non-Christian Religions, Nostra Aetate, promulgated on October 28, 1965 by the Second Vatican Council marked a special moment in the history of the Church and its relation to world religions. The Council, as seen from the outside, endeavored to witness God by a testimony rooted in the Christian tradition of centuries, but sensitive to the realities of change and human development. The work of the Council—*aggiornamento,* as it was called by Pope John XXIII—was to lead to an actualization, an active awareness, of the experience of God and his presence in the contemporary Christian historical context.

Such an inner renewal, inevitably open to illusion and romanticism, is familiar to Jews. The halakhic-rabbinic interpretation of the biblical experience of God and its actualization under ever-changing conditions of life is a continuous example of organic *aggiornamento* in Judaism. It started as a process of phenomenological commentary or expounded explanation of the Written Word under Ezra and Nehemiah after the Babylonian Exile and the return to the Promised Land. The word of God, concise, laconic, became an explained and detailed way of being, *halakhah,* a way of going and being. The experience of God in the rabbinic explanation of the basic biblical text became an *aggiornamento.* It is right up to our time a vivid, numinous dimension of God's presence in the active reality of daily ritual and personal sanctity. In the rabbinic *aggiornamento* the experience of God emerged as a daily experience of divine reactualization.

The *aggiornamento* initiated by the Vatican Council is a process of inner renewal that entails consideration of past religious experience and a reckoning of the soul in relation to other faith commitments. It includes, specifically, consideration and reconsideration of Judaism and the Jewish people. Negative Christian attitudes of centuries, the denial of Israel's destiny and vocation, required reflection going beyond the theological triumphalism of the Church Fathers and the ideas of medieval theologians.

Israel, God's chosen, existed and exists, witnessing God and the covenantal relationship, despite alienation and ostracism which culminated in the Holocaust, a devastating reality of total evil. The Holocaust reminds Christians and Jews of the historical necessity to recognize that direct and indirect involvement of Christians in the cultural milieu of the Western world made possible antisemitism in its most extreme manifestation. Though not immediately related to Christian thinking, the paganism of Nazi Germany was fed by the ideological reasoning of anti-Judaism in Christian theology and certain papal pronouncements. Christian spiritual negation of Judaism, a denial of Israel's vocation, was taken over, in turn, by totalitarian ideologues in order to deny and destroy Israel as a living community.

The Council's reconsideration of Israel was part of a concern over the very meaning of Christian testimony. Vatican II searched into the "mystery" of Christianity at this point in history, a search into the meaning of God's call. *Nostra Aetate* follows this inner examination as it relates to the main religious commitments, devoting a separate section to Judaism. Such a scrutiny does not imply pluralism but constitutes a sincere probing into roots and common concerns.

Nostra Aetate was prepared and written by Catholic theologians and religious experts and directed to the Catholic community. The original draft, and particularly the fourth section devoted to Judaism, underwent changes after many discussions. The proposal called forth the expression of profound differences among the bishops attending the Council. Conservatively oriented clergy and outside groups tried to obstruct consideration of Judaism altogether, using arguments familiar from medieval disputations. For some groups *Nostra Aetate* served as a pretext to criticize Vatican II and to allow non-religious organizations, for instance, the Arab League, and Arab diplomats, to attack the inter-religious dialogue and the State of Israel. A current of anti-Jewish theology was evident in articles and books—underlining God's rejection of Israel and Jewish involvement in the death of Jesus—distributed openly or clandestinely among the Council fathers. A text on deicide, written by Luigi M. Carli, Bishop of Segni, accused the Council of "historic distortion." Augustin Cardinal Bea responded with a scholarly document published in *Civiltà Cattolica* IV, 21, on November 6, 1965 (later published in English in *Thought* XLI, 160, Spring 1966).

I

The discussions at Vatican II entailed a constant dialogue of clarification, involving the expertise of Catholic theologians and specialists as well as Jewish personalities active in the inter-religious relationship. One of them, Dr. Joseph L. Lichten, played a central role.[2] As director of the Anti-Defamation League of B'nai B'rith's department of Intercultural Affairs, he represented the organization in Rome during the days of the Council. His sensitivity and knowledge of the Jewish-Catholic dialogue were of particular significance in informing Council members on the Jewish point of view regarding the main historical and religious problems involved in the dialogue. He presented a study-survey conducted for the Anti-Defamation League by the Survey Research Center of the University of California, inspired by Oscar Cohen and directed by Charles Glock and Rodney Stark, published later as *Christian Beliefs and Anti-Semitism.*[3] It has become a classic of socio-religious studies and undoubtedly influenced Vatican Council members.

Joseph Lichten pointed out the influence of the deicide charge on American Catholics:

> Perhaps as many as five million American Catholics, out of a total of forty-five million, see the Jews as principally responsible for the death of Jesus, and they are led thereby to a negative assessment of the contemporary Jew. The fact that those who believe and feel this way tend

to go to church more frequently underscores the need for the Catholic Church to intensify its efforts if it hopes to bring all Catholics to the principles of brotherhood which it espouses.[4]

Arthur Gilbert described the impact of the study at the Vatican Council:

So troubled were Catholic leaders by this startling revelation of Christian anti-Semitism that the Dutch Documentation Center for the Council volunteered to publish the findings and distributed them to every Council father, since the debate on the Jewish statement was surely to induce comments. Therefore, on September 17, the findings were placed in the mailbox of each Council father with a note by the Center Director expressing his hope that the document would serve the Council, the Church, and the lapse between Jews and Christians.[5]

The final Council vote on the Declaration showed the Church's special concern for this document, a turning point in Catholic understanding of Judaism and the Christian-Jewish relationship. In the final ballot on the Declaration as a whole, 2221 voted yes, 88 voted no, and 3 votes were void.[6]

The reactions to *Nostra Aetate* within the Jewish community were mixed, ranging from total negativism and prudent criticism to reserved acceptance and enthusiasm. Reservations were expressed on the very fact of a Catholic document on Judaism and dialogue. It reminded many, particularly after the European experience, of previous pronouncements by the Church. Those documents of the past were part of the ecclesiastical medieval environment that resulted in the repeated exclusion of Jews from public and national life. It was felt that the Vatican II Declaration on the Jews might be a modern, more sophisticated version of the *Constitutio Pro Iudaeis,* a bull by Pope Calixtus II (1119–1124). This papal document, which established a pattern of relationships with the Jewish people, served as a protective statute at a time of persecution by secular powers.[7]

Caution on *Nostra Aetate* was recommended in the inter-religious dialogue by Rabbi Joseph B. Soloveitchik, one of the most brilliant Jewish minds of this century, in his essay "Confrontation." In his recommendations to the Rabbinical Council of America he proposed a dialogue that respected each faith's commitments and avoided any theological discussion. He proposed discussions on humanitarian and cultural endeavors and man's moral values. His categorical resistance to theological dialogue was summed up as follows: "To repeat, we are ready to discuss universal religious problems. We will resist any attempt to debate our private individual commitments."[8]

Rabbi Eliezer Berkovits bitterly criticized dialogue of any kind, especially at this moment in time—the post-Christian era. He wrote:

> There is no reason on earth why Judaism should make itself available to fraternal dialogue with a religion which, by its very premises, declares others to be in error and, from the outset, destroys the basis of the true dialogical situation. . . . We reject the idea of inter-religious understanding as immoral because it is an attempt to whitewash the criminal past.[9]

There were, however, many voices favoring dialogue and stressing the importance of the Jewish-Christian relationship, particularly at this moment in history, after the Holocaust and Vatican II. On the American scene, this attitude resulted in special programs by ecclesiastical organizations and private agencies that devoted time and energy to illustrate to the community at large the spiritual and social transcendence of the inter-religious encounter. For this reason, American Catholic opinion on many questions regarding religious freedom and inter-religious relations was of decisive influence. Jacob B. Agus summed up the mood of search for mutual knowledge and meaning of those days when he said that the dialogue should be "mutually challenging, not necessarily mutually contradictory."[10]

In October 1974, Pope Paul VI instituted a Vatican Commission for Religious Relations with the Jews, which in 1975 issued *Guidelines and Suggestions for Implementing the Conciliar Declaration Nostra Aetate (n. 4)*. The document suggested changes in the approach to liturgy, teaching and education, and joint social action.[11] The document was an advance over *Nostra Aetate,* but not in relation to previously published guidelines published by episcopal conferences in the United States and Europe.[12]

II

Nostra Aetate is open to interpretation and committed reading, and that process deepens the dialogue. The statements of the U.S. National Conference of Catholic Bishops in 1975, of the French Bishops Committee for Relations with Jews in 1973, of the National Commission for Relations between Christians and Jews in Belgium of 1973, of the Catholic Church in the Netherlands of 1970, and of the Synod of Vienna in 1969 have all evolved from dialogue and encounter.

A Jewish reading of the Vatican Statement requires respectful consideration of the Catholic faith commitment. This must be done in perspective of Jewish religious thought and the covenantal relationship, but mindful of the Christian vocation. Certain temptations must be avoided, for instance, total negativism regarding the possibilities and future of the dialogue, based on past experiences. Another is self-pity for past persecutions and pains; those were very real, but self-righteousness is not an answer to the challenge of dialogue, one of the hardest challenges to a religious person. The right Jewish attitude in this situation requires self-reckoning and reconciliation.[13] It entails recognition of the dialogue partner as a subject of faith, a child of God. It also calls for a perception of Christianity's role in bringing God to the Gentiles, essentially to humanity in the rabbinic meaning of God's covenant with Noah, the biblical symbol for humanity.

Nostra Aetate (n. 4) begins with an explanation of the relationship of the Church to Judaism, referred to in the document as "Abraham's stock." The Church acknowledges that according to God's saving design the beginnings of Christian faith and election "are found already among the patriarchs, Moses and the prophets." All who believe in Christ "are included in the same patriarch's call, and likewise that the salvation of the Church is mysteriously foreshadowed by the chosen people's exodus from the land of bondage." The Church cannot forget that "she draws sustenance from the root of that well-cultivated olive tree onto which has been grafted the wild shoot, the Gentiles. Indeed, the Church believes that by his cross Christ, our Peace, reconciled Jews and Gentiles, making both one in himself."

The Vatican document indicates a way of relating to Israel. It does not repeat the attitude of past centuries, for instance, the concept that the Tanakh, the Hebrew Bible, is merely a preparation for Jesus' coming and mission, and that Israel lost its purpose and meaning in the divine plan.

The Vatican *Guidelines* of January 1975 emphasize the value of the Hebrew Bible:

An effort will be made to acquire a better understanding of whatever in the Old Testament retains its own perpetual value (cf. *Dei Verbum* 14–

15), since that has not been cancelled by the later interpretation of the New Testament.

The French bishops' statement of 1973 adds a dimension of understanding that opens new vistas in the relationship:

> According to biblical revelation, God himself constituted this people, brought it up, advised it of his plans, concluding with it an eternal covenant (Gn 17:7), and giving it a vocation which St. Paul qualifies as "irrevocable" (Rom 11:29). We are indebted to the Jewish people for the five books of the Law, the prophets, and the other Scriptures which complete the message. After having been collected by oral and written tradition, these precepts were received by Christians without, however, dispossessing the Jews.
>
> Even though in Jesus Christ the covenant was renewed for Christendom, the Jewish people must not be looked upon by Christians as a mere social and historical reality but most of all as a religious one; not as the relic of a venerable and finished past but as a reality alive through the ages. The principal features of this vitality of the Jewish people are its collective faithfulness to the one God, its fervor in studying the Scriptures to discover, in the light of revelation, the meaning of human life, its search for an identity amid other men, and its constant efforts to reassemble as a new, unified community. These signs pose questions to us Christians which touch on the heart of our faith: What is the proper mission of the Jews in the divine plan? What expectations animate them, and in what respect are these expectations different from or similar to our own?

The Vatican *Guidelines* indicate the permanence of Judaism, though they do not refer to the rabbinic commentary on the biblical word, the Mishnah and Midrash, and later rabbinical literature. These commentaries represent the halakhic tradition central to the Jewish commitment. The *Guidelines* do, however, point out that this post-biblical tradition was "deeply affected" by the coming of Christ:

> The history of Judaism did not end with the destruction of Jerusalem, but rather went on to develop a religious tradition. And, although we believe that the importance and meaning of that tradition were deeply affected by the coming of Christ, it is nonetheless rich in religious values.

III

The accusation of deicide has for centuries plagued the Jewish people and created a popular climate of dislike, even hatred. The death of Jesus was placed on the shoulders of the Jews by Church Fathers and medieval theologians. Annual passion plays and pre-Vatican II catechetical teaching continued the accusation.[14] *Nostra Aetate* refers to the matter without qualification, thereby creating a question of concern for the Jewish reader:

> True, the Jewish authorities and those who followed their lead pressed for the death of Christ; still, what happened in his passion cannot be charged against all the Jews, without distinction, then alive, nor against the Jews of today.

The reference to "Jewish authorities" pressing for Jesus' death is too vague and requires more detailed consideration. This is done by the Vatican *Guidelines:*

> Judaism in the time of Christ and the apostles was a complex reality, embracing many different trends, many spiritual, religious, social, and cultural values.

Some of the questions to be asked are: Who are the Jewish authorities in the Roman-dominated Jerusalem? Does the text refer to the high priest, a nominee of Rome? Or does it refer to the Pharisaic scholars of the Sanhedrin or perhaps the populist leaders of the Zealot movement? It is quite difficult to determine a central Jewish authority at that time. Rabbinic literature reflects the pluralistic nature of authority by accepting several opinions on the subject, discussed by the rabbis in the Mishnah and in the midrashic commentaries. Does *Nostra Aetate* include all the Jewish leadership of the time?

Underlying *Nostra Aetate* is the requirement to present the history of Jews and Judaism in a way that reflects the Gospel teaching:

> Although the Church is the new people of God, the Jews should not be presented as rejected or accursed by God, as if this followed from the Holy Scriptures. All should see to it, then, that in catechetical work or in the preaching of the word of God they do not teach anything that does not conform to the truth of the Gospel and the spirit of Christ.

These recommendations have been followed in the United States by the Department of Education of the United States Catholic Conference. Together with the Anti-Defamation League of B'nai B'rith, special courses on Jews and Judaism for Catholic teachers were developed. The educational program, *Understanding the Jewish Experience,* offers background information on Judaism from the earliest days to the twentieth century's experience, in the fields of theology, liturgy and history. The recent publication of *Abraham, Our Father in Faith,* edited by the Superintendent of Schools' Office of the Archdiocese of Philadelphia, and jointly republished by the National Conference of Catholic Bishops—Secretariat of Catholic-Jewish Relations and the Anti-Defamation League of B'nai B'rith, is part of this educational project. The booklet provides teachers on the elementary and secondary levels with background and classroom materials on Judaism that can be easily incorporated in the teaching of religion and the presentation of Jews and Judaism.

IV

The Council's concern with the historical reality of antisemitism was shown in the general discussions and the preparation of *Nostra Aetate.* The first draft had a line "condemning" antisemitism. Some Council fathers considered that the word "condemn" should only be employed by a Vatican Council in problems relating to dogma. Cardinal Bea, however, reminded the Council of the March 25, 1928 declaration by the Vatican Congregation of the Holy Office that specifically used "condemnation" in relation to the Catholic Church's position on antisemitism.

Nostra Aetate points out:

> Furthermore, in her rejection of every persecution against any man, the Church, mindful of the patrimony she shares with the Jews and moved not by political reasons but by the Gospel's spiritual love, decries hatred, persecutions, and displays of antisemitism, directed against Jews at any time and by anyone.

The Vatican *Guidelines,* ten years later, state clearly and strongly:

> Moreover, the step taken by the Council finds its historical setting in circumstances deeply affected by the memory of the persecution and massacre of Jews which took place in Europe before and during the Second

World War. . . . While referring the reader back to this document (*Nostra Aetate*), we may simply restate here that the spiritual bonds and historical links binding the Church to Judaism condemn as opposed to the very spirit of Christianity all forms of antisemitism and discrimination which in any case the dignity of the human person alone would suffice to condemn.

The Vatican *Guidelines* manifest growth in understanding and consideration not yet present in *Nostra Aetate*. Both documents fail, though, to recount the past with the centuries of theological contempt that educated generations of Christians to mistrust and hate the Jewish people, if not Judaism. A reckoning of the heart, a genuine act of reconciliation, requires the recognition of past mistakes and the expression of hope for renewal.

A similar phenomenon is obvious in the so-called *Puebla Document* of the third meeting of CELAM, the Latin American Bishops' Conference of February 1979 in Mexico. A draft of the document spoke of condemnation of antisemitism, but later versions, under the influence of certain groups, omitted that expression. The final version refers only to the Vatican II document on the subject. It is a serious omission considering the reality of antisemitism in certain Latin American countries and the constant danger of racism in those societies. Documents of bishops' conferences in the United States and Europe, however, follow the Vatican *Guidelines'* terminology and "condemn" the scourge of antisemitism.[15]

Nostra Aetate does not consider the nature and aims of the dialogue relationship, nor the meaning of the Catholic-Jewish dialogue. At the very beginning of the *Nostra Aetate* declaration Pope Paul VI states:

> In our time, when day by day mankind is being drawn ever closer together and ties are becoming stronger between different people, the Church is paying closer attention to the relationship with non-Christian religions. In her stands of fostering unity and love among men, indeed among peoples, she considers above all what men have in common and what draws them to fellowship.

The Vatican *Guidelines* of January 1975, after ten years of continuous dialogue, work and theological consideration, devote the first section to a definition of the term:

> To tell the truth, such relations as there have been between Jew and Christian have scarcely ever risen above the level of monologue. From now on, real dialogue must be established.

Dialogue presupposes that each side wishes to know the other, and wishes to increase and deepen its knowledge of the other. It constitutes a particularly suitable means of favoring a better mutual knowledge and, especially in the case of dialogue between Jews and Christians, of probing the riches of one's own tradition. Dialogue demands respect for the other as he is—above all, respect for his faith and his religious convictions.

In virtue of her divine mission and her very nature, the Church must preach Jesus Christ to the world (*Ad Gentes,* 2). Lest the witness of Catholics to Jesus Christ should give offense to Jews, they must take care to live and spread their Christian faith while maintaining the strictest respect for religious liberty, in line with the teaching of the Second Vatican Council (Declaration *Dignitatis Humanae*). They will likewise strive to understand the difficulties which arise for the Jewish soul—rightly imbued with an extremely high, pure notion of the divine transcendence—when faced with the mystery of the incarnate Word.

The paragraph underlines the need for dialogue within the perspectives of each religious commitment, avoiding syncretism or delusions due to an excess of good will or desire to achieve a pleasant and comfortable situation:

While it is true that a widespread air of suspicion, inspired by an unfortunate past, is still dominant in this particular area, Christians, for their part, will be able to see to what extent the responsibility is theirs and deduce practical conclusions for the future.

In addition to friendly talks, competent people will be encouraged to meet and to study together the many problems deriving from the fundamental convictions of Judaism and of Christianity. In order not to hurt (even involuntarily) those taking part, it will be vital to guarantee, not only tact, but a great openness of spirit and diffidence with respect to one's own prejudices.

The Vatican *Guidelines* clearly and strongly state:

Further still, these links and relationships render obligatory a better mutual understanding and renewed mutual esteem. On the practical level in particular, Christians must therefore strive to acquire a better knowledge of the basic components of the religious tradition of Judaism; they must strive to learn by what essential traits the Jews define themselves in the light of their own religious experience.

V

There is one aspect that both *Nostra Aetate* and the Vatican *Guidelines* do not consider in their striving "to learn by what essential traits the Jews define themselves in the light of their own religious experience." This trait is Zionism, an essential part of the Jewish vocation since biblical days (Genesis 12 and other texts). The exile and the return experience of Ezra and Nehemiah and the liturgical hope expressed in daily prayer and sustained in the High Holidays and Passover celebrations symbolize the Jewish people's relationship to the Promised Land. The experience of near destruction under Nazi slavery and other forms of totalitarian persecution and the creation of the State of Israel are central elements of contemporary Jewish identity. Those events must be taken into consideration in any attempt to understand the Jewish people and twentieth-century Judaism. Failure to do so is a serious flaw of both Vatican documents.

The documents of the American and French bishops, however, pay special attention to the centrality of Israel in the existence of the Jewish people. The American document of November 1975 points out:

> In dialogue with Christians, Jews have explained that they do not consider themselves as a church, a sect, or a denomination, as is the case among Christian communities, but rather as a peoplehood that is not solely racial, ethnic or religious, but in a sense a composite of all these. It is for such reasons that an overwhelming majority of Jews see themselves bound in one way or another to the land of Israel. Most Jews see this tie to the land as essential to their Jewishness. Whatever difficulties Christians may experience in sharing this view, they should strive to understand this link between land and people which Jews have expressed in their writings and worshiped throughout two millennia as a longing for the homeland, holy Zion. Appreciation of this link is not to give assent to any particular religious interpretation of this bond. Nor is this affirmation meant to deny the legitimate rights of other parties in the region, or to adopt any political stance in the controversies over the Middle East, which lie beyond the purview of this statement.

The document of the French bishops takes a broader dimension discussing theological and political implications;

> The dispersion of the Jewish people should be understood in the light of its history. Though Jewish tradition considers the trials and exile of

the people as a punishment for infidelities (Jer 13:17; 20:21–23), it is nonetheless true that, since the time when Jeremiah addressed his letter to the exiles in Babylon (29:1–23), the life of the Jewish people in the diaspora has also held a positive meaning. Throughout its trials, the Jewish people has been called to "sanctify the name" amid the nations of the world. Christians must constantly combat the anti-Jewish and Manichean temptation to regard the Jewish people as accursed, under the pretext of its constant persecutions. According to the testimony of Scripture (Is 53:2–4), being subjected to persecution is often an effect and reminder of the prophetic vocational.

Today more than ever, it is difficult to pronounce a well-considered theological opinion on the return of the Jewish people to "its" land. In this context, we Christians must first of all not forget the gift, once made by God to the people of Israel, of a land where it was called to be re-united (cf Gn 12:7; 26:3–4; 28:13; Is 43:5–7; Jer 16:15; Soph 3:20).

Throughout history, Jewish existence has always been divided between life among the nations and the wish for national existence on that land. This aspiration poses numerous problems even to Jews. To understand it, as well as all dimensions of the resulting discussion, Christians must not be carried away by interpretations that would ignore the forms of Jewish communal and religious life, or by political positions that, though generous, are nonetheless hastily arrived at. Christians must take into account the interpretation given by Jews to their ingathering around Jerusalem which, according to their faith, is considered a blessing. Justice is put to the test by this return and its repercussions. On the political level, it has caused confrontations between various claims for justice. Beyond the legitimate divergence of political options, the conscience of the world community cannot refuse the Jewish people, who had to submit to so many vicissitudes in the course of its history, the right and means for a political existence among the nations. At the same time, this right and the opportunities for existence cannot be refused to those who, in the course of local conflicts resulting from this return, are now victims of grave injustice.

Let us, then, turn our eyes toward this land visited by God and let us actively hope that it may become a place where one day all its inhabitants, Jews and non-Jews, can live together in peace. It is an essential question, faced by Christians as well as Jews, whether or not the ingathering of the dispersed Jewish people—which took place under pressure of persecution and by the play of political forces—will despite so many tragic events prove to be one of the final ways of God's justice for the Jewish people and at the same time for all the nations of the earth. How could Christians remain indifferent to what is now being decided in that land?

The Jewish reader might not agree with some of the concepts of the documents but the statements recognize the centrality of Israel in the existence of the Jewish people. The Jewish reader recognizes a sincere attempt to understand the totality of contemporary Judaism.

VI

The Christian-Jewish relationship has undergone a particular transformation. It has gone from argument to dialogue, from conflict to a meeting situation, from ignorance and alienation to encounter, a conversation between equals. The road is not a smooth one. There still are problems and misunderstandings, but mainly there is a desire to listen and to respond, to see the other as a person, not an object of contempt.[16]

The dialogue requires reckoning and reflection. Jews have to overcome two thousand years of memories, memories from the times of the New Testament experience, medieval disputations, the Inquisition, and present-day Christian ideological criticisms of Zionism and Israel. Jews have to overcome the castrating effects of images transmitted by generations and the concrete experiences of Christian triumphalism associated with political regimes of right-wing orientation. Christians have to overcome two thousand years of prejudice, of theological arrogance and spiritual contempt. Education and contemporary Christian reckoning of the soul, Vatican II and other Christian efforts are the means that will eventually open new roads of spiritual understanding.

Dialogue is both a process of inner cleansing and a search for truth. The inner cleansing is an attempt to see the other as a creature and part of God's special design for mankind. A respectful relationship, that at this point we call dialogue until a more precise word can describe this unique, special meeting, is never a confrontation but a common fervor, mindful of the different vocations. Real dialogue calls persons into being, into their own being but mindful in acknowledging the other as a person with a way and a commitment. Religious dialogue is a recognition of the other as person, and God as the common ground of being.

The promulgation of *Nostra Aetate,* the publication of the Vatican *Guidelines,* and the Episcopal documents on Christian-Jewish dialogue are good signs, signs of peace, signs marking the beginning of a prophetic time and a prophetic relationship. Jews and Christians have started a new time, a time of hope. The situation is difficult, as are all creative efforts, but religiously challenging. For the first time we perceive and acknowledge the other as a person, a brother in God, and a common path, the way of Christians and Jews witnessing God, a witnessing that embraces our total meaning.

Dialogue is a process of growth in depth. The first stage requires a basic knowledge of the other's faith commitment beyond prejudice and images. There is another stage, and this book is an expression of this maturation process that involves looking into ourselves to determine the real dimensions of the meeting of the two faiths, the meeting of Jews and Christians. There is the temptation to prophesy eschatological dreams that remain essentially a dream of the moment or part of a conversionary tendency. Dialogue requires search and patience. We need a time of meditation, of reflection and consideration for the future. Patience is required for the doubts, for the repetition of old situations, for excessive dreams, the result of unreserved enthusiasm. Reflection, careful committed reflection, and critical consideration are indispensable in the search for a joint vocation. The search into the meaning of God's special call is a search for the meaning of our faith encounter beyond syncretism and sporadic sympathies. Ours is a search for the mystery of a new dimension: the possibility to witness God together, not unified, but standing together in a time of general unbelief and ideological triumphalism. Ours is a search in humility for God's presence and call.

NOTES

1. Martin Buber, *Die Stunde und die Erkenntnis* (Berlin: Schocken, 1936), p. 155.

2. Joseph L. Lichten, "The Council's Statement on the Jews," in *Christian Friends' Bulletin* (December 1965).

3. Charles Glock and Rodney Stark, *Christian Beliefs and Anti-Semitism* (New York: Harper & Row, 1966).

4. Quoted in Vincent A. Yzermans, *American Participation in the Second Vatican Council* (New York: Sheed & Ward, 1967), pp. 573–574.

5. Arthur Gilbert, *The Vatican Council and the Jews* (Cleveland and New York: The World Publishing Company, 1968), p. 147.

6. *Ibid.,* p. 300.

7. Cf. Solomon Grayzel, *The Church and the Jews in the XIIIth Century* (New York: Hermon Press, 1966), pp. 76–78.

8. Joseph B. Soloveitchik, "Confrontation," in Norman Lamm and Walter S. Wurzburger, eds., *A Treasury of "Tradition"* (New York: Hebrew Publishing, 1967), p. 80.

9. Eliezer Berkovits, "Judaism in the Post-Christian Era," in *Judaism* (January 1966) p. 74.

10. Jacob B. Agus, *Dialogue and Tradition* (New York: Abelard-Schuman, 1971), p. 102.

11. Cf. Thomas F. Stransky, "The Guidelines, A Catholic Point of View," and Leon Klenicki, "The Guidelines, A Jewish Point of View," in *Face to Face: An Interreligious Bulletin* I (Summer 1975) 7–13.

12. All quotations from *Nostra Aetate,* the Vatican *Guidelines,* and the various bishops' conference statements are from: Helga Croner, comp., *Stepping Stones to Further Jewish-Christian Relations* (New York: Stimulus Books, 1977).

13. Cf. Walter Jacob, *Christianity Through Jewish Eyes* (Cincinnati: Hebrew Union College, 1974).

14. Cf. Augustin Cardinal Bea, *The Church and the Jewish People* (New York: Harper & Row, 1966).

15. Leon Klenicki, "The Presentation of Jews and Judaism in the Puebla Document," *A Report* (New York: Anti-Defamation League of B'nai B'rith, 1979). Cf. also John Eagleson and Philip Scharper, eds., *Puebla and Beyond* (Maryknoll, N.Y.: Orbis Press, 1979), pp. 250–262.

16. Cf. Hans J. Schoeps, *The Jewish-Christian Argument* (New York: Holt, Rinehart & Winston, 1963).

Appendix:
Declaration on the
Relationship of the Church
to Non-Christian Religions

Paul, Bishop
Servant of the Servants of God
Together with the Fathers of the Sacred Council
For Everlasting Memory

1. In our times, when every day men are being drawn closer together and the ties between various peoples are being multiplied, the Church is giving deeper study to her relationship with non-Christian religions. In her task of fostering unity and love among men, and even among nations, she gives primary consideration in this document to what human beings have in common and to what promotes fellowship among them.

For all peoples comprise a single community, and have a single origin, since God made the whole race of men dwell over the entire face of the earth (cf. Acts 17:26). One also is their final goal: God. His providence, his manifestations of goodness, and his saving designs extend to all men (cf. Wis 8:1; Acts 14:17; Rom 2:6–7; 1 Tim 2:4) against the day when the elect will be united in that holy city ablaze with the splendor of God, where the nations will walk in his light (cf. Rev 21:23f.).

Men look to the various religions for answers to those profound mysteries of the human condition which, today even as in olden times, deeply stir the human heart: What is a man? What is the meaning and the purpose of our life? What is goodness and what is sin? What gives rise to our sorrows and to what intent? Where lies the path to true happiness? What is the truth about death, judgment, and retribution beyond the grave? What, finally, is that ultimate and unutterable mystery which engulfs our being, and whence we take our rise, and whither our journey leads us?

2. From ancient times down to the present, there has existed among diverse peoples a certain perception of that hidden power which hovers over the course of things and over the events of human life; at times, indeed, recognition can be found of a Supreme Divinity and of a Supreme Father too. Such a perception and such a recognition instill the lives of these peoples with a profound religious sense. Religions bound up with cultural advancement have struggled to reply to these same questions with more refined concepts and in more highly developed language.

Thus in Hinduism men contemplate the divine mystery and express it through an unspent fruitfulness of myths and through searching philosophical inquiry. They seek release from the anguish of our condition through ascetical practices of deep meditation or a loving, trusting flight toward God.

Buddhism in its multiple forms acknowledges the radical insufficiency of this shifting world. It teaches a path by which men, in a devout and confident spirit, can either reach a state of absolute freedom or attain supreme enlightenment by their own efforts or by higher assistance.

Likewise, other religions to be found everywhere strive variously to answer the restless searchings of the human heart by proposing "ways," which consist of teachings, rules of life, and sacred ceremonies.

The Catholic Church rejects nothing which is true and holy in these religions. She looks with sincere respect upon those ways of conduct and of life, those rules and teachings which, though differing in many particulars from what she holds and sets forth, nevertheless often reflect a ray of that truth which enlightens all men. Indeed, she proclaims and must ever proclaim Christ, "the way, the truth, and the life" (Jn 14:6), in whom men find the fullness of religious life, and in whom God has reconciled all things to himself (cf. 2 Cor 5:18–19).

The Church therefore has this exhortation for her sons: prudently and lovingly, through dialogue and collaboration with the followers of other religions, and in witness of Christian faith and life, acknowledge, preserve, and promote the spiritual and moral goods found among these men, as well as the values in their society and culture.

3. Upon the Moslems, too, the Church looks with esteem. They adore

one God, living and enduring, merciful and all-powerful, Maker of heaven and earth who speaks to men. They strive to submit wholeheartedly even to his inscrutable decrees, just as did Abraham, with whom the Islamic faith is pleased to associate itself. Though they do not acknowledge Jesus as God, they revere him as a prophet. They also honor Mary, his virgin mother; at times they call on her, too, with devotion. In addition they await the day of judgment when God will give each man his due after raising him up. Consequently, they prize the moral life and give worship to God, especially through prayer, almsgiving, and fasting.

Although in the course of the centuries many quarrels and hostilities have arisen between Christians and Moslems, this most sacred Synod urges all to forget the past and to strive sincerely for mutual understanding. On behalf of all mankind, let them make common cause of safeguarding and fostering social justice, moral values, peace, and freedom.

4. As this sacred Synod searches into the mystery of the Church, it recalls the spiritual bond linking the people of the new covenant with Abraham's stock.

For the Church of Christ acknowledges that, according to the mystery of God's saving design, the beginnings of her faith and her election are already found among the patriarchs, Moses, and the prophets. She professes that all who believe in Christ, Abraham's sons according to faith (cf. Gal 3:7), are included in the same patriarch's call, and likewise that the salvation of the Church was mystically foreshadowed by the chosen people's exodus from the land of bondage.

The Church, therefore, cannot forget that she received the revelation of the Old Testament through the people with whom God in his inexpressible mercy designed to establish the ancient covenant. Nor can she forget that she draws sustenance from the root of that good olive tree onto which have been grafted the wild olive branches of the Gentiles (cf. Rom 11:17–24). Indeed, the Church believes that by his cross Christ, our Peace, reconciled Jew and Gentile, making them both one in himself (cf. Eph 2:14–16).

Also, the Church ever keeps in mind the words of the apostle about his kinsmen, "who have the adoption as sons, and the glory and the covenant and the legislation and the worship and the promises; who have the fathers, and from whom is Christ according to the flesh" (Rom 9:4–5), the son of the Virgin Mary. The Church recalls too that from the Jewish people sprang the apostles, her foundation stones and pillars, as well as most of the early disciples who proclaimed Christ to the world.

As Holy Scripture testifies, Jerusalem did not recognize the time of her visitation (cf. Lk 19:44), nor did the Jews in large number accept the gospel; indeed, not a few opposed the spreading of it (cf. Rom 11:28). Nevertheless, according to the apostle, the Jews still remain most dear to God because of their fathers, for he does not repent of the gifts he makes nor of the calls he issues (cf. Rom 11:28–29). In company with the prophets and the same apostle, the Church awaits that day, known to God alone, on which all peoples will address the Lord in a single voice and "serve him with one accord" (Soph 3:9; cf. Is 66:23; Ps 65:4; Rom 11:11–32).

Since the spiritual patrimony common to Christians and Jews is thus so great, this sacred Synod wishes to foster and recommend that mutual understanding and respect which is the fruit above all of biblical and theological studies, and of brotherly dialogues.

True, authorities of the Jews and those who followed their lead pressed for the death of Christ (cf. Jn 19:6); still, what happened in his passion cannot be blamed upon all the Jews then living, without distinction, nor upon the Jews of today. Although the Church is the new people of God, the Jews should not be presented as repudiated or cursed by God, as if such views followed from the holy Scriptures. All should take pains, then, lest in catechetical instruction and in the preaching of God's word they teach anything out of harmony with the truth of the gospel and the spirit of Christ.

The Church repudiates all persecutions against any man. Moreover, mindful of her common patrimony with the Jews, and motivated by the gospel's spiritual love and by no political considerations, she deplores the hatred, persecutions, and displays of anti-Semitism directed against the Jews at any time and from any source.

Besides, as the Church has always held and continues to hold, Christ in his boundless love freely underwent his passion and death because of the sins of all men, so that all might attain salvation. It is, therefore, the duty of the Church's preaching to proclaim the cross of Christ as the sign of God's all-embracing love and as the fountain from which every grace flows.

5. We cannot in truthfulness call upon that God who is the Father of all if we refuse to act in a brotherly way toward certain men, created though they be to God's image. A man's relationship with God the Father and his relationship with his brother men are so linked together that Scripture says: "He who does not love does not know God" (1 Jn 4:8).

The ground is therefore removed from every theory or practice which leads to a distinction between men or peoples in the matter of human dignity and the rights which flow from it.

As a consequence, the Church rejects, as foreign to the mind of Christ, any discrimination against men or harassment of them because of their race, color, condition of life, or religion.

Accordingly, following in the footsteps of the holy apostles Peter and Paul, this sacred Synod ardently implores the Christian faithful to "maintain good fellowship among the nations" (1 Pet 2:12), and, if possible, as far as in them lies, to keep peace with all men (cf. Rom 12:18), so that they may truly be sons of the Father who is in heaven (cf. Mt 5:45).

Each and every one of the things set forth in this Declaration has won the consent of the Fathers of this most sacred Council. We too, by the apostolic authority conferred on us by Christ, join with the Venerable Fathers in approving, decreeing, and establishing these things in the Holy Spirit, and we direct that what has thus been enacted in synod be published to God's glory.

Rome, at St. Peter's, October 28, 1965

I, Paul, Bishop of the Catholic Church

There follow the signatures of the fathers.

Notes on the Contributors

JOSEPH BLENKINSOPP is Professor of Old Testament at the University of Notre Dame. He taught previously at several institutes in England and the United States including Vanderbilt Divinity School, Hartford Seminary Foundation, and Chicago Theological Seminary. During the fall semester 1978, he was rector of the Ecumenical Institute, Jerusalem, and has also done archeological work in Israel. He did his doctoral work at Oxford University and has also studied at London University and the Biblical Institute in Rome. His most recent book is *Prophecy and Canon* (University of Notre Dame Press, 1978) and he contributes regularly to several scholarly journals. He is a member of the American Academy of Religion, Society of Biblical Literature, World Union of Jewish Studies, and other bodies.

LAWRENCE BOADT, C.S.P. is a member of the Paulist Fathers, an American Catholic religious order of priests, and professor of Scripture at the Washington Theological Union in Washington, D.C. He has written several articles on the nature of Hebrew poetry and ancient prophetic literature, and is an editor of the Paulist Press coordinating Jewish-Christian publications.

MARTIN A. COHEN, rabbi, is professor of Jewish History at the Hebrew Union College-Jewish Institute of Religion, New York. He has written extensively on biblical, rabbinic and early modern history. He has served as editor of three sections of the *Encyclopedia Judaica*. Dr. Cohen serves as co-chairman of the national committee on Interreligious Affairs of the Anti-Defamation League of B'nai B'rith. He is also co-editor of the Hispanic Bulletin, *Nuestro Encuentro*.

MONIKA K. HELLWIG teaches theology at Georgetown University in Washington, D.C. She is the author of a number of books, including *The Christian Creeds; Tradition: The Catholic Story Today;* and *Death and Christian Hope*; as well as some cassette lecture series on Christian faith, worship and theology. She was forced to flee Germany as a child and became interested in Judaism and Jewish-Christian relations when studying theology as an adult.

LEON KLENICKI, rabbi, is co-director of the Department of Interreligious Affairs of the Anti-Defamation League of B'nai B'rith. He is associate editor of *Face to Face: An Interreligious Bulletin* and co-editor of the Hispanic bulletin *Nuestro Encuentro.* He edited a Haggadah for interfaith liturgical usage, *The Passover Celebration,* and co-edited *Issues in the Jewish-Christian Dialogue* (Paulist Press). Rabbi Klenicki teaches Judaic studies at Immaculate Conception Seminary, New Jersey.

LEONARD S. KRAVITZ, rabbi, is Professor of Midrash and Homiletics at Hebrew Union College-Jewish Institute of Religion, New York. He has published articles in the *Journal* of the Central Conference of American Rabbis, *Judaism,* and *Hebrew Union College Annual.* He was ordained by the Hebrew Union College-Jewish Institute of Religion in 1954.

ANDRÉ LACOCQUE was born in Belgium and studied in Strasbourg and Montpellier, also at the Rabbinical School of Paris, and at the Hebrew University in Jerusalem. In 1957 he received a Ph.D. and in 1961 a doctorate in theology from Strasbourg University. Dr. Lacocque held various pastoral positions in France and Belgium and was Professor of Old Testament at the Protestant Theological Seminary of Brussels. Since 1966, he has been Professor of Old Testament at the Chicago Theological Seminary and director of its Center for Jewish-Christian Studies. He also lectures at Spertus College of Judaism, Chicago. Dr. Lacocque is a member of various learned societies and has received research and publications grants.

MSGR. JORGE MEJIA was born in Buenos Aires, earned a doctorate in theology from the Angelicum University in Rome and a licentiate in biblical studies from the Pontifical Institute there. He did post-doctoral studies at the Ecole Biblique et Archéologique Francaise in Jerusalem. Msgr. Mejia served as professor of Old Testament in the faculty of theology of the Catholic University of Argentina, as Secretary for Ecumenical and Interreligious Relations for the Latin American Council of Bishops, and as editor of the Catholic review, *Criterio.* Since 1977, he has been Secretary of the Vatican Commission for Religious Relations with the Jews in Rome. In addition, Msgr. Mejia is the author of two books, *Guía para la lectura de la Biblia,* and *Amor, Pecado, Alianza (Una lectura del Profeta Oseas).*

S. DAVID SPERLING is Associate Professor of Bible at the New York School of the Hebrew Union College-Jewish Institute of Religion. He was ordained by the Jewish Theological Seminary and is now a member of the

Central Conference of American Rabbis. A native of New York City, Dr. Sperling received his Ph.D. in Semitic Languages at Columbia University. He has contributed to various scholarly journals, as well as to the *Encyclopedia Judaica* and the *Interpreter's Dictionary of the Bible*. Most recently he has collaborated in the authorship of *Handbook of Hebrew Letters*, a study of ancient Hebrew epistles.

INDEX OF AUTHORS AND SUBJECTS

STIMULUS BOOKS are developed by Stimulus Foundation, a not-for-profit organization, and are published by Paulist Press. The Foundation wishes to further the publication of scholarly books on Jewish and Christian topics that are of importance to Judaism and Christianity.

Stimulus Foundation was established by an erstwhile refugee from Nazi Germany who intends to contribute with these publications to the improvement of communication between Jews and Christians.

Books for publication in this Series will be selected by a committee of the Foundation, and offers of manuscripts and works in progress should be addressed to:

Stimulus Foundation
785 West End Ave.
New York, N.Y. 10025